Contents

Introduction *Dermot A.*   5

Faith and Culture: The Challenge of Inculturation
  Dermot A. Lane   11

The Shapeless God of Israel:
An exploration of the aniconic tradition of biblical religion
  William Riley   40

Disclosing the passion for the possible:
Interpreting Sacraments as Life's Interpreters
  Anne Kelly   64

Music, Meaning and Mystery:
Towards a Theophany of Music
  Anne M. Murphy   85

Where Hope and History Rhyme:
The Poetry of Seamus Heaney
  John Devitt   107

The New Agenda of Unbelief and Faith
  Michael Paul Gallagher   133

Glimpsing the Divine:
Metaphor and Religious Thinking
  Andrew McGrady   151

The Media and the Church
  Donal Harrington   189

Morality and Culture in Dialogue
  ✠ *Donal Murray*   213

Contributors   233

*Dedicated to
all the students,
graduates,
staff,
members of the Board,
and Patrons of
Mater Dei Institute of Education
during the years 1966-1992*

Introduction

Dermot A. Lane

During the academic year of 1991-1992 Mater Dei Institute of Education celebrated twenty-five years of involvement in teacher education for post-primary schools. The Institute was founded in 1966 by John Charles McQuaid, Archbishop of Dublin, to ensure a supply of professionally qualified teachers of religion for post-primary schools in Ireland. While the Institute has remained faithful to the vision of its founder, it has also evolved and developed in response to the growing needs of the larger educational community which it seeks to serve.

As part of its Silver Jubilee celebration the Institute hosted a series of public lectures on the subject of *Religious and Culture in Dialogue*. The papers presented at this series of public lectures, plus a related paper given by Donal Harrington to the Mater Dei Summer School in June 1992, are now offered to a wider audience in the hope of making a small contribution to the current debate about the relationship that exists between religion and culture.

The recent appointment of Michael D. Higgins as Minister for Arts, Culture and the Gaeltacht has brought culture back to the centre of national consciousness. The creation of this new portfolio, and in particular the nomination of Michael D. Higgins, have been warmly welcomed. Within days of taking up his appointment the new Minister was talking about the energy, creativity and imagination that culture can bring to social and political issues. A significant dimension of this dynamism derives surely from the intrinsic relationship that obtains between culture and religion.

The issue of religion and culture is one of the most pressing questions facing Christianity today as it moves towards the next millennium. The relationship between religion and culture is omnipresent in educational, political and ecclesial discussion in contemporary Ireland. The neglect of culture in the Government's Green Paper on *Education For A Changing World* (1992), with the

5

exception ironically of what it calls 'the enterprise culture', is a matter of considerable concern among educationalists. The debate about Church and State which has surfaced in recent referenda is an expression of the wider question concerning the relationship between religion and culture. At the ecclesial level discussions abound, both at home and abroad, concerning faith seeking appropriate cultural expression. For example, a conference on 'Christianity and Culture in Europe: Memory, Awareness and Planning' was held in eastern Europe by way of preparation for the meeting of the European Synod of Catholic Bishops in 1992. Further, an ecumenical group in England has been discussing the relationship between gospel and culture over a period of at least six years. These discussions have given rise to the publication of working papers entitled *The Gospel and Contemporary Culture*, edited by H. Montefiore, London, 1992. This publication provided the background for the consultation on 'The Gospel and Culture' which took place in July,1992 at Swanwick, England. The 1991 Consultative Document in preparation for the Fourth General Conference of Latin American Bishops (CELAM) at Santo Domingo in October 1992 deals explicitly with the challenge of evangelisation and culture.

Part of the problem is that we live in an era of unprecedented change and this affects the way culture is perceived and the gospel is proclaimed. Indeed, many would argue, with considerable evidence to support their case, that we are at present caught in the midst of a paradigm change in relation to our understanding of the cosmos, science, philsophy, economics, the humanities and theology. Paradigm changes are a time of tension for both culture and religion; they also offer an unique opportunity for the crafting of new cultural forms and expressions of religious faith.

For example, it is quite clear that many of the assumptions underlying contemporary culture are alien to the spirit of the gospel: individualism, consumerism, secularism, and the split between facts and values. At the same time, it must be pointed out that there are openings within contemporary culture that are sympathetic to the good news of Jesus Christ: the universal concern for human rights and gender equality, the new quest for a social justice that respects the integrity of creation, the search for liberation and spiritual fulfillment. If the church fails to incarnate its message within new cultural categories, there is the distinct danger that the gospel will be discarded because of its association with dated cultural forms. One way foward in evaluating the mutually critical dialogue that must take place between religion and culture is the appeal to a new synthesis of theory and practice that effects a liberating praxis of salvation of all within community.

The papers that follow seek to address, directly or indirectly, some of the tensions and opportunities that surround the complex realtionship that exists between culture and religion. The approach is interdisciplinary, covering theological, biblical, liturgical, musical, literary, educational, and moral aspects of the relation between religion and culture. This choice has been influenced largely by the curriculum on offer in the Institute.

In his opening paper on 'Faith and Culture' Dermot A. Lane explores the teaching of the Second Vatican Council on religion and culture. In the light of this teaching, he outlines some of the theological questions arising from contemporary cultural changes: feminism, pluralism, modernity. In the course of his paper, he highlights the need for a method in theology to deal with the challenge of inculturation.

William Riley, in 'The Shapeless God of Israel', deals with Israel's ideological refusal to portray God in visual form. Riley suggests that this refusal has several implications for the dialogue between biblical religion and its contemporary culture.

Anne Kelly, in 'Disclosing the Passion for the Possible: Interpreting Sacraments as Life's Interpreters', brings a feminist hermeneutic to bear on the way we experience and celeberate the sacraments. She suggests that the sacraments should be allowed to interpret our experience just as much as we seek to interpret the sacraments. In this way the sacraments lift us out of routine and apathy; they also help us to rediscover our interconnectedness and relatedness; and they begin to sanctify the ordinary, everyday experiences of women and men alike.

Ann Murphy, in 'Music, Meaning, and Mystery', describes the juncture where these have met. It is possible, she suggests, to experience, in and through music, intuitions of meaning and intimations of mystery. Such experiences transcend proof, and persuade us to consider great music as a theophany, a manifestation of the divine.

John Devitt, in 'Where Hope and History Rhyme', shows how Seamus Heaney is deeply concerned about the divisions that plague contemporary Ireland. Devitt suggests that *The Cure at Troy*, Heaney's version of the *Philoctetes* of Sophocles, represents an important moment in the poet's development. In this work of Heaney, we hear the voice of the prophet, balancing the apparently irreconcilable claims of reality and justice.

Michael Paul Gallagher, in 'the Unbelief Agenda Now', examines various shifts in modern culture that produce a less militant unbelief to-day and he proposes a parallel change in the pastoral journey towards faith. Where sensibility is dulled by secular assumptions, what is needed is a ministry of disposition to awaken wonder, and this can lead on to a new drama of decision and then towards the threshold of revelation.

Andrew McGrady, in 'Glimpsing the Divine: Metaphor and Religious Thinking', proposes a paradigm of metaphorical religious thinking which acknowledges the distinctive analogical use of language which characterises religious discourse. He offers a report on empirical research correlating the metaphorical aspects of religious thinking with the operational aspects examined in previous research (such as Goldman 1962). Several important implications for the teaching of religion are also considered.

The context for the article on 'The Media and the Church' by Donal Harrington is the tense relationship between the two and need for serious dialogue between them. The article explores the suggestion that a useful prologue to dialogue might be for both to engage in self-questioning. The questions thus formulated lead into a statement of the challenges facing church and media as communicators – challenges that have notable similarities.

Bishop Donal Murray, in 'Morality and Culture in Dialogue', examines the areas of freedom, tolerance, and concern for the envirnoment. If the dialogue between morality and culture is to suceed, then we need a balanced view of the human self as relational, interdependent and responsible in conscience to the demands of truth.

By way of conclusion, I wish to thank the organising committee who planned this series of public lectures: Eoin Cassidy, Michael Drumm, William Riley, and Kevin Williams. Like all committees in the Institute, they worked beyond the call of duty in conceiving and executing the idea of a series of lectures on the theme of *Religion and Culture in Dialogue*. Appreciation must also be expressed to the students of the college who contributed enormously to making a sucess of each evening. Lastly but by no means least, there was Sr Marcellina O Sullivan who as always was untiringly attentive to the welcome and hospitality that make such public occasions memorable for all.

Dermot A. Lane
February, 1993

Faith and Culture:
The Challenge of Inculturation

Dermot A Lane

The question about the relationship between faith and culture is in one sense as old as Christianity itself. It arose in a particularly acute form in the first century when the early Church was faced with difficult questions about the admission of Gentiles into the Christian community without circumcision. It continued to exercise the early Church towards the end of the first century and well into the second century as the Church made her pilgrim way from a largely Jewish matrix into a Hellenistic culture. This same question haunts the Church to-day as she makes her painful way from being a predominantly European reality to being a world Church.

However, it must be admitted that the precise formulation of the question about the relationship between faith and culture is somewhat different from previous centuries. There are elements surrounding the issue to-day that were not present previously. These elements include, for example, the emergence of an Enlightenment shaped historical consciousness which is quite distinct from earlier times, the collapse of a unified and single metaphysical system, and the growing presence of cultural pluralism. These developments have influenced the way we understand culture to-day. The concept of culture includes not only arts and letters but also ways of life, value systems, the rights of people, beliefs and traditions shaping human identity.[1] Probably the single, most significant difference between the present and the past concerning faith and culture is the pace of change. To-day there is 'an acute sense of stress and disorientation induced by the experience of too much change in too short a time ... Above all, there is the fear that we may not be able to adapt at all: the premature arrival of the future frightens us precisely because it is premature and we are unprepared.'[2]

How then are we to describe the questions and problems relating to faith and culture to-day? One way is to recognise the embarrassment that we all experience from time to time concerning certain religious expressions and practices which no longer do justice to deeply held religious convictions. A tension is experienced between personal faith and the culturally conditioned expressions of that faith. How do we express our faith commitments in a language and framework that is not open to contradiction from modern science or perhaps ridicule by secular humanists or even caricature by the media? What is or ought to be the relationship between faith and culture? Is culture intrinsic to faith or are they two separate and distinct realities and therefore only externally related ...?

Another description of the problem concerning faith and culture is to look at the issue from the side of contemporary culture. Here many would want to agree with Paul Tillich's resolution of the issue when he says that 'Religion is the substance of culture and culture is the form of religion.'[3] This helpful formulation of the issue has come under attack by a new group of cultural critics, calling themselves post-structuralist or post-modernist or deconstructionists; they argue that there is nothing behind culture, that culture has no final referent. All that exists in culture are images, an endless play of signification without content or any point of reference to a transcendent source. It is at this particular juncture that the prophetic voice of George Steiner must be taken seriously. According to Steiner, the meaning of art, literature and music 'is, in the final analysis, underwritten by the assumption of God's presence.'[4] The issue here is surely the ambiguity of so much modern culture – much of which is antithetical to personal faith in a Transcendent Reality.

A third description of the debate concerning faith and culture arises out of the emergence in this century of a new global awareness. Within this global consciousness there is at the same time a growing variety and richness of different cultures. How does faith, Christian faith, relate to this pluralism of cultures? Can faith cope with the cultural pluralism of Africa, Asia and Latin America? The issue is no longer one simply of faith and culture but rather one of faith and cultures.

Recent Popes have grappled with the issue of faith and culture. For example, John XXIII could be said to have initiated the contemporary debate when, in his opening address to the Second Vatican Council, he introduced the distinction between the substance of the deposit of faith and the manner of its expression.[5] This corresponds more or less to the first level of the problem described above. Paul VI in *Evangelii Nuntiandi* points out that 'the split between the Gospel and culture is without doubt the drama of our time.'[6] This expression of the issue could be said to represent the second level of the problem described above.

In 1982 John Paul II established a Pontifical Council for Culture to promote dialogue between the different cultures and the Gospel. In his opening address he pointed out: 'Since the beginning of my Pontificate, I have considered the Church's dialogue with the cultures of our time to be a vital area, one in which the destiny of the world at the end of this century is at stake.' He concludes by saying that one of the functions of the Council for Culture will be the promotion of an 'encounter between the salvific message of the Gospel and the multiplicity of cultures.'[7] This concern of John Paul II corresponds to the third level of the problem of faith and culture expressed above.

In the light of this broad introduction to our theme, it seems to me that the general theme of this series of public lectures marking the Silver Jubilee of Mater Dei Institute in 1991/92, namely, 'Religion and Culture in Dialogue' is indeed well chosen. It is particularly appropriate for a Catechetical Institute to address this subject since it was in a catechetical document, *Catechesi Tradendae*, that John Paul II in 1979 first proposed a way forward in the debate about faith and culture by recommending the principle of inculturation as a way of describing the proper relationship between faith and culture.[8]

In the light of these introductory remarks I plan to approach my topic 'Faith and Culture: the Challenge of Inculturation' in four sections. I will begin with an outline of the drama of Vatican II in relation to faith and culture. I will then move on to work out some principles for a theology of inculturation. Thirdly, I will indicate the ingredients of a method for inculturation and, fourthly, I will address some of the more significant cultural shifts to-day and the challenge they present to Christian faith.

THE DRAMA OF VATICAN II AND THE POST-CONCILIAR CHURCH

If it is true to say that the key question at the First Vatican Council in 1869 was the relationship between faith and reason, then we must say that the central non-ecclesiological issue at the Second Vatican Council and in the Post-Conciliar Church is the relationship between faith and culture. There can be no doubt that something quite dramatic took place at Vatican II and there are various ways of interpreting this unique historical and ecclesial event. For some, Vatican II was an occasion of liturgical recovery and the biblical retrieval of lost elements within the Christian tradition. For others, it was a period of important Christian renewal and theological reform. For another group, Vatican II was an unfortunate and regrettable series of concessions to the so-called liberals and progressives. With the passage of time, it has become abundantly clear that the use of labels is the least helpful way of interpreting Vatican II.

Given the advantage of twenty-five years of historical hindsight, I believe with many others that the real issue at Vatican II was about the Church coming to grips with modernity. This engagement by the Church with the culture of modernity is summed up in *The Pastoral Constitution on the Church in the Modern World*, 1965. The Church exists in the world, not above or below the world but in the world; the kind of world it must serve is the *modern* world – not the pre-modern classical world. Slowly but surely the Church during Vatican II embraced the culture of modernity for the first time – a little like the embrace between a boy and girl on their first date. I use this image deliberately because it captures some of the awkwardness and even embarrassment of what happened at Vatican II. To appreciate fully this new encounter between the Church and modernity we need to look at the previous one hundred years during which the Church had deliberately refused to take this step.

What was outstanding about the style and shape of Catholicism in the previous century was the stout refusal by the Church to face modernity. This refusal can be seen in a series of different events which sought to enter into dialogue with the modern world, each of which was condemned by the Church.

The first of these took place in the 1860's in Germany when a group of intellectuals sought to open up dialogue with the modern world. Under the leadership of Ignaz von Döllinger they made a plea at a meeting in Munich in 1863 for academic freedom and the replacement of scholasticism by a more critical theology. This movement was condemned by Pius IX in a letter entitled *Tuas Libenter* which became known as the Munich Brief. This in turn was followed by the Syllabus of Errors a year later. This strong reaction against the modern world in turn was re-affirmed some five years later by the First Vatican Council (1869).

A second attempt was made by the modernist movement roughly between 1890 and 1910. This movement, which sought once again to engage the modern world by appealing to human experience and historical research, was condemned by the Encyclical Letter *Pascendi dominici gregis* issued by Pius X in 1907.

A third effort to come to grips with the modern world was initiated in France and was known as *La Nouvelle Théologie* of the 1940's. However, the spirit of this movement was at least challenged by the Encyclical Letter *Humani Generis* published in 1950 by Pius XII. During this hundred years the Church was reacting against the rising post-Enlightenment culture of modernity. The underlying issue was about the relationship between the Church and the world or, more specifically, the relationship or better the lack of a relationship between faith and culture. The reaction of the Church to the winds of the modern world was one of withdrawal.

The images used by different historians of theology to describe the relationship between the Church and the world, between faith and culture, during this period are instructive. Henri de Lubac, the French Jesuit theologian, who was later made a Cardinal and who died in 1991, talked about a theology in which 'the supernatural was exiled',[9] that is, the sacred was removed from the realms of nature, history and the secular. H. Richard Niebuhr in his important work on *Christ and Culture* describes the Catholic Church's relationship with culture in terms of 'Christ above Culture'.[10]

Gabriel Daly, the Irish theologian, likens the Church between the two Vatican Councils as 'a village encompassed by a high wall which separated the villagers from the surrounding jungle.'[11] Joseph Komonchak, the North American ecclesiologist, talks about the emergence of a 'Catholic sub-culture' in the nineteenth and early twentieth centuries[12] – meaning a sub-culture in contrast to the cultural monopoly of the Middle Ages and earlier.

This sketchy overview of the period preceding Vatican II helps us to understand and appreciate the vital significance of what actually happened at the Second Vatican Council. It must not be forgotten that the spirit of withdrawal by the Church from the modern world – a kind of *fuga mundi* – did, in fact, inform the first session of the Council. The spirit of opposition to the world was present in the preparatory schemata, especially in the documents on the Church and Revelation. What is significant is that a change of direction took place during the first session and that this significant shift was prompted largely by the direct intervention of Pope John XXIII. The language of *aggiornamento*, the image of opening windows, and the disagreement with 'the prophets of gloom' began to take effect and gather pace from the middle of the first session onwards. This shift gathered momentum and is reflected, often unevenly and sometimes inconsistently, in the final documents. The shift is symbolised in the overall thrust of the documents: the ecclesial recognition of other Churches, respect for the value of non-Christian religions, the affirmation of the principle of religious freedom, the acknowledgement of the importance of human rights and social justice, the endorsement of 'a new humanism', and a real concern for the salvation of the world. A new dialogue is established between the Church and the world but, above all, a positive relationship between faith and culture, is set in motion. A New Pentecost takes place.

The document which captures much of this most strikingly is *The Pastoral Constitution on the Church in the Modern World* – especially Part II, Chap. 2, which deals with 'The Proper Development of Culture'. The Council affirms that:
- there are many links between the message of salvation and culture (a.58);

- God spoke according to the culture proper to each age (a.58);

- the Church has ... utilised the resources of different cultures in its preaching (a.58);

- the Church ... is not tied exclusively to any race or nation, to any one particular way of life (a.58);

- culture must be subordinated to the integral development of the human person, to the good of the community and of the whole of mankind (a.59);

- the discoveries of modern science should be blended by the faithful with Christian doctrine (a.62).

Against the background of the previous hundred years, these general principles of Vatican II are striking; they symbolise a Church seeking to come to grips with the values of the modern age and anxious to enter into a genuine dialogue with contemporary culture. A new relationship is forged between the Church and the world, between faith and culture, between the signs of the time and the Gospel of Christ.

This new emphasis emanating from Vatican II moves quickly to the centre of the stage in the post-Conciliar Church – at times in tension with the past, on other occasions, in a creative interaction with the present. It was above all the large theological vision of Paul VI that held these development together in a creative unity. As with Vatican II, we can only outline in broad strokes the general direction of post-Conciliar development.

In 1969 Paul VI, on the occasion of a visit to Uganda, explicitly addressed the question of faith and culture. This address, often referred to as the Kampala Address, is significant because it talks about the adaptation of the Gospel to African culture and then goes on to affirm with nuance the value of cultural pluralism:

Your evangelistic work raises a question which remains very much alive and arouses a great deal of discussion, namely the adaptation of the gospel, the church, to African culture ... Must the church be European, Latin, Oriental, or should it be African?[14]

In response to his own question, Paul VI goes on to say that the language of faith is manifold and:

From this point of view, a certain pluralism is not only legitimate, but desirable. An adaptation of the Christian life in the fields of pastoral, ritual, didactic and spiritual activities is not only possible, it is even favoured by the Church. [15]

In 1973 the Congregation for the Doctrine of the Faith acknowledged in a document entitled *Mysterium Ecclesiae* that the formulae of faith are historically and culturally conditioned. [16]

In 1974 the international Synod of Bishops met in Rome to discuss the question of Evangelisation which resulted in the important document *Evangelisation in the Modern World* – probably the best treatment to date of faith and culture in a Church document. In this document Paul VI says:

What matters is to evangelise man's culture and cultures (not in a purely decorative way as it were applying a thin veneer, but in a vital way, in depth and right to their very roots) ... always taking the person as one's starting point. [17]

He then goes on to pose the hermeneutical challenge facing those who would evangelise cultures to-day - a challenge we will return to later on:

The individual Churches ... have the task of assimilating the essence of the Gospel message and of transforming it, but without the slightest betrayal of its essential truth, into a language that these people understand. [18]

In 1977 the Synod of Bishops on Catechesis brought different interventions from the floor on the subject of faith and culture, with particular references to the concept of inculturation. Out of this Synod came the Apostolic Exhortation, *Catechesi Tradendae (Catechesis in our Time)* written by John Paul II in 1979. It is in this document that the word inculturation is first used by a Pope:

The term *acculturation* or *inculturation* may be a neologism, but it expresses very well one factor of the great mystery of the Incarnation. We can say of catechesis ... that it is called to bring the power of the Gospel into the very heart of culture and cultures. [19]

The theme of Inculturation, now linked by John Paul II to the mystery of the Incarnation, is taken up frequently in subsequent Papal documents. [20]

In 1982 in his opening address to the Council for Culture, John Paul II strongly asserts the organic and two-way link between Christianity and culture:

> ... the synthesis between culture and faith is not just a demand of culture, but also of faith. A faith which does not become culture is a faith which has not been fully received, not thoroughly thought through, not fully lived out. [21]

Finally, in 1991 in his most recent Encyclical, *Centesimus Annus*, John Paul talks about the sustaining, purifying and enriching role of evangelisation in culture. [22]

This overview of the drama of Vatican II and the post-Conciliar period highlights how the church has come to view the modern world in a positive light and how this in turn has demanded the development of a new dialogue between faith and culture. Out of this dialogue comes the call for the inculturation of faith.

TOWARDS A THEOLOGY OF INCULTURATION

As we have just seen, the language of inculturation as a way of describing the relationship between faith and culture is quite recent in the teaching of the Church. One of the reasons why inculturation is a new issue for the Church is, as we have just seen, the recent recognition by the Church at Vatican II of the need to enter into dialogue with the modern world. Another reason why incult-uration is a relatively recent issue is that cultural differences in this century have created a new challenge to the meaning of the gospel in the twentieth century. These cultural changes have included the movement from a classical culture to a historical one, the shift from a pre-scientific culture to a scientific one and the emergence of a second enlightenment which now focuses not simply on the age of reason but on the question of practical reason – each of which is reflected directly or indirectly in *The Pastoral Constitution on the Church in the Modern World*.[23] To ignore these cultural changes is to end up giving answers to questions people no longer ask.

There is in effect a two-fold challenge – indeed risk – involved in inculturation. On the one hand, if inculturation does not take place, then the message of faith will simply end up addressing issues that belong to a bygone age. At best, faith will evoke feelings of nostalgia and, at worst, it will have nothing to say to contemporary questions. On the other hand, if there is too much inculturation so to speak, there is the possibility of losing sight of the theological significance of the Gospel and thereby reducing faith merely to worldly knowledge. The challenge of inculturation is one of addressing and transforming the contemporary situation without losing the newness of the Christian faith. The faith must be re-born in every age and culture.

We need now to examine the content of this challenge of inculturation. What is involved in the process of inculturation? How does inculturation take place? What is the goal of inculturation? To answer these questions, we must clear the way by outlining what inculturation is not, that is, we must begin by overcoming certain misunderstandings about inculturation.

In the first place, it must be pointed out that inculturation is not about the imposition of faith or the Gospel on the surrounding culture. This not uncommon approach is built around certain misunderstandings about the faith. The Gospel of Christ does not exist in some kind of *a priori* pure state or ahistorical pristine condition, waiting to be applied. Lying behind this common supposition is a merely propositional view of God's self-revelation. The revelation of God in creation, history and Christ is primarily about the personal self-communication of God in deeds and words. The content of revelation is primarily personal:

> The deepest truth about God and the salvation of human beings is made clear in Christ.[24]

Because this personal revelation of God exists only in human words and historical deeds, it must be acknowledged that revelation itself is already a culturally conditioned reality. To this extent, it can be misleading to talk about the essence of the Gospel as if it existed somewhere out there waiting to be applied to the different cultures around the world. The essence of the Gospel exists only as already inculturated in Jewish or Hellenistic or contemporary forms or probably a mixture of all three.

Further, it should be noted that inculturation is not simply about the adaptation of the Gospel to local circumstances. This point was made explicit by the 1985 Extraordinary Synod which goes out of its way to make a real distinction between adaptation and inculturation:

> Inculturation, however, is different from a mere external adaptation, as it signifies an interior transformation of authentic cultural values through integration into Christianity and the rooting of Christianity in various human cultures.[25]

Two points are worth highlighting in this quotation. The encounter between faith and culture is one that brings about transformation – an emphasis that keeps on recurring in Church documents about faith and culture.[26] Indeed, transformation is an important criterion of effective inculturation. The second point is that the movement between faith and culture can be from faith to culture and culture to faith.

The third preliminary point about inculturation is that it is not about the comfortable co-existence of faith alongside culture. Inculturation always invokes a process of interaction between faith and culture. Without this interaction – a continuous process of critical interaction – between faith and culture there is the real danger that the Gospel will become, as Newman put it, the dead faith of the living, instead of the living faith of the dead. How then are we to understand the process of inculturation if it is not imposition, if it is not adaptation, if it is not simply the comfortable co-existence of faith and culture?

To answer this question we must go back to the foundation of the Christian faith in the mystery of the Incarnation. The revelation of God in the reality of Jesus, which we sum up in the doctrine of the Incarnation, is the primary paradigm for understanding the process of inculturation. The Incarnation is about the creative coming together of God and humanity in Jesus of Nazareth at a particular point in history in a particular culture. It is this unique interaction between the divine and the human in Jesus that provides the model for understanding the relation between faith and culture. It is worth reflecting for a moment on the dynamic of the Incarnation, if we are to appreciate what is involved in the relationship between faith and culture.

21

The Incarnation is about the eternal Word of God becoming flesh in the particular person of Jesus of Nazareth. The Incarnation therefore is about the appearance of the universal within the particular, the entry of the absolute into the relative, the manifestation of the eternal within the temporal, the revelation of the Infinite within the finite. This means that the inculturation of faith is something that occurs in particular forms and expressions of culture. In other words, we must recognise the scandal of particularity that attaches to the mystery of Incarnation and continues to exist in the inculturation of Christian faith to-day in the different cultures of the world. Thus John Paul II in his address to the Bishops of Kenya in 1980 talks about the importance of recognising the African Christ:

> Thus, not only is Christianity relevant to Africa, but Christ, in the members of his Body, is himself African.[27]

Recognising the scandal of particularity that belongs to the Incarnation and therefore by implication to the process of inculturation will prevent imperialistic universalisations of the Gospel. Inculturation therefore is not, for example, about the universal Christianisation of African culture but rather the particular Africanisation of the Christian message.

A second point about the Incarnation that is instructive about the process of inculturation concerns the dynamic of the Incarnation. A full statement of the mystery of the Incarnation requires that we recognise the two-fold movement of God becoming human and the human becoming God in Jesus. God, to be sure, takes the initiative in the Incarnation, but it must be noted that this divine initiative evokes the perfect response of the human in Jesus. What is unique about the Incarnation is that Jesus embodies in his life the unity of God's descent into the heart of humanity and the ascent of humanity into the life of God. The Incarnation lights up our understanding not only of God but also of the human. As Edward Schillebeeckx puts it: 'Christology is concentrated creation,'[28] that is, the Christ-event is a microcosm of the continuous interaction between the divine and the human throughout the whole of life. In a somewhat similar manner, the incarnation of the faith in culture, which is what inculturation really means, can light up what is already there of divine presence in culture. Inculturation brings out what is best in culture or equally it can enable culture to realise creatively its full potential. The effect of the encounter between faith and culture in both instances, whether it be one of lighting up what is already there or re-shaping culture, is transformative.

A third point about the Incarnation that is of absolute significance for inculturation arises from the strictly theological meaning of this Christian doctrine. Because the Word was made flesh and dwelt among us in Jesus, we can say that the gulf between heaven and earth, between God and humanity, between the sacred and the secular, has once and for all been definitively overcome, so that now we glimpse heaven on earth, find God in humanity and discover the sacred in the midst of the secular. Through the Incarnation a new relation has been established between God and the world, between the divine and the human, between the natural and the supernatural. The Christian God is a distinctively incarnate God, present in all things throughout creation, throughout humanity, and throughout history.

It is above all else this staggering truth that enables culture, human culture, to mediate faith. Our universe in the light of the Incarnation is symbolic and sacramental and it is these qualities of the universe that gives culture its potential theological significance. The whole of life from the tiniest speck of cosmic dust to the personification of that dust in humanity is shot through symbolically and sacramentally with divine life. Consequently, we can talk not only about the potential theological significance of culture – but we must go further with Tillich and others and talk explicitly about a theology of culture.[29] The Christian doctrines of creation and Incarnation imply a theology of culture, because these two doctrines enable us to see the world as the sacrament of God. What this means in effect is that the dialogue between faith and culture is a two-way dialogue, with faith animating culture and culture contributing to faith. We must now examine this two-way dialogue between faith and culture. In particular, we must map out a method of inculturation that will take due account of the intrinsic importance of both faith and culture. This brings me to the third point of my paper.

INCULTURATION IN SEARCH OF A METHOD

If we are now clear about what inculturation is not and the links between Incarnation and inculturation, then we are in a position to move to the question of method. Once again, I want to take my point of departure from Vatican II in mapping a method of inculturation because, after all, it was Vatican II that turned the Church around in the direction of dialoguing with the culture of the modern world. It is clear that the documents of Vatican II do not contain any clear methodology. Yet some of the Council documents do contain hints of a methodology. For instance, *The Pastoral Constitution on the Church in the Modern World* does talk about the duty of the Church in terms of 'scrutinising the signs of the times and of interpreting them in the light of the Gospel.'[30] *The Decree on Ecumenism* does recognise the ecclesial reality of other Churches and *The Declaration on the Relationship of the Church to Non-Christian Religions* does acknowledge the presence of truths and values in other major world religions. There is, I suggest, at last the beginnings of a methodology in these statements, albeit undeveloped. There is a recognition by Vatican II of the existence of truth and values outside the Christian community, that is, outside the confines of the Church itself. Secondly, there is a call to enter into dialogue with the truths and values of other religions, that is, a call to open up a new dialogue between the Church and the world, between the Gospel and the contemporary situation. To say more than this would be to read into the Council documents that which is not there and that which was not intended.

These directions implicit in Vatican II echo Paul Tillich's celebrated Method of Correlation. According to Tillich, a correlation ought to exist in theology between questions and answers, between the Gospel and the contemporary situation, between the message of Christianity and the human search for meaning. Some have argued that Tillich's method of correlation is not sufficiently rooted in human experience as the source of all theology. What is perhaps more important is the overall framework Tillich proposes. Many Catholic theologians to-day, such as E. Schillebeeckx and David Tracy, would see theology in terms of bringing about mutually critical correlations between human experience and

Christian tradition, between the world of modernity and the Gospel of Jesus Christ. Within this revised method of correlation there is a mutually self-correcting movement between the Church and the world, between the Gospel and contemporary experience. The nature and character of the correlation between the message of Christianity and the contemporary situation can vary significantly from identity to non-identity to similarity-in-difference.[31] What is important is that the dialogue take place – however difficult or dissonant it may be. The question which arises at this juncture is how is dialogue to take place, how should the correlation be conducted, how is the conversation to be initiated and effected, especially between those who seem to disagree on fundamental issues? What kind of principles should inform the correlation? To answer this question, we must turn to the second movement of the method I am proposing, namely, the science of hermeneutics.

In the last twenty-five years or so, hermeneutics has moved to the centre of the stage in science, philosophy and theology. Hermeneutics is the art of understanding and interpreting different texts, events and human experiences. The human act of interpretation involves three realities: the phenomenon to be interpreted, the person interpreting that phenomenon and the interaction between these two realities.[32] One of the most appropriate ways to understand this interaction between the interpreter and the reality in question is the model of a conversation.

In particular, hermeneutics seeks to provide a way forward beyond the impasse of objectivism and relativism as well as the ever-increasing welter of pluralism, difference and otherness. Hermeneutics recognises the impossibility of the ever achieving Cartesian certainty in relation to the mastery of nature, the control of history, the meaning of classical texts promised by the detached epistemology of the Enlightenment. Above all, hermeneutics unmasks the illusion of impartial and value-free approaches to human understanding. Every interpreter brings a particular prejudice, a particular pre-understanding, to bear in seeking to understand a text or a tradition or the position of the other; likewise, every interpreter operates out of a particular subjectivity shaped by social location. It is only when these factors are recognised that real dialogue, genuine conversation, and effective communication can begin to take place. This means that there must be some acknowledgement of beliefs, values and commitment in our conversations with others. Further, there must be a willingness to listen, to seek to understand what is genuinely other and different, strange and alien to us within the conversation – even to the extent of allowing our own prejudices to be quest-ioned, challenged and, if necessary, transformed.[33] The essence of good conversation is the capacity to allow interruptions to take place and even determine the direction of the dialogue, especially when these interruptions come from outsiders and those on the margins of life.

This hasty summary of the principles of hermeneutics must be applied to the correlation that takes place between the Gospel and contemporary life, between the message of Christianity and the modern world. In particular, I want to suggest that this method of correlation and these principles of hermeneutics should inform the interaction between faith and culture. In other words, the relationship between faith and culture should be one of a mutually critical correlation that is guided by the basic principles of hermeneutical theory. Inculturation should follow the way of correlation and hermeneutics. But, it will be asked, are correlation and hermeneutics sufficient to cope with the 'conflict of interpretations' that are inevitable and the pluralisms that persist? In response to this question, we must answer 'no'. This brings me to the third moment of an adequate method for inculturation and that is the proposal of a liberating praxis as essential to the processes of correlation and hermeneutics.

There are many who would hold that the conversation between faith and culture must continue, especially when faced with the presence of so much pluralism. According to this viewpoint, the only adequate response to pluralism is more dialogue, conversation and communication. This particular perception of theology in general and of inculturation in particular must be called into question. The contribution of political, liberation and feminist theologies is to challenge an understanding of theology that is concerned only with conversation. These particular theologies opt for an emphasis that places the primacy on praxis. This option is inspired by a variety of considerations that can only be sum-

26

marised here: the practical character of Judeo-Christian faith, the re-location of religious experience within praxis and the post-modern challenge to assume responsibility in solidarity through praxis for the re-shaping of a more humane and just society[34] as well as respecting at the same time the integrity of creation.

In addition to this emphasis on praxis coming from liberation theologies, there are signs within liberal theology that a moment of liberating praxis is called for by way of response to the presence of pluralism.[35] For example, we find David Tracy arguing that

> What conversation is to the life of understanding, solidarity is to the life of action.[36]

Let me hasten to add here that these two quite distinct theologies, namely, liberation theology and liberal theology, are arriving at a common concern with the importance of praxis from quite different points of departure.[37] Leaving aside the real differences that exist, which I do not underestimate for one moment, there is nonetheless agreement that praxis, in particular a liberating praxis, is an essential moment in the mutually critical correlation between the gospel and the world and in particular in the dialogue between faith and culture. Without this commitment to a liberating praxis within the dialogue between faith and culture, there is the distinct danger of giving the impression that faith or culture somehow have at their disposal universal, timeless and disembodied truths of superiority. Likewise, if there is no commitment to a liberating praxis within the critical correlation between faith and culture, one must begin to question the authenticity and sincerity of the dialogue. Further, the experience of praxis in solidarity with others adds new insights to the dialogue. Ultimately, the goal of conversation must be the liberation of the participants in a way that affects not only their individual differences and otherness, but also transforms the structures and institutions that perpetuate such alienation and separation.

Under the rubric of a method for inculturation therefore, we are proposing three fundamental elements that should accompany the dialogue between faith and culture: a mutually critical correlation, the pursuit of the principles of hermeneutics within this correlation and a moment of liberating praxis as integral to the dialogue.

27

CHALLENGES FROM CULTURE TO FAITH IN IRELAND TO-DAY

In the fourth and final part of my paper I want to highlight some of the challenges coming from culture to-day for Christian faith. I do this in the belief that the crisis in the Church to-day is less a crisis of faith and much more a crisis of cultural mediation. Further, I wish to focus on the cultural issues facing Christianity in order to highlight one of the underlying theses of my paper, namely, that what is required to-day is an appreciation, or better a theology, of culture and not just a theology of a fixed faith *à la* K.arl Barth. The latter, it seems to me, betrays the theological implications of the Incarnation, namely, that the whole world and therefore culture have been affected by the Christ-event. The cultural issues I want to reflect on are feminism, pluralism and modernity. I have chosen these cultural issues because I believe these are the areas that will exercise the Catholic Church in Ireland well into the next millennium.

Of all the cultural challenges facing Christian faith to-day, by far the most important is feminism. With Roger Garaudy and so many others, I believe that:

> the greatest cultural revolution of all times (will be) the one which replaces a structure and a culture that have been worked out by the male half of humankind over thousands of years by a structure and a culture which will be the handiwork of the whole of humankind, comprising the female as well as the male component.[38]

The cultural rise of feminism in this century and its impact on areas of life as diverse as education and economics, ethics and politics, literature and religion, is a pointer to the importance of this new revolution: feminism is a world-wide movement seeking to overcome the division of human beings into categories of superiority and inferiority on the basis of sex and gender. Further, feminism reacts against the assumption that male experience is normative for understanding the whole human race, pointing out that the half cannot be taken to represent the whole. In addition, feminism seeks to transform the pervasive presence of patriarchy within human relationships, social institutions and political structures. This wide-ranging agenda of feminist theory and praxis raises searching questions for religion and, in particular, for Christianity. Indeed, for some feminists, Christianity is the cause of the problem and is therefore written off as irredeemably sexist and patriarchal. For others, Christianity is an important source of renewal containing within itself the seeds of woman's transformation and liberation. It is clearly beyond the scope of this paper to map out the resources within the Gospel that are pertinent to the women's movement. More modestly, I wish to put down some markers that might inform a cultural encounter between feminism and faith.

In the first place, it must be pointed out that the cultural challenge coming from feminism cannot be resolved simply by an 'add and stir' approach. Feminism is not 'a patch that can be sewn, inconspicuously ... over the rips and tears of division'[39] within the Church. The addition of 'sisters' to 'brothers' in the liturgy or the substitution of so-called female qualities for male qualities in our discourse about God is only a first step in a long journey. To do this only is to risk more aggravation and further alienation. Instead, what is required, as we have seen with every encounter between faith and culture, is the transformation of both faith and culture, a transformation that goes deep down into the attitudes, language and structures within the Christian community.

Secondly, feminism is a challenge for Christian faith that must be articulated primarily by women. This does not mean that men can remain indifferent. To the contrary, men must become involved in feminism because they are a fundamental part of the problem. If women have been discriminated against in society and Church, then this means that men have been given an inflated self-image. The liberation of women from exploitation will only fully succeed if and when men are also liberated from an exaggerated understanding of their status. The exploitation of women by men has diminished not only women but also men. To this extent, feminism is an issue affecting the whole of the Christian community and therefore can only be fully resolved by reference to the whole community.

A third marker that must be noted is that the key question in feminism is anthropology, that is, an understanding of what it means to be fully human. The centrality of anthropology in feminism has been recognised in recent Church documents.[40] Back in the early Seventies, Paul VI pointed out in a slightly different context that the Church is not tied to any particular anthropologies from the past.[41] Up to now, andro-centric anthropologies have been operating in our thinking and social praxis. These anthropologies are in need of a radical restructuring and transformation. The sources of such a transformation must surely include impulses coming from ecology and theological doctrines of creation and Incarnation. Many ecologists to-day point out that there is a connection between the exploitation of nature and the oppression of women. In making this connection, they call for the development of an anthropology that focuses on the human as linked to the earth. From a theological point of view, this anthropology must rediscover that all women and men are created equally in the image of God, and that all baptised Christians are 'one in Christ' and therefore bear equally the image of Christ: the doctrines of the *Imago Dei* and the *Imago Christi* must inform a renewed anthropology. To be equal in origin and in destiny is to be equal in history. Only when this transformation of anthropology through the cultural encounters between faith and feminism takes place can we begin to address the host of other issues arising from the women's movement.

Unless this kind of open dialogue and critical correlation between feminism and faith begins to take place at all levels within the life of the Christian community, there is the real likelihood that the next generation of women will be disaffected from the life of the Church. At present, there are indications that many of the newly emerging women's groups in Ireland have given up on the Church in terms of supporting their legitimate struggle to move beyond cultural stereotypes.

The second major challenge coming from culture to faith is pluralism. We live in a world of cultural pluralism and it is in this world of pluralism that the inculturation of faith must take place. For many, pluralism is a threat to the faith and for others pluralism within the unity of faith is a source of enrichment. The first of these two quite different attitudes to pluralism must be analysed if any real progress is to be made concerning the on-going inculturation of the Christian faith.

Those who object most to pluralism usually do so on the basis and assumption that there is one philosophy and one culture which is superior to all other philosophies and cultures. Apart from the obvious fact that it is impossible empirically and sociologically to prove this assumption, this particular position seems to forget that Vatican II and the post-Conciliar Church tells us quite explicitly that the faith cannot be tied to any one culture.[42]

Further, pluralism is experienced as a threat only by those who conflate the important distinction that exists between the personal act of faith and the content of that act of faith as expressed in different cultural forms. In particular, pluralism is perceived in negative terms by those who forget that the earliest expressions of Christian faith as found in the New Testament and in the Patristic period are, in fact, plural and diverse. For example, the New Testament gives quite diverse portraits of Jesus in the four Gospels and these in turn are expanded into different theologies in Paul and John. Similarly, in the Patristic period up to the sixth century and indeed beyond, we find different culturally determined theologies of the Christian faith. One thinks of the Alexandrian, Antiochean and Syrian schools of theology – not to mention the Augustianian, Thomistic and neo-Scholastic traditions right up to Vatican II.

diversity

What is quite remarkable about this great diversity of theological expressions within the Christian tradition is the capacity of the one and the same faith to hold together such diversity. The history of Christianity is shining with diversity-in-unity right up to Vatican II. The Second Vatican Council and post-Conciliar period in turn has produced its own diversity within unity. Recognition of this diversity can be found:

- in Pope John XXIII's distinction between the substance of the faith and the manner of expressing it;[43]

- in the acknowledgement by the Dogmatic Constitution on Divine Revelation that there can be 'development' and 'growth' in understanding the Apostolic tradition in the Church through the help of the Holy Spirit;[44]

- in the recognition of the Dogmatic Constitution on the

Church of 'legitimate differences' among particular Churches;[45]

- in the reference in the Decree on Ecumenism 'to differences in theological expressions of doctrine';[46]

- in the call which we have seen in the post-Conciliar period for inculturation;

- and lastly, did we not see already that Paul VI talked about a legitimate pluralism within the process of inculturation in his address in Kampala in 1969?

Fear of pluralism will only be fully overcome when we begin to realise that the Gospel of Christ from its birth within Judaism right up to the present is always a Gospel already inculturated in many and various cultures. The strength of the Gospel is precisely its creative capacity to co-ordinate an underlying unity within cultural diversity. After all, the fundamental thrust of the Spirit of Christ in the Church is to unify what is broken, to heal what is wounded, to gather what is scattered, and to integrate what is isolated in the world. This is how the author of the letter to the Ephesians describes the plan of God revealed in Christ as a plan to unify all things, in heaven and on earth, in Christ.[47]

On the other hand, there are limits to pluralism and the Church spells these out quite clearly. These limits require that the diversity of theological expression should be compatible with the Gospel of Christ, should promote an underlying communion within the Church and should respect the legitimate teaching role of the Church. The image that comes to mind to describe this relationship between diversity and unity is the image of the relationship between the conductor and the orchestra. The revelation of God in Christ is to cultural diversity what the conductor is to the orchestra. The source of unity within cultural and theological diversity is the person of Christ: his life, death and resurrection, and the outpouring of his Spirit upon the disciples and apostles gathered at Pentecost. Further, within the context of limits, it must be pointed out that the pluralism we are discussing here is a pluralism quite distinct from relativism. Pluralism does not necessarily mean relativism. A pluralism that is engaged in dialogue and correlation with faith is far from relativisitic; it is a pluralism seeking a centre of unity. Without some centre of unity, pluralism will lead to chaos.

The third and final challenge coming from culture to faith is the continuing challenge of modernity – which brings me back to where I started in this paper, namely, the embrace of modernity by the Church at Vatican II. There can be no doubting, no hesitating, no going back on the importance of what took place at Vatican II. The gains of this development are quite clear: the centrality of human rights, the importance of social justice, the principle of religious freedom, the development of democracy and so on. It would indeed be a strange faith and a strange Church that would not take account of the stirrings and developments of the modern world. But equally it would be a weak faith and a bloodless Church that would follow uncritically the ways of the modern world. This brings us to the central issue about the relationship between faith and culture. To what extent can the Church embrace modernity? To what extent can faith incorporate itself into the spirit and forms of modern culture?

To answer these questions, we must look once again more critically at the values and promises of modernity since the time of the Enlightenment. The age of reason must become critical of its own achievements and successes. When this happens, we begin to discover an underlying ambiguity within modernity itself. More and more commentators are pointing up the darkside of the culture of modernity.

It is one of the great ironies of the twentieth century that the cultural forces released by the Enlightenment – such as science and technology – which promised to liberate humanity, have, in fact, ended up threatening humanity.[48] To be sure, modern science and technology have brought great benefits to the world, but they have also brought at the same time some destructive consequences in their train: the exploitation of nature, the nightmarish build up of nuclear weaponry, the distortion of human communications in spite of advanced information technology, and a self-destructive consumerism. One commentator captures the dilemma quite accurately when he points out:

> Without science, technology and industrial growth we perish; but with them, it also seems, we perish.[49]

What is beginning to emerge from this brief analysis of modernity

33

is the following problem facing inculturation. At the very moment in history when the Catholic Church is reaching out to embrace the culture of modernity with all its promises, we are discovering at the same time that there is a dark and menacing side to modernity. Not only that, but the secular world is growing more and more suspicious of the so-called 'progress' promised by modernity. This, in brief, is one of the major challenges coming from modern culture to Christian faith. The way we respond to this particular expression of the problem of inculturation, I suspect, will influence our responses to all the other challenges coming from contemporary culture.

There are at least three temptations that should be avoided in dealing with this problem. The first temptation is to bypass the challenge of modernity and revert to a pre-modern classical expression of Christian faith. This approach ends up ignoring modernity in the hope that it will go away; it yearns nostalgically for a past golden age which we know never existed historically. In taking this approach, faith turns its back on the modern world and all the hard-won gains that came with modernity.

This particular temptation is one that faces Irish Catholicism at present. It has been said that the Catholic Church in Ireland over the last hundred years was so preoccupied with nationalist issues that it did not have time to face the challenges of modernity. As a result, faith in Ireland tended to be untouched by modernity. This particular diagnosis perhaps helps us to understand some of the antagonism in Ireland towards religion to-day. As the Nationalist question moves on to the larger canvas of membership in the European community, the critical spirit of modernity is now confronting a largely pre-Enlightenment faith. The result of this confrontation is a noisy clashing of cultures. It is this clash of cultures in Ireland that also helps to understand at present the unhealthy interest in fundamentalism, sects, the occult, apparitions and moving statues. A faith that has faced modernity will be less susceptible to the phenomenon of moving statues!

A second temptation facing faith is to become a purely counter-cultural force in the modern world. This particular response has some merit to it. For one thing, this response recognises what we have called the darkside of modern culture. Further, the counter-cultural response of faith brings out the important prophetic and critical dimension of Christian faith, refusing to accept the possessive individualism and consumerism that is so characteristic of modern culture. However, the problem with a counter-cultural approach is that it creates another culture, a sub-culture going back to the position of the Church before Vatican II. In effect, it refuses the challenge of inculturation, that is, the challenge to permeate contemporary culture so as to transform it, knowing that no culture is absolute or final. In particular, the counter-cultural option can all too often become 'an appeal for withdrawal from ... culture into sectarian alternative communities.'[50] When this happens, faith becomes a merely moralistic stance outlining what we are against, but rarely indicating what we stand for. Of course, it is important to protest against the modern world, to denounce the dehumanising dimensions of contemporary culture, but it is equally important to announce from within that culture what faith stands for. This annunciation must be done in the cultural forms of the day, otherwise we end up talking to ourselves.

A third temptation facing faith is to adopt a dualistic approach to modern culture. This option veers towards separating faith from reason, divorcing the divine from the human, and removing the sacred from the secular. In the end, the language and praxis of faith are spiritualised into an other-wordly domain, removed from all contact with the world.[51] When this happens, the faith in question is no longer the Christian faith which takes its point of departure from the mystery of the Incarnation – that central doctrine which affirms that the locus of God's presence is humanity and creation.

To resist these temptations is to begin to move in the difficult direction of inculturation. This means embracing the modern world in a spirit that is constructive and yet critical, that announces and denounces at one and the same time. There is no easy way around the culture of modernity. There is too much that is of lasting value within modernity, though equally there is much that is also menacing and destructive. It is only by inculturating Christian faith in the forms of modernity that we can begin to transform modernity itself of those elements which diminish human dignity.

Only then can we begin to discuss the possibility of an emerging alternative post-modern world.[52] Before this can happen, the painful encounter of faith with modernity must take place. It is our thesis that this encounter between faith and modern culture must follow the way of dialogue and inculturation opened up by Vatican II, giving rise to a critical correlation infomed by the principles of hermeneutics, and embracing at some stage within the dialogue an important moment of liberating praxis.

In the end, every act of inculturating Christian faith must involve a dying and rising, a dying to old cultural forms so so that the substance of the faith may re-appear in new cultural forms. One image that captures this process of inculturation within our changing cultures is the image of the life-cycle of flowers.[53] Flowers come and go within the creative cycle of dying and rising. Within that cycle, we should not forget that the flowers which once bloomed and have died now provide the soil from which new flowers will grow. It is just possible that at present we are in the midst of a creative dying of old cultural forms and are awaiting the rising of new cultural forms of Christian faith. Like all change, the transition is painful but the promised outcome is full of hope.

Notes

1. This broad description of culture is an amalgam taken from the UNESCO Conference on 'Cultural Policies' in 1982 and other sources.
2. C. Mooney, "Cybernation, Responsibility and Providential Design', *Theological Studies* 51 (June 1990) 287.
3. See P. Tillich 'On the Idea of the Theology of Culture' in V. Nuova, *Visionary Science: A Translation of Tillich's 'On the Idea of a Theology of Culture' with an Interpretive Essay*, Detroit: Wayne State University, 1987.
4. G. Steiner, *Real Presences*, London: Faber & Faber, 1989, p.3.
5. *Gaudium et Spes*, a. 62.
6. *Evangelii Nuntiandi*, 1975, a.19.
7. *L'Osservatore Romano*, 28 June, 1982, pp.1-8.
8. It should be noted that the term inculturation came into use in the late 'sixties and early 'seventies to describe the proper relationship between faith and culture. It was used in particular by the Jesuit General, Pedro Arrupe, in an important letter to the Society of Jesus.
9. Henri de Lubac, 'Causes Internes de l'Attentuation et de la Disparition du Sens du Sacré', *Théologie dans l'Histoire: II Questions Disputées et Résistance au Nazisme*, Paris: Desclée de Brouwer, 1990, p. 19-21.
10. H.R. Niebuhr, *Christ and Culture*, New York: Harper Torchbooks, 1951.
11. Gabriel Daly, 'Catholicism and Modernity', *Journal of the American Academy of Religion*, L111/3 (1985), p.777.
12. J. Komonchak, 'The Enlightenment and the Construction of Roman Catholicism', *The Annual of the Catholic Commission on Intellectual and Cultural Affairs*, 1985, pp. 47-48.
13. A more systematic account can be found in A Shorter, *Towards a Theology of Inculturation*, London: Chapman, 1988, pp. 177–238.
14. Quotation taken from Y. Congar, *Diversity and Communion*, London: S.C.M. Press, 1984, p. 189, or *La Documentation Catholique*, 51, 16 Sept. 1969, p. 756.
15. Ibid.
16. 'Mysterium Ecclesiae' in *Vatican Council II: More Post-Conciliar Documents*, A. Flannery (ed.), Dublin: Dominican Publications, 1962, pp. 428-440.
17. *Evangelii Nuntiandi*, a. 20.
18. *Evangelii Nuntiandi*, a.63.
19. *Catechesi Tradendae*, a. 53.
20. e.g. John Paul II, *Slavorum Apostoli, Apostles of the Slavs*, 1985; Address in the Cameroon, *L'Osservatore Romano*, 9 Sept. 1985.
21. *L'Osservatore Romano*, 28 June 1982, pp. 1-8.

22. *Centesimus Annus*, 1991, a. 50.
23. See, for example, articles 4, 5, 36 and 62.
24. *Dei Verbum*, a. 2.
25. *Synod Report, 1985*, D.4. The same point is reiterated in the 1986 *Instruction on Christian Freedom and Liberation*, from the Congregation for the Doctrine of the Faith, a. 96.
26. See, e.g. *Evangelii Nuntiandi*, a. 18; 'Dialogue and Proclamation' by the Pontifical Council for Interreligious Dialogue, *Origins*, 4 July 1991, a. 46.
27. AFER, vol. 22, no. 4, August 1980, 198.
28. E. Schillebeeckx, *Interim Report on the Books 'Jesus' and 'Christ'*, London: S.C.M. Press, 1980, p. 128.
29. See P. Tillich's essay, 'Über die Idee einer Theologie der Kultur (1919)', recently put out in a new English translation by Victor Nuovo, *Visionary Science: A Translation of Tillich's 'On the Idea of a Theology of Culture', with an Interpretive Essay*, Detroit: Wayne University Press, 1987.
30. *Gaudium et Spes*, a. 5.
31. See D. Tracy, 'The Uneasy Alliance Reconceived: Catholic Theological Method, Modernity, and Post-Modernity', *Theological Studies* 50 (Sept. 1989), p. 562-563.
32. D. Tracy, *Plurality and Ambiguity: Hermeneutics, Religion and Hope*, San Francisco: Harper & Row, 1987, p. 10.
33. See W. Jeanrond, *Theological Hermeneutics: Developments and Significance*, London: Macmillan, 1991.
34. For further elaboration of these considerations, see M. Lamb, *Solidarity with Victims*, New York: Crossroads, 1982; D. Lane, *Foundations for a Social Theology: Praxis, Process and Salvation*, Dublin: Gill & Macmillan, 1984.
35. Traces of this can be found in L. Gilkey 'Plurality and Its Theological Implications', *The Myth of Christian Uniqueness*, J. Hick and P. Knitter (eds.), London: S.C.M., 1987.
36. *Plurality and Ambiguity*, p. 107.
37. See D. Lane 'D. Tracy and the Debate about Praxis', *Radical Pluralism and Truth: David Tracy and the Hermeneutics of Religion*, W. G. Jeanrond and J. L. Rike (eds.), New York: Crossroad, 1991, pp. 18-37
38. *Pour l'avènement de la femme*, 1980.
39. S.M. Schneiders, *Beyond Patching: Faith and Feminism in the Catholic Church*, New York: Paulist Press, 1991, p. 4.
40. See John Paul II, *The Dignity of Women*, 1988, a. 1; *Christifidelis*, 1988, a. 50.
41. Paul VI, *Marialis Cultus*, 1974, a. 36.

42. See *Gaudium et Spes*, a. 42; *Evangelii Nuntiandi*, a. 20.
43. See *Gaudium et Spes*, a. 62.
44. *Dei Verbum*, a. 8.
45. *Lumen Gentium*, a. 13.
46. U.R., a. 17.
47. Eph 1:9-11.
48. E. Schillebeeckx, *Church: The Human Story of God*, London: S.C.M., 1989, p. 2-3.
49. L. Gilkey, 'Theology of Culture and Christian Ethics' in *Through the Tempest: Theological Voyages in a Pluralistic Culture*, J.B. Pool (ed.), Minneapolis: Fortress Press, 1991, p. 150.
50. J. Coleman, 'Inculturation and Evangelisation in the North American context', *Proceedings of the Catholic Theological Society of America*, 1990, p. 27.
51. See R. Haughton, 'Belief and Culture', *In All Things: Religious Faith and American Culture*, R.J. Daly (ed.), Missouri: Sheed & Ward, 1990, pp. 156-178.
52. For an outline of the shape and structure of a post-modern world, see D. Lane, *Foundations for a Social Theology: Praxis, Process and Salvation*, pp. 94-100.
53. This image has been taken from R. Haughton, art.cit.

The Shapeless God of Israel:
An exploration of the
aniconic tradition of biblical religion

William Riley

FROM AN ICONIC PERSPECTIVE

Pompey in the Holy of Holies

In the year 63 B.C., after subduing the nation of Judaea in an action that marked the end of Israelite autonomy for centuries to come, the conquering general Pompey committed an act which would have been considered unspeakable to any of the populace which he had just subdued: he entered the Holy of Holies of the Jerusalem Temple, a place which only the High Priest could enter in post-exilic religion, and then only during the solemn rites of the Day of Atonement.

What he found there was a chamber void of sacred images; on this point, both Jewish and Roman authors agree.[1] The deeper question is what did Pompey expect to find. Those who adhered to the faith of Israel were quite explicit that an image of their God was not to be fashioned through human art. However, this concept of a god without image or idol was so strange and outlandish to people in the Hellenistic culture that many thought that the Jews must be saying that they had no statue of their god because they had something to hide. Perhaps the studied remoteness of that inmost chamber in the Jerusalem Temple helped to fire the pagan imagination: what could be so shameful an image of God that Jews preferred to concoct a preposterous story of a god without shape or form? To those who thought about it, the conclusion was obvious: Israel worshipped its deity in the shape of an ass's head. The theory went further than that, of course, since no one, not even a Jew, would freely choose the ass as a symbol of God. The reason was historical: when the Israelites were coming out of Egypt and crossing the desert, they were dying of thirst, but an ass led them to an oasis and saved their lives, and so it became the image of Israel's god.

It was a good rumour. It explained mysterious behaviour and showed a whole nation in a bad light. It demonstrated some basic acquaintance with Israel's history. It was such a good rumour that it was barely touched by Pompey's discovery,[2] and even after it had served for centuries its anti-Semitic purposes, it was transferred (as many anti-Jewish rumours were) to the Christians.[3] The lie was believable, the truth was incredible.

Pompey's surprised discovery in the Holy of Holies illustrates a tension between the biblical religion of Israel and the wider Hellenistic culture in which Israel existed. In many respects, Israel accommodated Hellenism in terms of architecture, education and even language,[4] but on the point of portraying God in painting or sculpture there could be no compromise. This in itself poses an interesting point in the important theme which has been taken for this Jubilee Lecture series, that of Religion and Culture in dialogue, for although biblical religion has been influenced by various cultural factors coming to it from the wider world, on this point it seems to draw a line beyond which the influence of culture cannot go. The stubbornness of the aniconic or imageless tradition of biblical religion was incomprehensible and even offensive to those of other cultural and religious traditions; to both the Israelite and the non-Israelite, it provided a strong statement in its time and place which is worth exploring to see its possible implications for modern Christians.

Idols in the Pagan World

The commandment which framed Israel's rejection of representing the Deity by physical image is to be found in the Decalogue in words usually omitted from the abbreviated form in which we learn the Ten Commandments:

> 'You shall not make for yourself a carved image or any fashioning of that which is in the sky above, or the earth below or in the seas under the earth. You shall not make yourself bow down to them and you shall not serve them for I, Yahweh your God, am a jealous God visiting an ancestral sin on children of the third and fourth generation of those who hate me, but

> enacting steadfast love to the thousandth generation of those
> that love me and keep my commands.' [5]

Neither the wording nor the context of the commandment allows a conclusive argument to be made as to whether the prohibition on images was originally intended to refer to the worship of foreign deities or to the representation of the God of Israel – although the latter seems the more likely.[6] In any event, biblical religion soon embraced both prohibitions and rejected equally the claim of anything manufactured within or without Yahwism to represent godhood. Both prohibitions created a conscious rift between Israel and the religious atmosphere which surrounded it. In order to appreciate such a rift, it is necessary to investigate briefly the place and value of idols to Israel's neighbours.

Reading the Hebrew Scriptures might produce the feeling that there was a simple equation to be made between pagan gods and the idols made to represent them. Better knowledge of Egyptian and Mesopotamian cultures in particular have enabled us to see such an equation as a misrepresentation of the official theologies of these great civilisations. However, if we were then to conclude that the idol functioned primarily as a simple representation of the god, even primarily as a representation which had been dedicated exclusively for the purposes of public and private liturgies, then we might be making a mistake in the opposite direction.

Since ancient Near Eastern civilisations were notably lacking in systematic theologians, it can be difficult to discern the precise nature of the belief which underpinned the religions of these ancient superpowers. However, religious texts abound and sometimes give us insights into ancient beliefs as they were expressed in myth and ritual. One such Egyptian text is 'The Theology of Memphis ',[7] the original of which dates to the middle of the Third Millenium B.C., a period in which biblical texts and biblical scholars were even more scarce than systematicians! Perhaps surprisingly in a text so ancient, and one with a clear propagandising purpose at that,[8] the modern reader discerns a picture of the creator god Ptah which conveys immanence while carefully preserving the separate existence of the deity:

> he is in every body and in every mouth of all gods, all men,
> [all] cattle, all creeping things, and (everything) that lives, by
> thinking and commanding everything that he wishes. [9]

The text is of interest to our theme, for Ptah's work continued with the creation of temples and idols for each god. The *ka* of each god (that is, the spiritual part of beings which requires an image, form or body in which to exist) then took up residence in the idols:

> So the gods entered into their bodies of every (kind of) wood, of every (kind of) stone, of every (kind of) clay, or anything else which might grow upon [Ptah], in which they had taken form.[10]

The thinking with which we are brought face to face by 'The Theology of Memphis' might be summarised in this way: the gods are given existence by their creation by Ptah, but only in the creation of idols by Ptah do they receive the form which their *ka*'s require. One might also notice that the divine image is not the manufactured product of human endeavour; it is no less than the divine creation of Ptah.

'The Theology of Memphis' may speak of idols as divine creations, but other Egyptian texts attribute the fashioning of cultic images to the king.[11] A similar picture emerges from Mesopotamian texts which speak of the idols as clearly of human origin and kings could boast of having provided them for their gods;[12] but texts which give instructions to the Mesopotamian 'Mouth Washing' ritual demonstrate that mere human manufacture did not do justice to idols in the eyes of their devotees. The 'Mouth Washing' ritual transformed the image from being a finished product of human processes into being an idol fit for cultic use. After various rites conducted in the workshop where the idol was made, the artisans swore one by one that their counterparts among the gods had done the work on the idol and that they themselves really had no part in its fashioning. Incantations were made to restore the tree from which the wood was taken to its former stature, thus denying that the idol benefited from terrestrial resources. The statue was brought to the river bank where the tools which had been used in its manufacture were thrown into the river, returning them to the god Ea, and rituals involving the life-giving waters enacted the process of bringing the idol to birth. Further incantations followed which, together with the ritual of opening the idol's mouth that also occurred at this point, were intended to enable the idol to walk, open its eyes, smell incense, eat food and drink liquid – in short, to perform all of the functions which would be required of the god in its liturgical role. This ritual acknowledged that the god has a separate existence from the idol since the god was admonished to 'Tarry not in heaven', but the image was more than mere representation. It became, for its devotees, a living means by which the god could benefit from, and respond to, the human worship for which the idol was fashioned.[13]

What comes across from these brief glances of ancient Near Eastern religions is that the idols were meant to be far more than mere human fashionings; they represented a powerful living presence of the god whose effective presence to worshippers depended in large part upon the idol. As living presence, Egyptian idols took part in ancient mystery plays[14] and the idols of Mesopotamia and Aram moved in procession, engaged in the rites of sacred marriages and even paid visits to one another in their temple homes;[15] Ugaritic texts indicate that the same was true of the idols of Canaan.[16]

The ancient Near Eastern idols were treated as persons in many respects. They were invited, even enticed, to enter their temple dwellings.[17] Once in residence, the Egyptian idol was awakened and given breakfast,[18] and its Mesopotamian counterparts were supplied with a carefully stipulated supply of food. The gods of Uruk had voracious appetites; after putting away no less than eighteen rams, a large bull and a bullock, they still had room for a second morning meal of only twelve rams, one large bull, eight lambs, seven ducks, three cranes, four boars, fifty assorted birds and a half dozen eggs. Two relatively lighter meals were also provided in the evening. And, as if the quantity did not provide sufficient problems for those in charge of preparing the divine cuisine, some of Uruk's gods displayed an unexpected fastidiousness in what could be served: Shakkan could not be offered ram's meat, Harru would not touch bull's meat and the goddess Beletseri was not interested in fowl. The goddess Ereshkigal was nearly anorexic by the standards of the Uruk pantheon; she would look at neither beef nor poultry, leaving her little more than rams to sustain her.[19]

From this brief and patchy survey of evidence drawn from different cultures and even from different millenia, it is clear that Israel was rejecting a part of religious culture that was central to the religion of Israel's ancient Near Eastern neighbours and this continued to puzzle those who came into contact with Israel from the wider Hellenistic world.[20] This is all the more striking given Israel's willingness to accept other elements which were common to ancient Near Eastern religions such as priesthood, festival, temple, sacrifice and prophecy, to name but a few.

FROM THE ISRAELITE PERSPECTIVE

The fact that biblical religion rejected idols – whether of Yahweh or of other deities – is evident from a number of texts and has been identified as one of the few certain characteristic tenets of Yahwism.[21] There can be little doubt that the prohibition considerably antedates the texts which have come down to us; this leaves the modern investigator in the unhappy position of being unable to isolate the original reason for the prohibition. However, the material which we do have is considerable and represents the mature reflection on this prohibition, upholding it in the face both of Israel's attraction towards graven images and of other nations' inability to understand Israel's seemingly irreligious stance.

Idols in the Life of Pre-Exilic Israel

Of course, the question must be asked of how well Israel adhered to the prohibition on idols. Textual evidence from the Hebrew Bible would lead us to believe that the prohibition was not very closely adhered to at all in the pre-exilic religion. Thus, to cite but a few examples, Solomon worshipped the gods of his wives from Sidon, Moab and Ammon,[22] a temple to Baal – complete with idols – existed in Jerusalem under Queen Athaliah,[23] and Manasseh takes the biblical prize for a Judaean king engaging in the worship of idols.[24] The heart-broken description of the Jerusalem Temple in the last years before its destruction by the Babylonians to be found in Ezekiel is filled with strange cults and idols at the very centre of Yahwistic worship.[25] But those examples all have one thing in common: they all show Israel's pre-exilic interest in *foreign* deities; these examples have little to say about whether Israel ever portrayed Yahweh.

Textual evidence on that subject is not lacking either. The out-standing examples are related: the Pentateuchal account of Aaron's fashioning of the golden calf in Exod 32:1-6 and the Deut-eronomist's narrative in 1 Kgs 12:28-30 of Jeroboam's establish-ment of two shrines, each with its golden calf. In both instances, Israel is told in nearly identical words that the calf represents 'your gods, Israel, who brought you out of the land of Egypt.'[26] But the quest-ion remains whether the narratives show Aaron and Jeroboam as daring to represent Yahweh or as introducing new deities. On the one hand, the unambiguous plural for gods should probably be seen as implying new deities,[27] yet the procla-mation of a feast for Yahweh centred around the idol implies that it is intended as a representation of Yahweh.[28] Since most scholars agree that both narratives are part of a polemic against the North-ern Kingdom and its Yahwism,[29] some clarification should emerge when we situate them in that context.

Both of these stories are in harmony with the Southern Kingdom's disapproval of Northern religious practice. Whereas Jerusalem had piously preserved the aniconic tradition through its indica-tion of Yahweh's presence by supplying the cherubim throne of the Ark with no visible representation on it, faithless Samaria had defied basic principles of Yahwism by portraying the deity as a golden calf, just as the ancestors had done during the desert wan-derings – or so the Judaean perspective would have it. The more common explanation among scholars today is that Samaria, far from trying to make an image of Yahweh, was – like its southern counterpart – providing Yahweh with a pedestal to indicate the divine presence, (albeit in a way that may indicate some influence from the Baal cultus).[30] The fact that such uncompromising Yah-wists as Elijah and Elisha did not seem to find the shrines at Bethel and Dan offensive are an indication that the golden calves did not violate any aniconic sensitivity for them, just as non-divine imag-es of bulls and cherubim posed no problems for orthodox wor-shippers in the Jerusalem Temple.

The connection between the Jeroboam story and the Aaron narra-tive is more intriguing. On the one hand, the Aaron narrative may be an attempt to see the idolatrous tendency of the Northern tribes as stretching back to the time of the nation's very origins.

However, in that case one would expect to find something in the text which refers this act of religious rebellion to the Northern tribes alone, and no such limitation exists. A more plausible explanation can be found if the Aaron narrative is seen to have a foundation older than its Pentateuchal casting: its core may be a tradition which saw in the golden calves at Bethel and Dan sacred objects which, like the Ark or the Bronze Serpent, dated back to the Exodus itself.[31] The form of the story as we have it in Exodus would then be a Southern acknowledgement of the Northern tradition, but retold in a pejorative light. That pejorative light was justified by the abuse of these images, to which Hosea may bear witness,[32] and by a syncretic confusion between Baal and Yahweh in the minds of the Northern worshippers. [33]

The major evidence for the visual representation of Yahweh in official (i.e., royal) shrines thus seems to be polemical rather than historical,[34] and allows the generalisation that official Yahwism was true to its prohibition of the visual representation of Yahweh. This generalisation cannot be extended to unofficial cultic sites[35] nor to the mixture of foreign gods with the worship of Yahweh,[36] but still provides a powerful testimony to the importance of visual shapelessness in Israel's approach to the Deity. It is equally notable that, although the Hebrew Bible recognises that idols sometimes appeared in connection with the Yahweh cult as representations of various non-Yahwistic deities, such idols were uncompromisingly rejected by biblical religion at least from the time of the prophets onwards. The religion of the Hebrew Bible must therefore be distinguished from both the popular religion of the people which was often to be found in operation at the high places and the religion of monarchy and priesthood as it was manifested in the pre-exilic Jerusalem Temple.

Post-Exilic Perspectives on Idolatry
Yahwism did not hold to its aniconic principles in Stoic silence. Instead, Israel lashed out at the practice of portraying deities and the deities thus portrayed with vigour and contempt. The Scriptures of Israel contain far too many examples to enumerate here,[37] but it is worthwhile noting that some of the more elaborate examples date to the Exile and after, a period in which Israel seems to have terminated much of its former experimentation with

idols. Deutero-Isaiah, surely one of the most accomplished theologians in the Hebrew Bible, paints a simple picture of the folly of the idol-maker who kindles a fire with half a block of wood and yet worships the other half as his idol,[38] and taunts those whose idols are so powerless that they must be carried around.[39] But implicitly contrasted with the useless idol is the God who creates[40] and foretells[41] and causes to be,[42] but especially the God who remains hidden and yet accessible to all through his utterance.[43] There was even a place in the post-exilic cultus for singing the praises of Yahweh through a contrast of his power with the uselessness of the eyes, noses, ears, throats, mouths, hands, and feet of idols, as is evidenced by Ps 115.[44]

The deuterocanonical material contains interesting pieces related to idols. The Letter of Jeremiah, which appears in our Bibles as the sixth chapter of Baruch, takes up the theme of the powerlessness of idols and also contains glimpses of the senseless feeding and clothing of idols[45] and of priestly corruption.[46] All of the concerns of the Letter of Jeremiah are taken up in story form in the first narrative of Bel and the Dragon, which appears as chapter fourteen of Daniel. In this charming tale, Daniel shows King Cyrus that Bel (the Babylonian Marduk) does not in fact consume the twelve bushels of flour, forty sheep and fifty gallons of wine presented to him daily, but that the priests and their families steal this nightly for their own use. Bel is not only proved to be lifeless and powerless, but handed over to Daniel who destroys both idol and temple.

The most elaborate treatment of idolatry is contained in the Book of Wisdom at the very threshold of the New Testament era. The author of this work not only presents the usual picture of the senselessness of idol-making,[47] but even ponders the origins of this strange phenomenon of idolatry – perhaps it all started with a grieving parent who wishes to remember a deceased child,[48] perhaps it was a community which wished to honour a far off ruler.[49] Most illuminating of all the material related to idols in this Hellenistic Jewish work is the connection which the book explicitly makes between the false imaging of God and the false standards of morality:

Then it was not enough to be mistaken about the knowledge of God,
But, living in a great battle of ignorance,
They speak of such evils as peace...
They do not yet keep either their lives or marriages pure,
But either lie in ambush to bear each other off or injure one another through adultery.
Everything is mixed together - blood and murder,
Theft and treachery, corruption, faithlessness, sedition, perjury,
Confusion about good things, forgetfulness of kindness,
Defilement of minds, sexual perversion,
Disorder in marriages, adultery and licentiousness.
For the veneration of idols that should not be named
Is the beginning and cause and goal of every evil thing.[50]

The theme, of course, is familiar, and was used by St Paul (who may well have been acquainted with the Book of Wisdom) to great effect in Rom 1:23-32, and also, in a somewhat different sense, by the rabbis.[51] Wherever its ultimate origin is to be located, the connection between idolatry (which is necessarily a false imaging of the Deity) and immoral living is one that goes to the very heart of the biblical vision. To rephrase the insight which Wisdom and the Letter to the Romans share, we could say that these Scriptures from the Hellenistic world assert that pagan religion has indeed influenced culture, but all to the bad: a false theology has produced a false culture; one can test the theology of a people by examining the ethos which it effects among them.

PUTTING SHAPE ON THE SHAPELESS GOD

The intolerance of our own age for engaging in a critique of the belief or morality of others makes it difficult to appreciate how the author of Wisdom – or St Paul, for that matter – can connect immoral living with a false notion of God. But this connection can be traced even further to the dynamism that characterises biblical religion.

Still, one must express some sympathy with those who yearned for a visual representation of the Deity. For some people, it can be one of the most difficult aspects of faith that no comprehensible image, visual or otherwise, can contain the Godhead. John Cassian tells a story which illustrates this difficulty graphically. During his visits to the Egyptian hermits in Scete at the turn of the fifth century, Cassian was unfortunate enough to land in the midst of a theological wrangle between the Bishop of Alexandria and the hermits. The bishop had used the occasion of the Epiphany letter announcing the dates of Lent and Easter to denounce the heresy of the Anthropomorphites that God has a physical body. The hermits were incensed, accused the bishop of heretical novelties and prevented the letter being read in most of the churches of Scete. A visiting theologian was enlisted by the priest of one church to explain the truth of the matter. He must have been very learned indeed, for he finally convinced the ring-leader, one Abba Sarapion, to consent to orthodox belief. To use Cassian's own words, the priest

> ...and the rest of us felt great joy at his assent; joy that the Lord had not allowed a man of such age and goodness, who had erred in simple ignorance, to end his days unorthodox in the faith.

> When we stood up to give thanks to the Lord in prayer, the old man felt mentally bewildered at having to pray, because he could no longer sense in his heart the anthropomorphic image of God which he had always before his mind's eye when praying. Suddenly he broke into bitter weeping and sobbing, and throwing himself prostrate on the ground with groans, cried: 'Woe is me! They have taken my God away from me, and I have none to grasp, and I know not whom to adore or to address.'[52]

One must pity Sarapion as he takes that painful first step on the long road of the *via negativa* – the acknowledgement that every human concept about God is ultimately inadequate, a road that might well have begun in the imageless tradition of Israel. Yet the *via negativa* intersects at many points with the *via positiva* – the concession that even our inadequate statements express *something* about God and that our nature demands that faith be given even such inadequate expression.[52a]

Linguistic Imaging

Both *via negativa* and *via positiva* may come together in Israel's naming of God. Even though much research has gone into the name Yahweh, scholarship generally admits that 'a confident etymology of the divine name cannot be given',[53] and so we cannot be certain about its original meaning. The name is generally seen in light of the statement 'I am who I am' in Ex 3:14 and thus would be translated as 'He who is'. But even here there are difficulties.[54] It should be noted in the context of our topic that the statement in Ex 3:14 does not sound like the giving of a name; it sounds rather like the refusal to answer an impudent demand to know the name of God! One is left with the impression that the name of God is meant to be enigmatic, perhaps embodying an acknowledgement of humanity's limitations in probing the depths of the divine.[55]

On linguistic grounds, a different approach to the meaning of the divine name commends itself: it can represent a causative form and thus mean 'The One who causes to be' or 'The One who causes to happen'.[56] A non-linguistic argument for this dynamic naming of God can also be found in Ex 3; when Moses questions the divine call, God offers him the sign that 'when you have brought the people out of Egypt, you will serve God on this mountain'; the only sign God is offering that Moses will lead the people to freedom will be after the fact – God gets things done!

The power and the danger of naming the divinity, even by a name revealed by none other than the Deity, was later expressed in the near total prohibition on even pronouncing the divine name. The same was not true of other verbal images of God. Anyone familiar with the psalms recognises that God is spoken of through a wide range of images such as rock,[57] fortress,[58] water,[59] the sun,[60] a winged being,[61] a father[62] – yet to sing or shout any of these was not felt to be as perilous as whispering the divine name itself.

Which is not to say that verbal and mental images of God were thought to be without their dangers – quite the opposite! Two of the most attractive literary productions in the Hebrew Bible, the tragedy of Job and the comedy of Jonah, could be said to revolve precisely around the disaster that can result from such imaging of God. In the case of Job, the sin of the three friends lies in their distorted and manufactured image of God. But Jonah is a different matter, for he is clearly a theologian of some competence whose mistake is to feel that – because he has grasped his image of God (and he can even give scriptural justification for that image) – he has in some way comprehended the mystery of God. [63]

'Knowing' God

Long before Job and Jonah were written, Hosea struggled in a morass of faulty images of God. Perhaps this is what gives the Book of Hosea its striking concern with 'knowing' Yahweh.[64] Any reader of the book will recognise that Hosea's anguish is not caused by religious indifference, but by religious fervour – a plague of religiosity had infected Hosea's people. In response, the prophet insisted on fixing religious attention firmly on the true God rather than on the false images which were being passed off as Yahweh in the popular religion. Rejecting a 'knowledge' of God that consists simply in form and ritual, knowledge of a god who could be predicted and manipulated,[65] Hosea makes it clear that authentic knowledge of God is nothing less than faithfulness and covenant love expressed in the keeping of the commandments.[66] Knowledge of God in this prophetic book is not intellectual, cultic or mystical; only the experiential has any claim to being true knowledge of God, and the only sure route to the experiential knowledge of God is living the covenant.

Hosea's hearers do not seem to have rallied to his call. After all, it was more fun to celebrate feasts, offer sacrifice and engage in fertility rituals than to keep the commandments in the eighth century B.C., just as talking about theology can seem more appealing than the living of theology at the turn of the twenty-first century A.D. Yet Hosea did make his mark, and that mark imprinted itself forcefully in the Christian Scriptures of the New Testament, as we shall see presently.

Humanity as the Image of God

But first, a familiar text is beckoning. One can not consider the question of the aniconic tradition of Israel without making reference to Gen 1:26 which speaks of humanity being created in the image of God. The translation which is most generally used in the liturgy (*Jerusalem Bible*) echoes a long tradition of translation in rendering the relevant phrase as 'Let us make man in our own im-

age, in the likeness of ourselves'; a more literal translation might
read: 'Let us make humanity in our image as our likeness'.[67] The
language of this passage could be dangerous, for the Hebrew
words used incline the reader to think in terms of a physical image. In a later time, this was to be the very passage in which the
Anthropomorphites of Egypt thought that they had found their
basic biblical justification; it could even have been the passage
which had inspired the heresy. The connection between humanity
and the image of the Deity did not originate in this passage, of
course. Israel's neighbours often made idols in human form and
told stories of their gods which reveal that this was the basic way
in which gods were thought to exist.[68] The context of the passage
in Genesis makes it clear that physical (or even spiritual)
resemblance to God was not intended; rather, humanity stands as
the image of God in authority over creation.[69]

Something interesting happens to this term in the New Testament. St. Paul shows that he is familiar with the language from
the first creation narrative which speaks of humanity as the image
of God.[70] But the image of God really finds its authentic human
expression for Paul in Christ, 'who is the image of God',[71] or,
more elaborately in the Letter to the Colossians, 'who is the image
of God Unseen, firstborn of all creation'.[72] According to Paul's
theology, Christ as image of God has the creational role of being
the model for humanity's more authentic re-creation in the divine
image, in the eschaton certainly,[73] but more immediately in the
present through a continuing process of change.[74] In the Letter to
the Colossians, the Christ event is seen to have radically altered
human creaturehood; as in First Corinthians, creation must be divided into the purely natural old creation and the new creation
which takes place in Christ.[75] In the Letter to the Colossians, the
primary effects of this are in the here and now: we live according
to the new nature which is in the image of the creator.[76] Humanity's title of 'image of God' has thus been interpreted as being
chiefly a moral title which has only been fully realised in Christ –
the new model for a new humanity.[77] To some extent, the shapeless God of Israel has taken shape for Paul in Christ and the question of imaging God has long ceased to be the question of how God
is to be pictured in art or spoken of in metaphors; the central

concern for imaging God is how to become the living images of God by patterning ourselves on Christ.

The First Letter of John

As one might expect, idols were still as repulsive to Paul the Christian as they had been to Saul the Pharisee.[78] However, it is none of the Pauline correspondence but rather the First Letter of John which contains the resounding warning: 'Little children, be on your guard against idols!'[79] and which places this warning as a concluding crescendo to the entire letter. The conclusion might strike the reader of this epistle as somewhat odd, given the fact that nowhere else in the letter is there any indication that pagan worship had been a particular problem for the community for which this letter was written.

However, the First Letter of John does demonstrate a keen interest in the knowing of God. This interest arises in part from what the author's opponents have been saying as they sow discord, doubt and falsehood among the community. Even though we cannot form a perfect picture of what these troublemakers believed and preached, the letter quotes and refutes enough of their claims and catchphrases to allow us to have some idea. They claimed that they had no sin;[80] they claimed to live in God[81] and to be illumined by the light;[82] they denied the traditional faith in Jesus as Messiah and Son of God come in the flesh;[83] they claimed to love God even though they showed a distinct lack of love for other Christians.[84] And, of course, they claimed to know God.[85]

The opponents' claim to know God seems to have particularly annoyed the author of First John, for the letter stresses who and what we as Christians know. Perhaps the author saw the turmoil and self-doubt that the easy, self-assured gospel of the opponents caused among individuals and groups in the community and wanted to respond by giving his community the assurance that they had something worth holding onto. The argument contained in the letter is lengthy, well constructed, wonderfully pastoral in its tone and concern, and not without its subtleties. Yet it would be true to the letter to summarise the argument in a few words: knowing God always shows itself in one certain way – the person who knows God keeps the commandments, the one who knows and loves God loves all other Christians.[86]

The warning against idols now falls into place. Unlike Paul, the First Letter of John does not have to concern itself with statues of carved stone or cast metal. Instead, the idols are far more insidious; the idols are false teachings and false claims about God which distract from the only true routes to experiencing God[87] – through Jesus and through the special ἀγάπη which characterises the Christian community, the ἀγάπη which is exemplified in the life of Jesus.[88]

Even though Pauline theology and Johannine theology are quite distinct in many respects, on this question we can note a certain convergence which we have also seen in Hosea. The human tendency to portray God in wood, stone, precious metal or philosophical abstraction can be ultimately misleading, for God cannot be adequately represented or captured by any of these means. 'No one has ever gazed upon God', as First John wisely reminds us.[89] But still, God is truly known by those who keep the commandments and follow Jesus' example of love.

Conclusion
Because it drew a limit to the effect that culture could have on religion, the aniconic tradition of Israel was often viewed as a quirk and an oddity, but it has had a profound and valuable effect on our religious awareness as twentieth century Christians. Israel's refusal to accept any definitive physical representation of God allowed biblical religion to embrace a wide range of verbal images to speak of God and to relate to God, yet with the constant insistence that the Deity is always more than any image that humanity can devise or utter. Because of their inherent limitations, every verbal image has the potential to become an idol when it pretends to capture even a large part of the essential mystery of God in comprehensible language. And so biblical religion moves its adherents away from a puny and distant God who can be captured by human artistry or human philosophy, deflating the arrogance of human statements about God with the insistent reminder of Exodus 3:14, 'I am who I am', and with many indications that God does not feel bound either by the statements of theologians or by the expectations of worshippers! Having abandoned the gods of idols and abstractions, of superstitions and sophistications, we

have some hope of coming to the God of human experience. We might even hear afresh the challenge of the biblical tradition: to know God through the covenant, to become the image of God by conforming to the example of Christ, to put shape with our own human lives on the shapeless God of Israel.

Notes

1. Tacitus, *Hist.* 5.9. A fragment of Livy's lost account of Pompey's Syrian campaign probably reflects this incident as well: 'They do not state to which of the gods the Temple at Jerusalem belongs nor is there any image there, for they do not think that the God has any shape.' (Quoted in M. Whittaker, *Jews and Christians: Graeco-Roman Views* (CCWJCW 6, Cambridge: Cambridge University Press, 1984), p. 124. Josephus does not state (as Tacitus does) that Pompey entered the Holy of Holies, probably for apologetic reasons, but does mention the entry into the Temple and the lack of religious image; cf. *Ant.* 14.4.4.

2. Although Tacitus relates the story of Pompey entering the Holy of Holies and discovering nothing, he still holds to vestiges of the image of the ass; see *Hist.* 5.3-4 which gives the fact of the statue and its existence in the Jerusalem Temple (as well as 5.5 which denies the existence of any statue at all in the Temple). In his apologetic efforts, Josephus had to acknowledge and refute the wide-spread story of the idol of an ass; cf. *Apion* 2.7.

3. This is most graphically demonstrated by the early third century graffito from the Paedagogium on the Palatine, and now in the Palatine Museum. Cf. J. Finegan, *Light from the Ancient Past*, 2 (Princeton: Princeton University Press, 1959), p. 373. The third-century apologist Minucius Felix has his pagan spokesperson Caecilius allude to the rumour in stating: 'I am told that under some foolish persuasion [the Christians] worship the consecrated head of a filthy animal.' (*Octavius* 9, translated in M. Whittaker, *Jews and Christians: Graeco-Roman Views*, p. 174.)

4. A survey of evidence for both the primary and secondary use of Greek in the Jewish communities of Palestine can be found in J. A. Fitzmeyer, 'The Languages of Palestine', CBQ 32 (1970), pp. 501-531, and in M. Hengel, *The 'Hellenization' of Judaea in the First Century after Christ* (translated by J. Bowden, London: SCM, 1989), pp. 7-18.

5. Ex 20:4-6 (| | Dt 5:8-10). The prohibition against carved images is to be found elsewhere in the legal traditions, notably in the parallel narration of the covenant in Ex 34 ('You shall not make cast gods'

– Ex 34:17) and in the curses of Dt 27 ('Cursed be each one who makes a carved image or a casting, an abomination to Yahweh, the work of an artisan's hands, and who sets it up in secret' – Dt 27:15; the phrase *to'aboth Yhwh* which has been translated as 'an abomination to Yahweh' might also be translated as 'an abomination of Yahweh').

6. The original form of the commandment probably read simply: 'You shall not make for yourself a carved image', the remainder being a later expansion. In this case, the singular (seen also in Dt 27:15) should be seen as referring to the attempt to represent Yahweh whereas the plural of Ex 34:17 or Lv 19:4 most likely referred primarily to foreign deities. Cf. W. Zimmerli, *Old Testament Theology in Outline* (English translation, Edinburgh: T. & T. Clark, 1978), p. 120, and J. P. Hyatt, *Exodus* (NCBC, London: Marshall, Morgan and Scott, 1980), p. 211.

7. Translated by J. A. Wilson in *Ancient Near Eastern Texts Relating to the Old Testament* (henceforth *ANET*, edited by J. B. Pritchard, third edition with supplement, Princeton: Princeton University Press, 1969) pp. 4-6.

8. The text seems to have been composed to give Memphis's god Ptah a suitable prominence in the Egyptian hierarchy after Memphis had assumed its position as capital of Egypt. S. H. Hooke, *Middle Eastern Mythology* (Harmondsworth, Middlesex: Penguin, 1963), pp. 72-73.

9. *ANET*, p. 5.

10. Ibid.

11. This is illustrated by the text translated by J. A. Wilson, 'Tut-ankh-Amon's Restoration after the Amarna Revolution', *ANET*, pp. 251-252, which boasts that, among the king's other achievements, 'He fashioned his father Amon upon thirteen carrying-poles, his holy image being of fine gold, lapis lazuli, [turquoise], and every august costly stone...He fashioned Ptah, South-of-His-Wall, Lord of Life of the Two Lands, his august image being of fine gold, [upon] eleven [carrying-poles]...Then his majesty made monuments for the gods, [fashioning] their cult-statues of genuine fine gold from the highlands...' The stela inscription concludes that such activity was the very purpose of Tut-ankh-Amon's creation: 'He [Amon] fashioned him in order that He (Himself) might be fashioned.'

12. Cf., e.g., the accomplishments of Samuditana in this regard cited in A. Spycket, *Les statues de culte dans les textes mesopotamiens des origines à la Ire Dynastie de Babylone* (*Cahiers de la Revue Biblique* 9, 1968), pp. 88-90, and those of Hammurabi in A. L. Oppenheim, 'Texts from Hammurabi to the Downfall of the Assyrian Empire', *ANET*, pp. 269-271.

13. The 'Mouth Washing' ritual is reconstructed from the available fragments by T. Jacobsen, 'The Graven Image' in *Ancient Israelite Religion* (edited by P. D. Miller, P. D. Hanson and S. D. McBride, Philadelphia: Fortress, 1987), pp. 15-32.

14. J. A. Wilson, 'Religious Drama in Egypt', *ANET*, p. 329;

15. Cf. H. Ringgern, *Religions of the Ancient Near East* (translated by J. Sturdy, London: SPCK, 1973), pp. 85 and 165.

16. Cf. M. C. A. Korpel, *A Rift in the Clouds: Ugaritic and Hebrew Descriptions of the Divine* (Münster: UGARIT-Verlag, 1990), p. 91.

17. R. D. Barnett, 'Bringing the God into the Temple' in *Temples and High Places in Biblical Times* (edited by A. Biran, Jerusalem: Hebrew Union College, 1981), pp. 10-20.

18. Cf. J. A. Wilson, 'A Ritual for Offering Food', *ANET*, p. 325; *idem*, 'The Daily Ritual in the Temple', *ANET*, pp. 325-326.

19. A. Sachs, 'Daily Sacrifices to the Gods of the City of Uruk', *ANET*, pp. 343-345.

20. The influence of Stoic and Epicurean philosophy upon Greek and Roman authors leads to a more sophisticated approach to theological matters, and both the Stoic and the Epicurean approaches are represented at length in Cicero's *de natura deorum*; the situation is further confused by the importation of cults from the East and the innovation of worship of the emperor. The result is that 'It was a matter of debate whether the statues were or were not thought to be the gods themselves'; R. Grant, *Gods and the One God: Christian Theology in the Græco-Roman World* (London: SPCK, 1986) p. 46. However, occasional comments and reports make it clear that the common devotees thought of idols in ways that were very similar to their ancient Near Eastern counterparts. Thus we know at least some images were thought to have been fashioned without human manufacture (as was the famous Artemis of Ephesus; for a story of an unmanufactured head of Pan cf. Cicero, *de divinatione* 1.13.23), the gods could be most powerfully provoked by a word directly spoken into an idol's ear (Seneca, *Ep.* 41.1) and idols were fed, groomed and carried in procession as part of their worshippers' devotion (cf., e.g., fragments from Seneca's lost *de superstitione* as quoted in Augustine, *de civ. dei* 6.10; Lucretius, *de rerum natura*, 2.618-628, translated in M. Whittaker, *Jews and Christians: Graeco-Roman Views*, p. 231). An explicit position of Varro reported by Augustine (*de civ. dei* 7.5) is reminiscent of the Egyptian gods' relationship to their idols: '...quorum qui simulacra specie hominis fecerunt, hoc videri secutos quod mortalium animus, qui est in corpore humano, simillimus est immortalis animi...' (...those who have made the images of those [gods] in human

appearance thus seem to have followed the fact that the soul of mortals, which is in the human body, is very similar to the immortal soul...); however, the reminiscence is really superficial, since Varro as a good Stoic is really proposing that images are only aids to the mind in visualing the true gods (which are the world-soul and its parts). The position of non-philosophers is probably better represented by the summary statement of R. MacMullen, *Paganism in the Roman Empire* (London: Yale University Press, 1981), p. 59: '...inhabitants of the Apologists' world thought first to touch the gods through images, because that was where the gods lived; or at least, to images they could be brought by entreaty, there to listen and act. Whether or not they fitted exactly, whether they looked like their portraits in stone or wood, they were to be found inside.'

21. W. H. Schmidt, *The Faith of the Old Testament* (English translation, Oxford: Basil Blackwell, 1983), pp. 77-78.

22. 1 Kgs 11:4-8.

23. 2 Kgs 11:18 (| | 2 Chron 23:17); cf. also 2 Chron 24:7 which can be translated: 'For Athaliah – that wickedness! – her sons broke down the House of God and even all the holy things of the House of Yahweh they made into Baalim.'

24. 2 Kgs 21:2-7 (| | 2 Chron 33:2-7). The Deuteronomistic Historian apportions much of the blame for the fall of Jerusalem to the idolatrous sins of Manasseh; cf. 2 Kgs 21:10-13.

25. Ezek 8:3-17.

26. Ex 32:4; 1 Kgs 12:28.

27. B. S. Childs in his textual and philological notes on Ex 32:4 in *Exodus* (OTL, London: SCM, 1974), p. 556, correctly points out that *'eloheka* can be either singular or plural. However, Childs fails to mention that all of the words governed by *'eloheka* in the verse indicate that the plural is intended. The invocation of a 'plural of majesty' expressed not only in the noun but in the related verbs and adjectives seems to be more a case of special pleading than of attested idiom.

28. Ex 32:5. Aaron's feeble excuse in 32:24 ('They gave [their gold] to me, I threw it into the fire and out came this calf.') seems to deny Aaron's ultimate responsibility for the fashioning of the calf in a way reminiscent of the 'mouth Washing' ritual and may be seen to reinforce the nature of the calf as idol.

29. J. G. Janzen, 'The Character of the Calf and Its Cult in Exodus 32', *CBQ* 52 (1990), pp. 597-607, has produced a study of the Exodus text (in isolation from the text in Kings) which situates Ex 32 against the Canaanite background. In this way Janzen argues that the calf is a representation of the conquering deity and thus a rival to Yahweh

(and Moses). Janzen does not directly address the question of the supposed Yahwistic or non-Yahwistic identification of the deity thus represented.

30. Cf. H. Ringgern, *Israelite Religion* (translated by D. Green, London: SPCK, 1969), p. 70, J. Gray, *I & II Kings* (OTL, London: SCM, 1977), p. 315, and C. Conroy, *1-2 Samuel, 1-2 Kings* (OTM 6, Wilmington: Michael Glazier, 1983), p. 169.

31. J. P. Hyatt, *Exodus*, pp. 299-300; W. Zimmerli, *Old Testament Theology in Outline*, p. 122.

32. Hos 13:2.

33. Hos 2:18 [EV 2:16]; cf.H. W. Wolff, *Hosea* (tranlated by G. Stansell, Hermeneia, Philadelphia: Fortress, 1974), pp. 49-50.

34. The same can be said for the less widely known narrative of Micah and his idol told in Jgs 17-18 which, in its present composite form, tells how idolatrous worship of Yahweh originated in the territory of Dan; cf. R. G. Boling, *Judges* (AB 6a, Garden City: Doubleday, 1975), pp. 254-267. Gideon's ephod (Jgs 8:27) was certainly condemned and may have been designed for the adornment of an idol, although this is not stated; cf. W. H. Schmidt, *The Faith of the Old Testament*, p. 80.

35. The evidence from the unofficial (Yahwistic) cultic sites allows different interpretations. Thus W. Harrelson, *From Fertility Cult to Worship* (Missoula: Scholars Press, 1969), p. 59, states that 'Even though the pillars (*massaboth*) and the poles (*'asherah*) were present at early shrines, these were not identified as representations of God.' However, others interpret references to *'asherah* as a reference to Yahweh's consort goddess; moreover, the excavation of one Israelite 'high place' has yielded a bronze bull figurine, and another has uncovered a similar figurine of a seated deity. Cf. A. Mazar, *Archaeology of the Land of the Bible 10,000-586 B.C.E.* (ABRL, New York: Doubleday, 1990), pp. 350-352.

36. The evidence of Ezek 8 has already been referred to. The letters of the Jews in Elephantine show that the worship of Yahweh was accompanied by the worship of Ishumbethel and Anathbethel, though it has been suggested that this pagan worship was not performed by Yahwists; cf. H. L. Ginsberg, 'Contributions to the Cult of Yaho', *ANET*, p. 491.

37. Some examples can be found in the very vocabulary used in reference to idols. The paronomastic *'elilim* ('nonentities') is particularly worthy of note (cf., e.g., Lev 19:4; Ps 96:5 and Is 2:8). J. Gray, 'Idol', *Interpreter's Dictionary of the Bible* 2 (edited by G. A. Buttrick, Nashville: Abingdon, 1962), pp. 673-675.

38. Is 44:9-20; cf. 40:18-20.

39. Is 46:1,5-7.
40. Is 40:28; 41:18-20; 42:5; 43:1,15; 44:24; 45:12; 45:18; 48:12-13; 51:13.
41. Is 41:26-29; 42:9; 44:6-8; 45:21; 46:8-10; 48:3-5.
42. Is 41:4; 44:25-45:7; 46:11; 50:2-3; 55:10-11.
43. Is 45:15-17,19; 48:16.
44. The precise dating of Ps 115 is problematic, but a post-exilic date is the more likely. Cf. A. Weiser, *Psalms* (OTL, translated by H. Hartnell, London: SCM, 1962), pp. 714-715, L. C. Allen, *Psalms 101-150* (WBC 21, Milton Keynes: Word, 1987), pp. 109-110 and C. Stuhlmueller, *Psalms 2* (OTM 22, Wilmington: Michael Glazier, 1983), p. 139. Given the tendency of the pre-exilic cultus to harbour idols within the Temple precincts, the use of this psalm seems much more suitable to the Second Temple period.
45. Bar 6:9-12,30,72.
46. Bar 6:28,33.
47. Wis 13:10-19.
48. Wis 14:15.
49. Wis 14:16-21. J. M. Reese, *The Book of Wisdom – Song of Songs* (OTM 20, Wilmington: Michael Glazier, 1983), p. 151, proposes that these ponderings in Wisdom on the origin of idolatry may be dependent upon similar musings by the historian Euhemerus whose writings are extant only in fragments.
50. Wis 14:22,24-27.
51. The rabbinic material is often directed towards the Jew who was tempted to idolatry; idolatry was seen in that context as the breaking of the entire Torah rather than as the breaking of a single command. Cf. the material quoted in E. P. Sanders, *Paul and Palestinian Judaism* (London: SCM, 1977), pp. 134-135.
52. John Cassian, *Conferences* 9.3; translated by O. Chadwick in *Western Asceticism* (LCC 12, London: SCM, 1958), p. 235.
52a. In considering the *via negativa* and the *via positiva*, one must recognise not only the inadequacy of our statements about God, but also their elusive validity. As Aquinas states, 'Intellectus negationis semper fundatus in aliqua affirmatione.' (*Questiones disputatae de potentia Dei*, q. 7, art. 5). Aquinas himself expressed this double quality of our statements about the divine by emphasising analogy as a fundamental means by which human speech expresses knowledge of God; cf. *Summa Theologica* I, q. 13, art. 1, 5, 10 and 12. I am indebted to Dermot Lane for these references.
53. E. Jenni, 'יהוה Jhwh Jahwe', *Theologisches Handwörterbuch zum Alten Testament 1* (edited by E. Jenni and C. Westermann, Munich: Chr. Kaiser, 1984), p.702.
54. For an outline of the evidence and some of the difficulties from one

who accepts the divine name to mean the 'Existing One', cf. R. de Vaux, 'The Revelation of the Divine Name YHWH', *Proclamation and Presence* (edited by J. I. Durham and J. R. Porter, London: SCM, 1970) pp. 48-75. F. M. Cross, *Canaanite Myth and Hebrew Epic* (London: Harvard University Press, 1973), pp. 68-69, suggests that the use of the relative *'asher* in Ex 3:14 indicates that the statement cannot predate the Iron Age, demonstrating that the formulation is a later reflection upon the meaning of the divine name (and such suggested etymologies of personal and place names in the Hebrew Bible are far from scientific).

55. W. Harrelson, *From Fertility Cult to Worship*, pp. 17-18.

56. Many of the arguments for this position are summarised by R. de Vaux, 'The Revelation of the Divine Name YHWH', pp. 59-62; cf. also W. F. Albright, *From the Stone Age to Christianity* (Garden City: Doubleday, 1957), pp. 258-261, and F. M. Cross, *Canaanite Myth and Hebrew Epic* (London: Harvard University Press, 1973), pp. 65-70; D. N. Freedman-M. P. O'Connor-H. Ringgern, 'יהוה *YHWH*', *Theological Dictionary of the Old Testament 5* (edited by G. J. Botterweck and H. Ringgern, translated by D. E. Green, Grand Rapids: Eerdmans, 1986), pp. 500, 511-514 (which builds an impresive philological case for the causative understanding of *Yhwh* from Amorite evidence).

57. Ps 62:2.

58. ⋅ Ps 91:2.

59. Ps 42:2-3 (EV 42:1-2)

60. Ps 108:2-6 (EV 108:1-5)

61. Ps 91:4.

62. Ps 68:6 (EV 68:5).

63. Cf. C. McCarthy-W. Riley, *The Old Testament Short Story* (MBS 7, Wilmington: Michael Glazier, 1987), pp. 129-131, 139.

64. The verb 'to know' (*yd'*) is used with the Deity as object in Hos 2:22; 5:4; 6:3 (2x); 8:2; 13:4; the expression 'knowledge of God' (*da'ath 'elohim*) occurs in Hos 4:1 (cf. also 4:6) and 6:6.

65. Cf. Hos 6:3.

66. Hos 4:1-2. H. W. Wolff, *Hosea*, p. 67; F. I. Andersen-D. N. Freedman, *Hosea* (AB 24, Garden City: Doubleday, 1980), p. 336.

67. H. Wildberger, *'selem* Abbild' *Theologisches Handwörterbuch zum Alten Testament* 2, p. 559.

68. Cicero was aware of the idea that humanity was made in the physical form of the gods, an idea which he proposes and disposes of in *de natura deorum* 1.32-37. In 1.37, he uses the phrase 'deus effigies hominis et imago'; the Vulgate speaks of 'hominem ad imaginem et similitudinem nostram' in Gen 1:26.

69. Gen 1:27-28. Cf. Ps 8:6-7 (EV 8:5-6). B. Vawter, *On Genesis: A New Reading* (London: Chapman, 1977) pp. 54-60; M. Maher, *Genesis* (OTM 2, Wilmington: Michael Glazier, 1982), pp. 29-30.

70. Cf. 1 Cor 11:7 (where Paul surprisingly narrows the notion of image to refer primarily to the male, a position which is not justified by the language either of the Hebrew Bible or of the Septuagint).

71. 2 Cor 4:4. Paul is deliberately using language from Genesis to show that creation receives its fulfilment in Christ and the gospel, as is clear from his continued use of Gen 1 in 2 Cor 4:6.

72. Col 1:15. The question of the authorship of the Letter to the Colossians remains a matter of debate. If not Pauline, it is at least 'post-Pauline', continuing and developing themes of Pauline thought.

73. In 1 Cor 15:49-50, the Christian hope is expressed in terms of bearing the image (*eikon*) of the 'Heavenly One'. Cf. also Rom 8:29-30.

74. 2 Cor 3:18: 'All of us, reflecting the glory of the Lord with unveiled faces, are being transformed as the very image from glory into glory, just as the Lord Spirit [effects].'

75. Cf. 1 Cor 15:44-53.

76. Col 3:5-10.

77. The use of the title for Christ in both 2 Cor 4:4 and Col 1:15 cannot be strictly limited to its moral aspect (although the moral aspect is very important in the context of the discussion of the Law in Second Corinthians). Col 1:15-20 uses the title 'image of God' to introduce Christ as pre-existing and cosmic rather than to emphasise the moral aspect of Christ. That the moral aspect is not alien to Col 1:15 can be discerned by the use of similar language in Col 3:10.

78. Cf., e.g., Rom 1:22-25; 1 Cor 8:4-6; 10:14,19-21; 12:2; 2 Cor 6:16; 1 Thess 1:9.

79. 1 Jn 5:21.

80. 1 Jn 1:8.

81. 1 Jn 2:6.

82. 1 Jn 2:9.

83. 1 Jn 2:22-24; 4:2-3,14-15; 5:1,5,10-12.

84. 1 Jn 4:20-21.

85. 1 Jn 2:4. That the knowledge is of God is intended and not knowledge of Jesus is indicated by the choice of pronouns in the Greek; cf. R. Bultmann, *The Johannine Epistles* (tranlated by R. P. O'Hara, Hermeneia, Philadelphia: Fortress, 1973), pp. 24-25.

86. 1 Jn 2:3-4,9-10; 3:10-24; 4:7-12,20-21; 5:1-3.

87. R. Bultmann, *The Johannine Epistles*, pp. 90-91.

88. 1 Jn 2:6; 3:16-18.

89. 1 Jn 4:12; cf. Jn 1:18.

praxis → the practical as
opposed to theory
practical experience

Disclosing the passion for the possible: Interpreting Sacraments As Life's Interpreters

Anne Kelly

> *Every angel is terrifying.*
> *And so I hold myself back and swallow the call-note*
> *of my dark sobbing. Ah, whom can we ever turn to*
> *in our need? Not angels, not humans,*
> *and already the knowing animals are aware*
> *that we are not really at home in*
> *our interpreted world.* [1]

INTRODUCTION

The crisis of our times has been described as a crisis of interpretation. Conflicting interpretations of what it means to be human, to be religious fight for our attention. In place of old traditional certainties and absolutes we face a climate of pluralism as many different sets of answers and indeed new questions are posed to the fundamental human issues. We are coming to realise how no human experience is uninterpreted experience. We could almost say that to be is to be interpreted.

At the heart of any religious tradition is its symbol system. When religious traditions cease to draw on their symbolic depths they gasp for breath, they die. At the heart of christian identity has always been the way christians have celebrated themselves. The stories, symbols, metaphors that are found in christian celebration are the language of christian identity. Just how we interpret and understand this language, the language of christian sacramental celebration is the subject of my paper. And it is not simply how we interpret this language that I am interested in but how in fact this language also interprets us. If we are the language we speak then I believe that the language of christian identity is the poetic language of christian sacraments.

symbols

At the heart of the christian experience of God is the call to conversion. Where our sacramental celebrations refuse to be open to this they are to be profoundly questioned. Adverting to the over-institutionalisation, clericalisation, sexism and remoteness of sacramental celebrations radically questions whether celebration (as presently experienced) in fact leads away from the basic christian awareness of the sacramentality of all life. The inabilty of people to discriminate between symbol systems, the loss of their capacity as symbol makers, the increasing gap between cult and culture, radically questions the way christians have celebrated and continue to celebrate themselves in our institutional churches.

Our critical questioning and our hermeneutics of suspicion alerts us to the predominance of male experience, male language, images, stories in how christians have celebrated themselves. The church's anamnesis in relation to women is more akin to a situation of radical amnesia. The silence surrounding women's experience, in language, texts and sacred spaces questions this amnesia. The church's failure to remember women has meant a silencing of a whole part of God's revelation. Hearing from a new centre demands a fidelity to this new naming and a correction of the distortions produced by a refusal to hear women's naming of themselves in relation to the sacred.

The challenge to christians to embody and become what they celebrate has different implications for women and men, for rich and poor. Questions of who has been empowered in these celebrations can no longer be ignored in today's critical climate. Where women have been negated in their sexuality and bodiliness and rendered silent and invisible in a patriarchal church one wonders whether our sacramental celebrations celebrate the presence or the absence of God. The absence of praxis as integral to the celebrating community questions whether in fact we have any right to continue celebrating while perpetuating injustice in the very structures of the celebrating community. Thus the interruptive stories of women, of the poor, of suffering, of the earth itself will be part and parcel of our developing framework. The need to develop communities of interpretation and transformation seems vital to complete our investigations.

And so with many questions as a critical frame for our enquiry we must ask whether the traditional celebration of our lives can nurture and inspire the passion for the possible? Can the traditional symbols and stories carry the burden of the questions we bring to them. Can the myth of the christian story carry the new interpretations demanded of it ? Or will we continue to celebrate in isolation from the questions?

Interpreting sacraments as life's interpreters demands that we develop an appropriate interpretative framework and hermeneutics. This I will do by considering the contemporary interest in hermeneutics and situating the question of theological method in relation to it. Moving on to a presentation of some key aspects of Paul Ricoeur's interpretation theory I will then use this interpretative framework as a method for interpreting christian sacramental celebration. My conluding remarks will ponder whether sacramental celebration can become a time and place which discloses the passion for the possible.

INTRODUCTION TO HERMENEUTICS

The kind of critical questioning that I have been inviting you to join in is in itself an expression of the current interest in interpretation or hermeneutics. Coming from the Greek hermeneuein (to interpret), hermeneutics refers to the 'intellectual discipline concerned with the nature and presuppositions of the interpretation of human expressions.'[2] It is a theory of interpreting verbal and aesthetic expressions.[3]

Interest in hermeneutics has surfaced in sources as diverse as literary criticism, sociology, history, anthropology, philosophy and theology. At least three different factors have contributed to this developing interest; namely new theories of human behaviour in psychological and social sciences, the development of an epistemology of language, and the contributions of the major philosophers Heidegger, Hegel and Wittgenstein. [4]

Hermeneutics is essentially concerned with the nature of a text, what it means to understand a text, and how interpretation and understanding are determined by the presuppositions and beliefs of the audience to which the text is being interpreted.[5]

We see them as we are

We are invited through an exercise of hermeneutics to pay attention to the language, history and culture that shape all interpreting. In fact it has been said that we don't see things as they are, we see them as we are.

In a theological context hermeneutics refers to a theory of text interpretation and to the development of the criteria for such interpretation.[6]

Theological method as critical correlation
The contemporary challenge to how one does theology (or thinks theologically) has been framed in terms of critical correlation.[7] David Tracy has articulated his understanding of fundamental theology specifically in regard to this critical correlation between human experience and the Christian fact.

One thinks theologically by a critical fidelity to the sacred texts of a tradition, through a critical dialogue employing the best of what contemporary philosophy and the human sciences have to offer. This task requires the development of criteria of adequacy and appropriateness in order to explore these meanings. Tracy suggests the use of phenomenology to explain meanings in human experience and language and the use of hermeneutics which is critical in attitudes of retrieval, restoration and suspicion, in order to explore the meanings in the Christian texts/tradition.

The contemporary crisis of interpretation is most evident in what we do with our 'exemplary written texts.'[8] Adverting to David Tracy's development of the notion of the classic we can find some interesting insights. The classic is a text which has helped form a culture and can include texts, symbols, events, persons, rituals. The classic comes to us bearing an excess and permanence of meaning, yet resisting any definitive interpretation. Thus revisiting the classic texts may disclose new meaning and possibilities, similar to what B. Kennelly and S. Heaney have done with their plays based on classical Greek stories.

The Christian classic – the story of Jesus Christ and the various ways the embodiment of this story has helped shape the culture of christian identity over time comes to us bearing within it a similar excess of meaning yet resisting definitive interpretation. What does it mean to believe in the revelation of God in Jesus Christ?

How do we interpret this revelation ? What are the grounds for meaning and truth? Theological method is concerned with establishing grounds for the credibility of the revelation of God in Jesus Christ.[9]

Theological method applied in the area of sacramental theology looks to the way that christians have celebrated themselves, looks to their classic rituals, and is concerned with the conditions under which 'the Church's claims for its prayer [are] to be rendered credible.'[10] Fidelity to contemporary human experience, its questions and new interpretations alongside a revisiting of the classic texts of our tradition which carry the people's memory over time is vital in developing sacramental theology.

Thus having highlighted the place of hermeneutics in the development of theological method I will now move on to a consideration of Paul Ricoeur's interpretation theory which I think is of particular relevance for interpreting and understanding christian sacramental experience.

PAUL RICOEUR'S INTERPRETATION THEORY[11]

Symbol fullness of language

Paul Ricoeur's hermeneutics offers us some very constructive ways of interpreting christian sacramental celebration. At the outset we must note that for Ricoeur his philosophy of critical reflection begins with symbols and the fullness of language therein.[12] Symbol represents for him the fullness of language. It gives rise to thought through metaphor and narrative and is received and interpreted within communities of interpretation.

Where we find symbolic language

Ricoeur in his interpretation theory presents us with the different fields in which we find symbols namely the fields of psychoanalysis, poetics and religion.[13] For Ricoeur there is no such a thing as symbolic language without interpretation.[14] Thus there arises very soon the need for a hermeneutics of symbols. It is only by interpreting that we can hear again. It is interpretation which brings us to the level of second naiveté, the level at which we can appreciate the depths of symbols, the level at which we can hear again.[15]

How we interpret it – regressively or progresisvely

In his dialogue with Freud[16] Ricoeur faces the reality that symbols can be interpreted in different ways, either regressively or progressively. The ambiguity of symbols, their many sidedness means that we are engaged in a conflict of interpretations. This overdetermination of symbols, their many meanings and possible interpretations,[17] has led Ricoeur into a dialogue with Freud's interpretation of existence as desire. Here we find conflicting interpretations of symbolic discourse. It is precisely the conflict of a reductive versus a restorative hermeneutics.[18] Where Freud interprets symbols in an archaeological and regressive way Ricoeur interprets them in a teleological and progressive way. One looks backwards to childhood, the other forward to the future. Nonetheless Ricoeur is prepared to acknowledge that symbols carry this double vector both repeating our childhood and probing our adult life.[19]

Polysemy/language/surplus of meaning

It is helpful at this stage to advert to the concept of polysemy which is an important one when it comes to interpreting symbols and symbolic language. This concept of polysemy is the property of words which allows them to have more than one meaning.[20] Ricoeur distinguishes different uses of language in relation to his understanding of polysemy He distinguishes ordinary language which tries to reduce polysemy, scientific language which tries to eliminate polysemy and poetic language which through metaphor exploits polysemy in a creative use of language that is concerned with semantic novelty. Metaphor has the power to increase our language, to redescribe reality, and to open up new worlds.[21]

In every symbol there is a surplus of meaning. Symbols plunge us into life itself. The language of metaphor and narrative which interprets symbols can never fully exhaust the meaning of a symbol. Language only captures the foam on the surface of life.[22]

RELIGIOUS TEXTS

Text discloses possible worlds

Ricoeur believes that identity is shaped by texts read, interpreted and loved. While texts for Ricoeur initially were restricted to written texts he later expanded his understanding to include meaningful action, and people's lives – in short anything which has left a trace and has similar readability characteristics as the written text. The text discloses possible worlds.

Understanding a text for Ricoeur means allowing the text to disclose a possible world and orientating oneself within it. Thus understanding and appropriation of texts invite one in the direction of thought opened up by the text. Similar in ways to Gadamer's fusion of horizons, the world of the text interprets the world of the reader. 'Texts speak of possible worlds and of possible ways of orientating oneself' within them.[23] Understanding the text means allowing it to disclose its world. It involves a letting go, and a receiving back of an enlarged self from the text. Perhaps the kind of experience one might have in theatre where the play interprets our world by disclosing another possible world. Where the text discloses a new world we are invited to let go before it and to receive its newness. This experience for Ricoeur is revelatory. Whether the texts are poetic or religious they have revelatory power.

The mytho-poetic

Ricoeur believes that a community is sustained by its mytho-poetic core.[24] This core constitutes the imaginary nucleus of a culture. It is hidden, an opaque kernel which is only indirectly recognisable through what is said, by what and how one lives, and by the distribution between different functional levels of a society. The mytho-poetic bears within it the identity of a people. The mytho-poetic is always the bearer of something which exceeds its own frontiers; 'it is the bearer of other possible worlds.'[25] It has structural and historical dimensions in its tendency towards sedimentation and innovation. It carries within it various levels of interpretation and reinterpretation. It is the task of a religious tradition to enable creative re-appropriation of this mytho-poetic core.

Interpreting religious texts

Religious texts are the symbolic or poetic language of the christian tradition. The key question we must ask is how they can function to awaken the imagination of the possible?

Interpreting and understanding religious texts is similar to interpreting and understanding other poetic texts. Religious texts can also disclose possible worlds. They offer a radical interpretation of our lives and invite us to live from a new centre. The world disclosed by the religious text offers an invitation to live from the newness and possibility captured in metaphors like becoming a new creation, living in accordance with the reign of God, or writing the new covenant on our hearts. Through the language of parable, the language of surprise and reversal, we are invited to live from a new centre which promises abundance of life.

The human being is sustained by this mytho-poetic core by which he or she is created and recreated. In a religious tradition confronting the world disclosed by this mytho-poetic is to face possibility, is to encounter what Ricoeur calls the grace of imagination, the surging up of the possible.[26] Thus for Ricoeur revelation is concerned with the calling into the heart of existence the imagination of the possible.

INTERPRETING SACRAMENTS

The hermeneutical spiral

As I move into this part of the paper I would like to stress the mutually interpretative nature of theology, sacrament and life. There is no presuppositionless start to how we think and act theologically in our relation to our understanding of and participation in the sacraments and our living lives of faith.

This inherently hermeneutical nature of all experience is as true of our attempts to live as a people faithful to a religious tradition as it is of one's being in the world. The inherently linguistic, social and historical aspects to this being in the world equally apply to our understanding of being and becoming Christians. Language, society and history are as much a part of the fabric of the being of a Christian. I believe that the symbols, language, narratives, memory and history that shape Christian identity are to be found primarily in Christian celebration of the sacraments. How one reflects and thinks theologically about these experiences and how one lives from them is the particular hermeneutical spiral out of which Christian identity is shaped over time. Whether one begins with life, celebration, or reflection, when engaging in a hermeneutics of sacraments is almost irrelevant. To begin anywhere is to begin in the middle, at some point on the spiral.

Christians transformed through their encounter with the God of Jesus Christ have ritualised this conversion experience and initiated others into the community of believers. Baptism, confirmation and eucharist have been the defining rituals of the Christian community. Whether one celebrated first and catechised later[27] or in recent times catechised first and then celebrated, Christians have always celebrated and sustained their identity primarily through rituals of initiation and belonging, and to a lesser extent through rituals of healing and commissioning.

Theological reflection on the meaning of this sacramental activity takes place within a tradition. Sacraments carry the memory of a people over time. They function like the Classic, bearing an excess of meaning, and carrying within them varying layers of interpretation. Sacraments as the bearers of meaning and memory carry a community's experience and reflection over time. Thus theological reflection on sacraments and a community's celebration of sacraments does not take place in a vacuum. A hermeneutics of Christian sacraments while affirming this relationship to the past must also be critical and suspicious as to how this tradition has been received and interpreted.

Sacraments as symbolic language
Following Ricoeur's analysis we can identify the language of Christian sacraments as that of symbol, a language of polysemy and ambiguity, bearing within it an excess of meaning. The symbols, metaphors, myths and narratives that we encounter in christian celebration is the language that grounds us. It is the language that speaks the people we are. As Aidan Kavanagh says, like words in a sentence it is the repeated utterance that makes us who and what we are.

A symbolic language allows for many interpretations, hence the plurality of models of interpretation of sacrament that we find today. Shifting consciousness begets new theologies. New meaning is then sought in the traditional symbols and narratives. This in turn affects celebration and the changes sought therein, which in turn leads to new praxis.[28] Equally, new consciousness and new theology reflecting on the God-human world relationship may seek new modes of celebration and action hitherto not catered for.

This may lead to frustration, disillusionment or disappointment where one eventually comes to see the symbol system as no longer celebrating the transformation believed in and sought by the participants' new awareness. [29]

Sacraments as the mytho-poetic

This raises the question of the tendency of a symbol system to-wards sedimentation rather than innovation. Sacraments function as the mytho-poetic core, because they constitute the imaginary nucleus of the Christian culture and carry the identity of the people. It is never purely conceptual and is not exhausted by praxis. The core of a community's identity is never received directly but is always embodied in some way, always mediated through the power of critical reason, through the language of metaphor and narrative, and through lived testimony and critical praxis. The Christian community is one whose symbol system has changed and evolved over time. As it is experienced today it carries within itself different layers of interpretation. [30] For the Christ-ian, critical appropriation of this mytho-poetic-core will call attention to how we can reinhabit the primeval world of symbol and myth through a critical distanciation, but will also need to be aware of the her-meneutics of suspicion through which any critical reflection must pass.

The dual function of the mytho-poetic in carrying identity and disclosing new possibilities demands a constant vigilance. There will always be a tendency to try to control symbols, [31] whether this is done in the interests of politics, culture, sex, race or class (whether it occurs unconsciously or consciously). This tendency towards becoming part of the 'structural' fabric of a society will often mean a resistance to the other aspect of the mytho-poetic, namely its innovatory or disclosive possibilities. A hermeneutics of the Christian sacramental imagination as the mytho-poetic core of Christian identity must pay attention to this tendency.

Equally well the mytho-poetic as the bearer of possibility must be remembered. How one can learn to listen to the symbols and myths at the heart of the Chistian imagination is often spoken of today in terms of evangelisation. One has to awaken the desire for faith, at the heart of a person's life. The starting point for contemporary women and men may be as fundamental as the need they experience for belonging and intimacy. These needs often triggered by 'limit' experiences of tragedy, suffering or joy push the individual back to a mytho-poetic core which discloses meaning.

Crisis of the symbolic imagination

Today's cultural context is characterised by symbolic poverty. Overall we encounter a flattening out of symbols, and a pragmatism that is uneasy in the realm of symbolic discourse. Symbolism is 'the very life's breath of religion when symbols lose their power, the religious traditions they inspire gasp for breath.'[32] The watering down of symbols, flat lifeless celebrations, the inability to discriminate between symbol systems, the loss of a community of interpretation, increasing privatisation of religion and secularisation of life all contribute to the crisis of the symbolic imagination.

The hermeneutics of suspicion applied to all our symbol systems makes it more difficult to know what it is we wish to affirm in symbolic discourse. Are our symbols interpreted regressively or progressively? Are they understood in terms of preservation or transformation of the status quo? Are they perceived to be socially constraining or liberating? Whether we can come to dwell at the level of a second *naiveté* in the realm of the symbol is something that contemporary celebration of the sacraments will have to address. What is the movement in the way we celebrate the sacraments that enables us to move, as Ricoeur suggested, from living in symbols to thinking from symbols.

Befriending Our Symbols

A story is told about the dancer Martha Graham who danced for a group of people and afterwards reporters were asking her what her dance meant. Darlings, she is reputed to have said, if I had known what it meant I wouldn't have danced it. The language of sacrament, of ritual is the symbolic or poetic language of the christian community. While it is the language we must speak it is the language that also speaks us. It is the language that we think we use but which in fact uses us. We do not speak ritual language when all else has failed, when we feel mindless or superstitious. We engage in ritual or symbolic behaviour when the experience we are undergoing demands it of us, drags it out of us.

74

Greetings from "Hillview Farmhouse"

Hillview Farmhouse

Milltown, Killarney, Co. Kerry, Ireland. Tel: 066-67117

Hillview Farmhouse on the main airport/Ring of Kerry route.
Golfing, Fishing, Mountain Climbing and Beaches nearby.
Ideal touring centre for Ring of Kerry, Dingle and Killarney, Ireland.

It is similar to the experience some years ago of the football fans in response to the disaster at Hillsborough in England. After the disaster fans flocked in procession to the site, their behaviour highly ritualistic, colours of the teams, mascots, tickets, procession, silence, tears, gestures, holding each other, storying and remembering their friends. At the deepest level that the experience had touched people ritual was the only language that could touch the pain. Ritual finds us then where we are most deeply feeling, being human and catches us up in its ancient rhythms. Patterning ourselves to its rhythms, its movements, at the depths of our human experience we can sense newness and possibility. Ritual can and does disclose the passion for the possible.

Contemporary crisis in regard to ritual and sacramental celebration is at one level caused by the innability of people to feel at home in the whole realm of the symbolic. We have not allowed ouselves to appreciate the very lives we live in order to discover our power as symbol makers. Tad Guzie adverts to the challenge to befriend one's symbols as having roots in everyday life where raw experience, becomes lived experience through story and festivity. Appreciating this pattern of experience, story and festivity as what makes our human lives more fully human is according to Guzie the very rhythm that makes life human. It is the basic dynamic that we must rediscover and explore in order to be able to participate in the symbolic language of the christian community.

Taking the ordinary and the everyday as ingredients in sacramental celebration invites us to perceive the sacredness of all of our lives. The sacramental nature of all of life for the christian means that God is in fact to be found in the 'bits and pieces of everyday life'. Rediscovering the depths of our human lives as graced to the core by the gift and presence of God adverts us to sacredness at the core and prepares us to continue to acknowledge and affirm this in our sacramental celebrations. Breaking bread around a table of mutual love and forgiveness is sacred long before we come to the sacramental celebration. It is the very sacredness of such sharing that allows it to become a symbol for us of the breaking through of divinity, in the community of followers of Jesus Christ. Taking the bits and pieces of our ordinary everyday lives and allowing them to speak to us of God is at the heart of developing a christian sacramental imagination.

Letting symbols speak

A second stage in the befriending of symbols is the challenge to contemporary celebration is to let the symbols speak.[33] To plunge our initiates into the saving waters of baptism by total immersion says more than the dribble or two of water poured from a cracked cup.[34] Oil that flows from beautiful containers may speak more eloquently of the love and power of God poured out than a furtive poking in a tiny box for a smear of hardened grease. To see bread that is broken and shared, to share a cup of wine around a table may alert us more to the reality we celebrate when the bread looks like bread and the wine is really poured and shared.

Polysemy of symbols

Letting symbols speak also calls for attention to the polysemy of symbols in order that we allow their many sidedness to suface. Whether it is bread or wine, water or oil, the richness is lost when we limit their meanings. When we think of bread broken and shared in the eucharist we should not simply think of something to be swallowed and adored. We lose the richness, the polysemy. Bread as the fruit of the earth plunges us back into our rootedness in nature. As the product of human labour it reminds us of our interconnectedness. As the basic food of life it reminds us of our interdependence. People without daily bread challenge our use of bread as a symbol in the eucharist. The bread evokes the manna in the wilderness, the bread of affliction, David taking the bread from the tabernacle, the bread of the Passover, the bread Jesus broke with his friends, the bread he promised for the life of the world . The breaking of the bread evokes all these meanings. The invitation is to allow the polysemy of the symbol to surface. In doing so we explore the muliple meanings, and can be challenged in new ways to imagine newness and possibility.

The challenge to allow the symbols to become interpreters of our lives also asks what this breaking of the bread has meant in the christian community and what it might mean. If we celebrate ourselves in memory of Jesus as bread broken and shared we are in turn invited to become broken and shared for each other. The challenge to become bread for the world is also it seems incumbent on the christian community who allows itself to be interpreted by the symbol. We cannot celebrate the presence of God in bread and not care about the earth, about bodiliness and about starvation. Allowing the symbol to question the community means asking painful questions about the exclusion of women from the blessing and breaking of bread. It also questions the community as to why so many marginalised people do not feel welcome at the breaking of the bread.

In fact rather than being the answers these symbols are as Aidan Kavanagh says the questions that continually rake one's life, making it a life of God rather than merely about God. Consenting to live according to the symbols, while prompted by the liturgical celebration, requires a community faithful to living the symbols they have celebrated, both inside and outside the liturgical celebration. Thus we make the move from thinking from symbols to living from them, allowing them to become interpreters of our lives.

Hermeneutics of suspicion
A hermeneutics of suspicion is not content to make grand sweeping statements about sacramental celebration which stand ideologically above contradiction. It pushes us back to the community of interpretation. It alerts us to the fact that the complexity of symbolic discourse allows symbols to function in different ways.

Symbols can function symbolically and allow us 'to be in a world of simple desire, interpretive ambiguity, indigenous cultural expression, and random significance and still connect our experiences and desires with the holy communion of God's chosen but ordinary people.'[35] Equally they can function 'diabolically when they sunder apart the tradition of the community from the ordinary experience of everyday. When ritual actions become absolute and perfectionist , impatient of ambiguity, and divisive, then the present needs of real people are irrelevant and unimportant.'[36] They can also function negatively when co-opted by sexism, colonialism, cultural domination, social injustice and racial alienation. Perhaps at times our celebrations and our symbol systems are lies behind which we hide. 'Is it possible that more than occasionally our sacraments are false signs, symbolic lies behind which we institutionally hide from the truth ?'[37]

Liturgical praxis

David Power has adverted to what he calls 'liturgical praxis' as 'a new consciousness at the eye of worship.'[38] He puts it succinctly, 'It is the engagement with life that we need to bring to worship, the readiness to be challenged to self-understanding by an affirmation of the holy that gives perspective to the appropriation of new social and inner experience.'[39] In listening to the new voices he urges worship to beome free from the pseudo-sacral, to move beyond dualistic and hierarchical perceptions, to gather back the bodily, earthly and cosmic and to retrieve the spirit of Wisdom.

The full power of the revelatory newness of the Christ event which we remember and celebrate in our liturgies is incomplete if severed from the lives of real people in real communities. This is not simply saying that we must live what we celebrate but that the call to a liberative praxis must enter into the very fabric of what we celebrate. The sacramental text discloses the newness of the world imagined by the praxis of Jesus. It must invite participants to risk opening themselves to living from the same centre – the praxis of Jesus in the service of the reign of God. It must nurture and inspire in participants a desire and passion for this world. And this world should be embodied as much in the celebrating community as outside of it. Where Jesus imagined and lived a discipleship of mutuality and equality our liturgies, our remembering should allow the same kind of mutuality and equality to question our lives and our celebrations.

Sacraments as interpreters of our lives

Allowing the symbols to become intepreters of our lives fundamentally comes down to allowing ourselves to experience conversion. The process for individuals and for the church is a slow and painstaking one. Many feel silenced and invisible in the language, texts and structures of Christian liturgies as they are presently celebrated. Their disappointment at the inability of the 'institution' to hear their voices has led to anger and disillusionment. Many have sought other contexts and communities that are more authentic attempts to live the gospel call to conversion and wholeness of life. I am thinking here of the womenchurch movement which sees itself in Exodus from the patriarchal institutional churches which deny them access to the fullest expression of their christian identity.

CONCLUSION: DISCLOSING THE PASSION FOR THE POSSIBLE

Along with Adrienne Rich I would like to say that 'a wild patience has taken me this far.'[40] There is little doubt in my mind about the vital part that worship must play in the life of the christian. As Dysart, the psychiatrist in Peter Schaeffer's *Equus* says 'Without worship you shrink, it's as brutal as that'. This shrinking of our lives, the failure to realise the full potential of our humanness, the failure to imagine the breaking through of divinity, can only leave us empoverished and longing. How we celebrate ourselves however can equally well destroy or nurture our faith.

The liturgical space, the times of celebration must become times when we imagine newness and possibility. Beyond the paralysis of imagination, beyond the cynicism and apathy of the age, beyond the brokenness and despair we must dare to imagine a space where hope and history rhyme.

What shape would our worship have to take for this new imagining to occur. In our memory as a people we share the dangerous memory of Jesus Christ – a dangerous memory that dares to imagine newness by going through pain and suffering. Never by-passing the pain, the yearnings of all of creation, we are driven back, in the words of Carter Heyward, 'to speak the Word that spills among us: Without our touching there is no God. Without our relation there is no God. Without our crying, our yearning, our raging, there is no God.'

Our sacramental celebrations must become spaces which nurture and inspire the passion for the possible. In speaking out our lives the symbols and stories invite us and challenge us to let go like Heaney's description of children iceskating

The ice was like a bottle. We lined up
Eager to re-enter the long slide
We were bringing to perfection, time after time

Running and readying and letting go
Into a sheerness that was its own reward:
A farewell to surefootedness, a pitch

Beyond our usual hold upon ourselves. [41]

Beyond our usual hold upon ourselves. The liturgical space has the potential to lure us into a new way of being, where we genuinely surrender to being interpreted by God. But it is the God of the prophets who imagines newness and not the domesticated God of the established order. It is the God who is imaged out of the experience of women and men in relation with the earth itself. In our traditional churches we have not yet dared to imagine in this new way. Where all voices are heard, where the newness sought is not simply adding on the experience of those hitherto excluded but one that demands that we see in a new way.

Is there any point in continuing to celebrate as we do at present? Do we abandon ritual in order to create the conditions that make the cult more authentic. Or do we continue to celebrate hoping that our rituals will inspire us to a conversion of heart? Perhaps it is not a question of either or but of many options. The new pluralism of our times must recognise the validity of many different ways of worshipping. The tradition can inspire many ways of imagining and dreaming. How we relate the new to the old may only be discovered through time. Heaney's invitation to see the old heavy, dull brown settle bed in a new way reminds us that

> Whatever is given
> Can always be reimagined, however four-square plant-thick,
> hull-stupid and out of its time
> It happens to be. [42]

The reimagining will take us into new places and ask us to recognise many different forms as authentic expressions of christian worship.

Recreating the links between liturgy and life means a rediscovery of our essential interconnectedness and relatedness. In a old/new ethic of relationality and care we can rediscover our connections with our own bodiliness, with each other and with the earth itself.

Our worship must invite us 'into the heartland of the ordinary'[43] where we can 'bless the ordinary', and 'sanctify the common'.[44] If it invites us to dance it must recognise that the dance will sometimes be dancing with tears in our eyes. And perhaps it is only those outside the system of power that can challenge it with the reality of forgotten, ignored or undeserved pain. Our christian lives, our collective memories have not all been ones which would lead us to rejoicing. The pain of the centuries, the barbarities and atrocities of the past hundred years alone, the silencing, exclusion and invisibility of women, the destruction of the earth, the increasing gap between the rich and the poor, should lead us to prophetic grieving and resisitance. If our liturgies, and celebrations have their fingers on this pulse of human life and suffering they will lead to grieving out of which can come newness. When we weep with Rachel for her children who are no more then we can move with Sarah to rejoice at the fulfilment of the promise. Where our liturgies and celebrations do not have this engagement with life and specifically with the dark underside of our pain our liturgies will breed apathy, depression and paralysis.

If we risk allowing the symbols to become interpreters of our lives, we risk being invited into a new way of being. Developing *M Fox* such communities of interpretation and transformation where many different voices are heard, inspiring many new kinds of imagining, visioning and dreaming is the challenge facing us as christians. Allowing our pain, and brokenness to enter our celebration in lamentation and grief alongside our dancing and joy is vital if we really want to be transformed and healed by the story we celebrate.

It is an invitation into the deep affirmation of life that is at the heart of the christian story of incarnation. Allowing the symbols to invite us into this space of affirming life cannot take place by ignoring the negative, the destructive, the dark times. Perhaps it is time to remind ourselves of the words of Thomas Kilroy in *Talbot's Box* 'I think meself the darkness is Gawd'. And yet through it the affirmation of life is essential. Bendan Kennelly writes in his poem 'Yes' about how 'I love the word / And hear its long struggle with no.' He continues

Say "yes" to life ??

> The only agelessness
> Is yes.
> I am always beginning to appreciate
> The agony from which it is born.
> Clues from here and there
> Suggest such agony is hard to bear
> But is the shaping God
> Of the word that we
> Sometimes hear, and struggle to be.[45]

81

Notes

1. Rainer Maria Rilke, Duino Elegies, The First Elegy, *The Selected Poetry of Rainer Maria Rilke*, (Picador Classics: London, 1987) p.151

2. Van A. Harvey, 'Hermeneutics', from *The encyclopaedia of religion*, Vol. 6 (Mircea Eliade,(Editor in chief), Macmillan Pub.Company: New York, 1987) p.279.

3. W. Jeanrond, 'Hermeneutics', from *The new dictionary of theology*, (Joseph A. Komanchak, Mary Collins, Dermot A. Lane (Editors), Gill and Macmillan: Dublin,1987) p.462.

4. Van A. Harvey, 'Hermeneutics', from *The encyclopaedia of religion*. p.280; W. Jeanrond, 'Hermeneutics', in *The new dictionary of theology*, p.462.

5. Van A. Harvey, 'Hermeneutics', from *The encyclopaedia of religion*, p.279.

6. W. Jeanrond, 'Hermeneutics', from *The new dictionary of theology*, p.462.

7. D. Tracy, *Blessed rage for order: the new pluralism in theology*, (Seabury Press: New York, 1975) Ch.2.

8. D. Tracy, *Plurality and ambiguity: hermeneutics, religion, hope*, (SCM Press: London, 1987) p.11.

9. R. Latourelle, 'A new image of fundamental theology', in *Problems and perspectives of fundamental theology*, (René Latourelle, Gerald O'Collins, eds.) (Paulist Press : New York, 1982) p.37.

10. P. Fink, 'Towards a liturgical theology', *Worship* 47, No.10, Dec 73, p.601-609, p.602.

11. The main text of Ricoeur's used for this article is Paul Ricoeur,*Interpretation theory: discourse and the surplus of meaning*, (Christian University Press:Texas 1976)

12. Paul Ricoeur, *The symbolism of Evil*, (Beacon Press: Boston 1967), p.348. The conclusion to this book(p.347-357) gives a good introduction to Ricoeur's early work on symbol.

13. Paul Ricoeur,*Interpretation theory*, p.53-54.

14. Paul Ricoeur writes 'There exists nowhere a symbolic language without hermeneutics; wherever a man dreams or raves, another man arises to give an interpretation; what was already discourse, even if incoherent, is brought into coherent discourse by hermeneutics.' *The symbolism of Evil*, p.350.

15. Paul Ricoeur, *The symbolism of Evil*, p.351.

16. Paul Ricoeur, *Freud and Philosophy: an essay on interpretation*, (Yale University Press: New Haven and London, 1970)

17. Paul Ricoeur, in *The Philosophy of Paul Ricoeur: an anthology of his work*

(Charles E. Reagan & David Stewart (Editors), .Beacon press: Boston,1978) p.99, and Paul Ricoeur, *Freud and Philosophy*, p.7 The anthology gives a good selection of Ricoeur's early writings and serves as a very useful introduction to his work.

18. Paul Ricoeur, in *The Philosophy of Paul Ricoeur*: p.89, and Paul Ricoeur, *Freud and Philosophy*: p.504

19. Paul Ricoeur, *The conflict of interpretations: essays in hermeneutics*, (Northwestern University Press: Evanston, 1974) p. 326-330

20. Paul Ricoeur, in *The Philosophy of Paul Ricoeur* : p.124 & fol.

21. Paul Ricoeur, in *The Philosophy of Paul Ricoeur* : p.133

22. Paul Ricoeur,*Interpretation theory*: p.63

23. Paul Ricoeur, in *The Philosophy of Paul Ricoeur* : p.144

24. Paul Ricoeur, in *The Philosophy of Paul Ricoeur* : p.237

25. Richard Kearney, 'Myth as the bearer of possible worlds: Interview with Paul Ricoeur' (*The Crane Bag*, Nos 1&2, 1978, p.260-266) p.260

26. Paul Ricoeur, in *The Philosophy of Paul Ricoeur* : p.237

27. As was the case with much 4th century Mystagogical catechesis .

28. Urban Holmes, 'Ritual and the social drama', *Worship* Vol 51, Nu.3, May 1977, p.197-214, p. 210.

29. This is particularly in evidence in relation to liberation and feminist theological analysis.

30. R.Kearney, *Dialogues with contemporary continental thinkers : the phenomenological heritage, Paul Ricoeur, Emmanuel Levinas, Herbert Marcuse, Stanislas Breton, Jacques Derrida*, (Manchester University Press, 1984) p.25.

31. R. Kearney, 'Religion and ideology', *Irish Theological Quarterly*, Vol.52, Nos 1/2, 1986, p.109-126, p.116.

32. J . W. Heisig, 'Symbol'. *The encyclopaedia of religion* ,Vol. 14 (Mircea Eliade,(Editor in chief), Macmillan Pub.Company: New York, 1987) p.198.

33. J. Gelineau , 'The symbols of Christian initiation', in *Becoming a Catholic Christian : A symposium on Christian initiation* (William J. Reedy Editor, Sadlier: New York ,1979) p.327-337.

34. A. Kavanagh, 'Initiation: baptism and confirmation'. in *The sacraments, readings in contemporary sacramental theology*, (Michael J. Taylor, Editor, Alba House: New York, 1981) p. 81-94.

35. Paul J. Philibert, 'Readiness for ritual:psychological aspects of maturity in Christian celebration', *Alternative futures for worship*, Vol. 1, (Peter E.Fink SJ, Editor, The Liturgical Press: Collegeville, Minnesota, 1987) p.63-121, p.81.

36. Paul J. Philibert, 'Readiness for ritual:psychological aspects of maturity in Christian celebration', *Alternative futures for worship*, Vol. 1, p.81.

37. J. Martos, *Message of the Sacraments*, Vol 1, *The catholic sacraments*, (Gill and Macmillan: Dublin, 1983) p.205.

38. D. Power, 'Liturgical praxis: a new consciousness at the eye of worship', *Worship*, Vol 61, No.4, July 1987, p.290-304, p.290.

39. D. Power, 'Liturgical praxis: a new consciousness at the eye of worship', *Worship*, Vol 61, No.4, July 1987, p.290-304, p.290.

40. Adrienne Rich, 'Integrity', *The fact of a Doorframe: Poems Selected and New 1950-1984* (W.W. Norton and Company: New York,1984), p.273

41. Seamus Heaney, 'Squarings xxviii', *Seeing Things*, (Faber and Faber: London, 1991), p.86

42. Seamus Heaney, 'The Settle Bed' , *Seeing Things*, p.28

43. Seamus Heaney, 'The Journey back', *Seeing Things*, p.7

44. Eavan Boland, 'Envoi', *The Journey and other poems*, (Carcanet: Manchester,1987) ,p. 43

45. Brendan Kennelly, 'Yes' , *A Time For Voices selected Poems 1960-1990* (Bloodaxe Books, Newcastle upon Tyne, 1990) p. 24

Music, Meaning and Mystery: Towards a Theophany of Music
Anne M. Murphy

The three words – music, meaning, mystery – connote three discrete entities which are yet intimately connected in the process of musical communication. It is my central concern in this paper to examine the concept of the connectedness of music, meaning and mystery in this context of musical communication and to demonstrate its actuality.*

Constructing the Theory: The Artist and the prophet
Constructing a theory of connectedness between music, meaning and mystery is more than a musicological exercise. Its concerns go beyond those of aesthetics and phenomenology. It attempts to place the technical data of music, which can be uncovered by empirical analysis, within a broad human and cultural context. In such a context musicological techniques can combine with other disciplines which, in the words and according to the counsel of Professor Denis Arnold, 'intrigue both the mind and the spirit'. [1]

As a musicologist with theological leanings, the particular cross-fertilisation which intrigues my mind and spirit is that of music and faith. The dialogue of faith and art is no new concept. Evidence from earliest civilisations and cultures bears witness to the cathartic and transcendent role of art in human attempts to express the emotional tensions related to the high points of living and dying - ultimately a religious context.

If we can accept Karl Rahner's definition of the adjective 'religious' in a broad sense, as applicable to all that 'gives concrete expression to (woman's and) man's infinite transcendence',[2] then we can infer that every instance of such transcendence has a religious dimension. In this broad sense, human nature, by virtue of its innate creativity, may be said to be religious. Human creativity – as the expression of hopes, of needs, of desires – witnesses to that instinct within the human spirit which energises women and men to see beyond the limitations of temporal existence and to rise above them. Human creativity is a statement of belief that life is meaningful. The object of this belief may be anything, – be it divine, human, or belonging to the realm of ideas or ideals, – which confers on life a significance beyond the indications of observable reality. Human creativity is a statement of hope; it concretises in sign and symbol, word and image, the human craving for permanence and value, a craving in fact for immortality.

The creative artist has always been at the forefront of the search for meaning and significance. It is perhaps the vocation of the artist to express this searching dimension of being human. The creative artist is the spokesperson, often unawares, whose art can offer to fellow human beings a perspective on the ultimate questions of life and death. Through his or her giftedness, the artist becomes the prophet and visionary whose art evidences what David Tracy calls 'the instinct for the essential.' [3]

Even in a century such as ours which has experienced and continues to experience what has been described as 'a crisis of meaning' the role of authentic art, according to the aesthetic theory of Theodor Adorno, even in negation, is always to posit meaning; this, Adorno maintains, is 'because art cannot escape, of its very nature being loaded with significance'. [4]

One of the most explicit and thorough accounts of a personal artistic credo in this century is revealed in the writings of the composer Arnold Schoenberg (1874-1951). At the heart of his philosophy is the belief that 'the process of artistic creativity is a way of participating in the universal struggle between matter and spirit'.[5] Schoenberg believed in the artist's God-given mission to be 'the first to comprehend new ideas and communicate them to the public'. To Schoenberg the musician is at the forefront of such a task since 'music can capture a truth which is beyond words'; to Schoenberg the 'sole concern of serious music [is] that spiritual reality which notes can express'.[6] This is not pious rhetoric. 'Spiritual reality' refers to that element of the 'essential' in a work of art which embodies some grain of eternal truth and beauty and as such has a 'disclosive and transformative power' for all those who experience it.[7] This is the hallmark of greatness and value in art.

The work of art, therefore, whatever the medium or form, is a con-cretisation of the transcendent dimension of human nature. It gives validity, authenticity, and credibility to the possible easing and eventual resolution of all conflict and yearning. Of the art of music in particular, George Steiner has written in *Real Presences*:

> Music has celebrated the mystery of intuitions of transcend-ence from the songs of Orpheus, counter creative to death, to the *Missa Solemnis*, from Schubert's late piano sonatas to Schoenberg's *Moses und Aron* and Messiaen's *Quatuor pour la fin du temps* . Countless times, this celebration has had manifest relations to religion. But the core-relation far exceeds any spec-ific motive or occasion. In ways so obvious as to make any statement a tired cliché, yet of an undefinable and tremendous nature, music puts our being as men and women in touch with that which transcends the sayable, which outstrips the analysa-ble. Music is plainly uncircumscribed by the world as the latter is an object of scientific determination and practical harness-ing.[8]

Music: Science and Art

The Polish composer Lutoslawski (b. 1913) has written of the rela-tionship of art and science within music. His words are relevant to this particular investigation and will perhaps offer some illumina-tion on that which relates and that which distinguishes the scien-tific and artistic elements in music:

> Science and art, the two areas of human activity, the two prod-ucts of the human spirit which, it would seem, are so utterly different from each other, yet have many traits in common ... The goal of science is obvious to all of us, it can be defined by one word: knowledge. But whenever I try to define the goal of art, my thoughts encounter a cloud of mist beyond which noth-ing can be discerned clearly. No definition is satisfactory, all seem to miss the crux of the matter, all are im-precise and unes-sential. Yet the goal is obvious to all who are given to experi-ence art and even more so to those who create it ... [The] role of a scientist is to investigate, probe and reason, all intellectual work and effort. The work of an artist has been generally asso-ciated with intuition, imagination and emotion. And rightly so, for no one will deny that the results of ecstatic states – or in the

popular idiom – moments of in-spiration, are clearly evident in the greatest works of art. These moments may be described as a state of readiness of the creative imagination for signals that flow from some unknown source, whose result is the sudden emergence of something that had not existed a moment earlier. But, I believe that I am not wrong when I say that without inspiration there would be no knowledge in the world. The work of a scientist abounds in moments of inspiration. We the people outside the world of science are aware of this from the history of science, from the biographies of the great scientists and from the history of scientific discoveries.

Nor would a creative artist be able to attain outstanding results in his labour without possessing a certain degree of wisdom. Hence the artist's labour possesses similar elements to that of a scientist, namely, to investigate, probe and reason. [9]

The problems of musical analysis.
Music analysts have been described with some acerbity as: 'The Zealots of explanation' who 'want to deny the arts their mystery' (Denis Donoghue). I prefer to think of musicologists and analysts as scientists who seek to probe and uncover evidence from human experience which deepens our understanding of the phenomenon of music, extends its cathartic and therapeutic potential, and increases its accessibility leaving the art of music richer, not poorer. This understanding would appear to be in keeping with the ultimate aim of musicology defined by Charles Seeger as follows:

> to contribute to the general study of man/woman what can be known of man/woman as music maker.[10]

The dictionary tells us that the act of analysis belongs in the realms of science, of physics and chemistry. In such a sphere analysis is an activity which examines minutely the constituent elements of an object; it attempts to ascertain the elements of a compound. Analysis also belongs, the same dictionary tells us, in less scientifically verifiable matters when it attempts to find and show the essence of a treatise. When a sentence is resolved into its grammatical constituents we describe that activity also as analysing. Analysis in a musical context encompasses both of the above types of sifting of evidence; the music analyst attempts to identify the grammatical elements of the music as a first step towards revealing the essence of the music as a meaningful communication.

The mystery of music as language

It is something of a 'mystery' that the precise and scientifically verifiable phenomena of musical language, – the pitches, durations, timbres, and dynamic values – should in combination be capable of moving the listener in a way that is beyond that which is measurable either in terms of technical expertise or intellectual understanding. That music can and does move us in this way is beyond dispute: how it does so is less easily definable. It seems to me that it is the fascination of the possibility of uncovering something of this mysterious 'how' which lies at the root of all the analytical theories and methods with which the history of music is strewn. 'Music is a code in which the deepest secrets of humanity are written'[11]; and secrets always fascinate and tantalise, and evoke curiosity.

Music: the language of mystery

Musical analysis inhabits very complicated terrain. I have used such terms as 'mystery', 'meaning', 'essence' – all nebulous terms, despite attempts to define them. But the creative artist, however tangible the raw materials of the art, belongs in this territory where shadow and substance interact. The musician composer whose work music analysts are attempting to understand, is something of a visionary and a prophet gifted with that 'instinct for the essential' mentioned earlier. Consciously or unconsciously the creative artist is engaged in the revelation of meaning through his/her art form, and walks constantly in the realms of mystery, – the mysteries of the art and the mysteries of life and of religion with which art in all its forms is so engaged. Again I invoke the eloquence of Steiner:

> Music and the metaphysical, in the root sense of that term, music and religious feeling, have been virtually inseparable. It is in and through music that we are most immediately in the presence of the logically, of the verbally inexpressible but wholly palpable energy in being that communicates to our senses and to our reflection what little we can grasp of the naked wonder of life. I take music to be the naming of the nam-

ing of life. This is beyond any liturgical or theological specificity, a sacramental motion. Or, as Leibnitz put it ; 'music is a secret arithmetic of the soul unknowing of the fact that it is counting'.[12]

There is a close relationship between music and mathematics, between music and physics, but the role of the music analyst is much more than that of statistician. There is an interpretative function for the analyst who seeks to explore the dialogue of events which occurs in the musical work. The complexity of the function arises from the fact that the musical entity is both art and science. Any speculative investigation into a musical composition must take into account both its scientifically verifiable data of rhythm, melody, and harmony, and its more numinous artistic and perhaps philosophical dimensions.

Music and Meaning: From Means to Meaning

Morris R. Cohen, in his book *A Preface to Logic* , writes as follows:

anything acquires meaning if it is connected with, or indicates, or refers to something beyond itself, so that its full nature points to, and is revealed in that connection.[13]

The application of the above statement to the investigation of meaning in music reveals an interesting chain of relationships and connections. In summary of the results of this investigation, the total phenomenon of musical experience is perceived and diagrammatically represented in figure one as resulting from the triadic inter-relatedness of composer, music, and listener. The process of communication of meaning in such experience, therefore, involves the following in triadic dialectic:

i) *a communicator*: the composer as creator of the music; craftsperson and artist.

ii) *a communication*: the music as created object or message; science and art.

iii) *a recipient of communication*: re-created by the musical message; listener and interpreter.

Figure 1: The triadic dialectic of musical communication

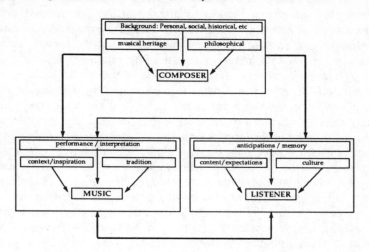

Levels of meaning: form and content

It is the burden of this paper that while music has no precise semantic of its own it is nonetheless a language which communicates meaning on levels beyond the terms of its physical properties.

The object of investigation in any musicological undertaking will therefore encompass not only the technical process of communication through music, that aspect of music which we might identify as the form, but also the content of the communication in question as a human phenomenon. The form of music is constituted by all that gives it intelligible shape. The form of music embraces all of those elements or processes whereby information is transmitted and received in terms of the melodic, rhythmic and harmonic signs and constructs which constitute the vocabulary of music. The content of the communication initiated through the formal musical elements may be identified in purely musical, that is, in absolute terms, or in extra-musical or referential terms. The separation of form and content is an academic exercise and purely theoretic. 'In music form is content, content form.' [13]

91

Excursus: An Irish jig or a military march will communicate in terms of toe-tapping rhythms; a Viennese Waltz, given the right context, will have us swirling around a dance floor, – or wishing we could; the content/meaning of such music is to be found within its own terms of reference, in this case predominantly those of its rhythmic patterns. But transfer both of these rhythmic patterns to the context of Berlioz's 'Symphonie fantastique' and the communication of meaning goes beyond the purely technical data of rhythm. The waltz here vividly portrays the grace and movement of a ballroom scene, but central to the communication is the image of the lovesick hero and the ever-out-of-reach beloved. The march too is more than the sum of its rhythmic patterns, it is the nightmare march to the scaffold of the hallucinating hero. The total meaning of both waltz and march can only be communicated and understood in the fusion of both absolute and extra-musical elements, that is, in the fusion of form and content. I have taken somewhat watertight/ simplistic examples to illustrate the two possible positions with regard to the attribution of meaning to music. Most music is not so easily categorised, nor should it be. The most satisfactory musical analysis recognises the co-existence of the purely musical and the extra-musical in a musical work.

Theorists and critics have made this area of meaning in music a battleground. The two main protagonists may be fairly accurately referred to as 'purists' or 'absolutists', on the one hand, and 'referentialists' on the other. The former claim that 'musical meaning lies exclusively within the context of the work itself' while the latter contend 'that music also communicates meanings which in some way refer to the extra-musical world of concepts, actions, emotional states and character'.[14] I believe that the absolutist and referentialist theories are not mutually exclusive. A purist adulation of form and structure for its own sake in much musical analytical writing, and the accompanying suspicion of any extra-musical connection or reference, would appear to be a reaction against the excessive subjectivism and romanticism displayed by many writers in aesthetics during the last century. It is not suggested that grammatical content can or should be ignored, but 'what is most important', according to Mahler, 'is not the notes'. Deryck Cooke elaborates on this statement when he writes: 'Content is ... the current of the composer's emotion of which the notes are the musical transformation.'[15]

Excursis: A brief look at some compositional realisations of the physical properties of a common chord will offer an indication of the difficulties to be overcome in undertaking, (if such a task were possible), to relate sound patterns to definitive meaning.

Example 1 on page 102 shows a collection of musical quotations which have one thing in common; they all derive wholly or in part from the same notes, the notes which form the chord of C major. If the chord of C had one meaning only, that meaning which might be attributed in relation to, and in terms of its scientific properties, then all of these quotations should convey the same meaning. But they do not.

For the sake of clarity, I have taken the very simple example of the notes of the chord of C major, but the same process might be carried out with many chord combinations. The musical quotations show just some of the many musical statements from our familiar repertoire which have been constructed from the same sound relationships. The result of the rhythmic, melodic and harmonic permutations and combinations is that these extracts 'mean' quite different things, communicate quite different messages, and lead to quite different musical journeys. Some of the musical quotations use the notes of the chord as a skeletal framework and add the intervening notes as passing decoration, but the underpinning tonal structure, at least in the opening measure, is that of the chord of C major.

Restrictions of space make it impossible to discuss the inspiration, compositional context and intent behind the music represented here. But if I refer you back to the diagram (fig 1, p. 91) of the triadic dialectic involved in musical communication, and if I say that these few quotations range from the simplicity of Mozart's 'Ah, vous dirai-je Maman', which we recognise as 'Twinkle, Twinkle, Little Star', through Bach and Haydn, to the prophetic mutterings of Beethoven, and the majestic romance of Schubert's Great C major Symphony, then I think my point about musical semantics and levels of meaning will be made.

A contemporary critique of the 'pure music approach' suggests that mere technical analysis contributes neither to musical appreciation nor to the science or art of aesthetics, confusing, as it does, the means of music with the end. The critique goes on to state that the real meaning or significance of a piece of music is not easy to fathom and 'demands much more time and concentrated effort than merely listing the technical means of expression; and it requires intuition'.[16]

This position is in harmony with Adorno's in its extension of the traditional philosophical definition of the truth content of a work of art as the 'identity of concept with object in cognition'. This 'identity theory' is embraced in Adorno's theory of 'immanent' analysis but transcended in that for Adorno the use of the term 'immanent analysis' 'means more than simply uncovering the 'facts of the work's structure as an end in itself'. Adorno's dialectical notion of truth, derived from Hegelian logic, 'recognises that truth lies not only in the identity of concept and object but also in their *non-identity*'. This contradiction is central to Adorno's negative dialectics. When applied to music:

> [it] leads to a second level of analysis which seeks to reveal the contradictions of the autonomous musical work through situating it in its social and historical context. [17]

The number and variability of the elements which are involved in musical communication are evidence of the non-absolute, open-ended character of musical meaning or message. The complexity of the dialectical approach to analysis could perhaps throw doubt on the traditional assumption of aesthetics that a work of art can be understood at all, 'in the limited sense of closed meanings'.[18] Perhaps this is part of the paradoxical nature of art, its enigmatic character 'which has characteristics of the *Vexierbild*, a puzzle which has potential but not a final solution ... [it] demands philosophical interpretation'.[19] Such qualities as, for example, the truth or beauty of a work, do not reside exclusively in the subjective imaginative life of the listener, or perceiving subject; they are apprehended *in* the music and, as such, this apprehension presupposes, rather than creates, their existence in the objective 'out there' of the music. Interpretation is a valid and necessary dimension of musical communication and pertains to the role of the listener.

The listener who is re-created by the music is the continuum whose presence is implied in all discussion of the triadic dialectic of musical communication. The listener is the third and vital partner in the chain of musical communication, the critical responsive link. The listener is the evaluating agent, not of objective factors of value or greatness, – however one might define them – but of the quality of the empathic response initiated by the music in the psychological and emotional world of thoughts, memories, feelings and expectations. The differences in responses are related more to the private world of the individual listener than to the original musical stimulus. There is, therefore, an openness in the attribution of meaning in musical analysis. There is in this openness, 'a halo of uniqueness' around every musical experience respecting what Adorno calls music's 'magical origin'.[20] Music represents rather than embodies something absolute. 'The meanings of the meaning of music transcend', Steiner has written. 'It has long been, it continues to be, the unwritten theology of those who lack or reject any formal creed.'[21]

An advocate of the referentialist approach to musical analysis has written as follows:

It will be asked on what basis and by what standards one is to assess [musical] significance, and it will be objected that anything but a technical analysis must be purely subjective. The whole aesthetic process is the perception of meaning, and what meaning can there be in key changes and the like? Art is an *introverted* form of perception and necessarily subjective, whereas the analysis of the mere means of expression is extroverted and materialistic. Art itself is a subjective expression, not in the sense of being purely individual, but in a collective sense and in the sense that all perception presupposes a subject as well as an object. As Jung says of subjective perception: 'it means more than the mere image of the object', and 'introverted sensation apprehends the background of the physical works rather than its surface. It is seeing things *sub specie aeternitatis* ... this is specifically characteristic of the artist [who reaches] into the past and future, while extroverted sensation seizes on the momentary existence of things open to the light of day. As we live in an extroverted age and society, there is an overwhelming prejudice in favour of the superficial. [22]

The phrase *sub specie aeternitatis* seems especially suited to the artistic endeavours of composers of religious music; their goal would appear to lie beyond the surface of things sensible and to be more attuned to that which is eternal.

The criticism of the superficiality of contemporary living is a particular challenge. As a Christian I hold a deep conviction that life and death – both – belong in essential harmony within that state of divine relatedness which is being human. As a Christian educator, I believe passionately in the disclosive and transformative power of great art to reveal something of the mystery of this harmony, something of the meaning of this often dissonant counterpoint of light and darkness which is life and death. I cannot offer chapter and verse as proof of this power in any particular instance. But anyone who has ever been moved by picture, poem, or symphony, will understand that such an epiphany of hope and meaning is beyond 'immanence and verification' [Steiner]. This is a theophany transcending considerations of formal faith or culture. The experience is like that of Job who heard His 'songs in the night'. It is to touch the hem of the eternal. In the expression of meaning the artist creator translates the material world, heightens or even transforms our awareness of it and shows it in 'the context of a higher reality' [23] which is mystery.

It is to this broad analytical theory that I subscribe, and to its approach cautiously aspire. I realise the complexity and the pitfalls of fragmentation inherent in its interdisciplinary method. However, standard technical analysis would seem to stop short of the real significance of music as a meaningful communication. This would seem particularly to be so in the case of religious music perceived as 'a revelation of truth' – to borrow Hegel's phrase regarding human art. (I also use the term 'religious' here in accordance with the definition of religious offered earlier in this paper.)[24] 'A truth beyond words', was how Schoenberg described the object of such revelation. The revelation to be enjoyed in Bach's Brandenburg Concertos may have little to do with that which we might label as explicitly or even implicitly 'religious', but it is more than the sum of crotchets and quavers, however competently analysed. Beethoven's Last Quartets are more than his expansion of the formal and expressive conventions of his musical inheritance, however eloquently described. And Mahler's symphonies are more than the juxtaposing of banal tunes with sublime melody, and more than the counterbalancing of the dissonance of despair with heart-easing resolution.

In examining the progression from means to meaning in musical communication, the task would appear to be to disclose the essence of the total experience of the music. Musical analysis is a rigorous academic discipline, the object of which is to discover the organic coherence and essential unity of a work, and through thoroughness, clarity and an inspired leap of the imagination to uncover meaning which is beyond facts. Uncovering the facts of a work's structure, or 'immanent analysis', to use Adorno's term, is not an end in itself. It is in the dialogue and complementarity of the scientific and artistic dimensions of the music that the mysterious essence of the total experience of the music can in some measure be revealed. Such a revelation, however partial, is of music's meaning, – the meaning of its own mysterious nature as itself revelatory of Mystery.

This is therefore, the particular philosophy of meaning in music from which I am attempting to formulate a theory of the connectedness of music, meaning and mystery. On the basis of this theory I believe that it is possible to understand and recognise religious music as a theophany, a manifestation of the divine.

Music, Meaning and Mystery
At the musicological juncture where music, meaning and mystery meet, we may experience in the music intuitions of meaning and intimations of mystery. Such experiences transcend proof, and win us over to an acceptance of music as mystery; mystery wherein fact and value recognise one another and embrace.

The words of Thomas Mann indicate the scale of the fact *versus* value dilemma within the phenomenon of the art of music, and expose something of the nature of both the fact and the mystery that is music.

> Music is a great mystery ... by virtue of its sensual spiritual nature and the amazing union it achieves between strict rule

and dream, good form and magic, reason and emotion, day and night, it is without a doubt the most profound, most fascinating, and, in the eyes of the philosopher, most disquieting phenomenon..... Music is a theology of number, an austere godlike art, but an art in which all demons are interested and which of all arts, is most susceptible to the demoniac. For it is both moral code and seduction, sobriety and drunkenness, a summons to the highest alertness and a lure to the sweetest sleep of enchantment, reason and anti-reason – in short, a mystery with all the initiation and educative rites which ever since Pythagoras have been part and parcel of every mystery; and the priests and masters of music are the initiates, the preceptors of that dual being, the divine-demoniac totality of the world, life, mankind and culture. [25]

The most persuasive and powerful factor at my disposal in the construction of a theory of the connectedness of music, meaning and mystery is music itself. The difficulty was, and is, one of the embarrassment of riches from which I might choose to illustrate my argument. I have chosen to let mystery be the guiding principle, the mystery of all mysteries which tantalise the intellect – the mystery of death and afterlife.

The mystery of death in life, and life after death has fascinated and inspired composers down through the centuries. It is with the musical end result of this encounter between the artist and mystery, the musical expression of struggle with belief and unbelief, hope and fear, mortality and immortality, time and eternity, that I bring this paper to a close. I would like to speak briefly about two works, Gerard Victory's *Ultima Rerum*, and Mahler's *Resurrection Symphony*.

Gerard Victory's Requiem work, *Ultima Rerum*, received its first performance in March, 1984, and was warmly received as the first major Requiem by an Irish composer. It was, above all its merits, the eclecticism of the work – 'a Requiem with Hindu, Moslem, Navajo Indian, mystic poet, old Irish and Norse injections'[26] – which commanded attention and interest.

Ultima Rerum, stretches over a broad canvas of musical styles and embraces sacred and profane texts widely differing in time and thought. The disparate elements are elegantly woven together within the traditional Requiem structure of the Roman Ritual. The initial impact of the coherence and overall unity of the work was summed up by one critic in the words: 'Its subject is human thought and the after-life, and ... there is no doubt that there is for [Victory] an after-life.'[27]

This comment would appear to identify and perhaps commend *Ultima Rerum* as no more than a personal testament. I believe it is, because of its public quality and the universal relevance of its speculative content, considerably more than a personal *credo*.

If, as is a conviction of this study, the artist is the prophetic spokesperson for all people, having both the obligation and the prerogative to interpret reality through creativity, then his/her testament of belief, whatever its object, assumes a public quality and a universal significance.

The metaphor of journeying, sailing on storm-tossed seas, courage and exploration, is the thematic 'ground bass' of *Ultima Rerum*. The cross-cultural significance of its imagery familiarly portrays the excitement of the great adventure and the joy of finding a safe harbour of rest at the end of the many journeyings, spiritual and temporal, which it encompasses. Gerard Victory, as Vaughan Williams before him in his *Sea Symphony* (1910), found inspiration in Whitman's *Passage to India*. Perhaps the source of hope and courage proclaimed by *Ultima Rerum* is the truth enshrined in the closing lines of Whitman, a truth which confers in every communal and personal odyssey something of an *imprimatur*: 'are they not all the seas of God?'

In *Ultima Rerum* it would seem that there is room for everyone. It is Christian and non-Christian, sacred and profane, it is belief and unbelief, hope and despair, meaning and nihilism. Its meaning, perhaps even its inadvertent message, lies in the harmonisation, both musical and philosophical, which it creates from the disparate elements which are its inspiration. Among these elements are a variety of the fruits of human speculation on the mystery of life and death. The compelling dynamic of *Ultima Rerum* is towards resolution, towards redemption, towards a sense of universal salvation which is revelatory. Such revelation extends the horizons of the human spirit, and discloses the transcendent and the divine as mystery – that mystery which, as Gabriel Marcel describes, 'attracts as towards the light'.[28] Such revelation is articulated in any art form in which faith, hope and art enter into dialogue, not in theological propositions but rather as the broken lights of creativity and prophecy. Such intimations of mystery are harvested by the intuitive skill and giftedness of the artist, and then offered as food for our starved spirits seeking resurrection and renewed life.

The Austrian composer Gustav Mahler (1860-1911) was something of a tortured spirit who agonised over life and its apparent emptiness and futility. Yet despite this, and what some would call his morbid fascination with the subject of death, his musical testaments are overwhelmingly in favour of life and its significance. This is particularly true of his Second Symphony, the *Resurrection Symphony*. Deryck Cooke has described the programme of this symphony as a 'symbolic description of a psychological mood sequence: a sense of outrage at the omnipresence of death, a haunting awareness of the fragility of life's happiness, and a feeling of disgust at the mechanical and aimless triviality of everyday life, followed by a turning away to faith in God and belief in resurrection and eternal life'.[29] Cooke suggests that these moods reflect the struggle to respond to the challenge to find some significance in a life which is doomed to extinction. Whether or not the listener is convinced by the religious concepts in which Mahler finds resolution for his symphony, the sheer power of the music is itself a resurrection experience. It is an affirmation of faith and inspiration in life itself as of value and significance, despite a multiplicity of indications to the contrary in the pain and weariness of daily living.

The fourth movement of the *Resurrection Symphony* is a serene hymn-like setting of the poem '*Urlicht*'. Mahler has said of this invocation of primeval light that it 'throws a bright light on what has gone before ... The matinal voice of faith sounds in our ears: "I am of God, and to God will return."'

The overall key structure of this symphony has significance in its symbolic tonal architecture. It is founded in the dark ruminations of C minor and reaches its sublime conclusion in the relative major key of E flat, – its tonal resurrection. The final movement spreads before us the kaleidoscope of emotions through which the music has led us. The struggle and despair has given way to the triumph of faith and hope. The hushed chorus out of the silence has declared: 'Rise again, yea, thou shalt rise again ... He who called thee will grant thee immortal life'. The solo voice adds: 'O believe, my heart ... what thou hast lived for, fought for, will be thine ... thou hast not lived in vain, suffered in vain'. In this last extract we pick up the music as the choral voices adjure us: 'Cease from trembling! Prepare thyself to live!'

The music soars upwards in waves of sound towards light, eventually becoming, in the final bars, a wordlessly powerful affirmation of life.

We are, as Steiner has written, 'Close neighbours to the unknown ... the artist and [his/her] respondent know "there is something in us that can be without us, nor cannot tell how it entered into us." The artist and poet and musician translate this insight into living and lived form.' [30]

Music such as we have heard tonight is a theophany, a shining through of God, named or unnamed. It is the shining, deep and often hidden in our humanness, of which Steinbeck speaks:

> Our dear race, born without courage but very brave , born with a flickering intelligence and yet with beauty in its hands. What animal has made beauty, created it, save only we? With all our horrors and our faults, somewhere in us there is a shining. That is the most important of all facts. *There is a shining.* [31]

Example 1

BACH
Well-tempered Clavichord, Book I, Prelude No. I

Fugue No. I

MOZART
Variations in C, K. 265, Pft.

Symphony No. 28, K. 200, 1st Movement

Concerto, K. 299, Fl., Harp & Orch., 1st Movement

Sonata, K. 329, Organ & Orch. (In One Movement)

Symphony No. 34, K. 338, 1st Movement

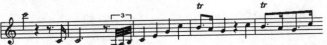

Concerto, K. 467, Pft. & Orch., 1st Movement

Sonata, K. 545, Pft., 1st Movement

Trio, K. 548, Pft., Vn. & Cello, 1st Movement

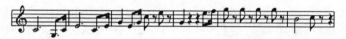

Symphony No. 41, K. 551, "Jupiter", 1st Movement

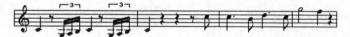

HAYDN
Symphony in G, "Surprise", 2nd Movement

1st Movement

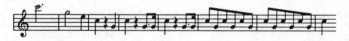

4th Movement, 2nd Theme

Symphony in C, "Toy", 1st Movement, 1st Theme

1st Movement, 4th Theme

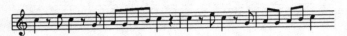

2nd Movement, 1st Theme

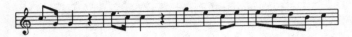

BEETHOVEN
Symphony No. 1, Op. 21, 1st Movement, 1st Theme

1st Movement, 2nd Theme

SCHUBERT
Symphony No. 7, "Great", 1st Movement

4th Movement, Introduction.

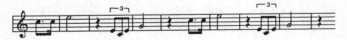

Glossary of Terms: Music, Meaning, Mystery

Music: the art of combining sounds with a view to beauty of form and expression.

Meaning: that which is meant; it is attributed to that which has import, purpose, design, significance.

Mystery: hidden or inexplicable matter; religious truth divinely revealed, especially one beyond human reason.

Each of the above definitions implies a certain duality within its specifications.

i) Music is to be understood in terms both of its form and of that which is expressed by that form. In this paper music is understood as a vehicle of human communication; a resource with the potential to enrich human life on many different levels with equal validity, according to the nature and levels of the response to it.

ii) Meaning is attributed in relation to purposeful form or design, but also in terms of the recognition of the significance of that form which is beyond scientifically verifiable formal data. There would appear to be the possibility of concordance between levels of meaning under this heading with levels of response referred to in paragraph (i) above.

iii)   Mystery would seem to embrace that which is hidden and also that which is revealed, or at least revealed as beyond complete explication. In the course of this paper the term 'mystery' will have a dual function and purpose: firstly to refer to the mysterious language of music as a vehicle of communication, and secondly to refer to those realities of religious faith with whose mystery much of the repertoire of music concerns itself.

Notes

1.   'The Profession of Musical Scholarship'. *Modern Musical Scholarship*, Oriel Press Ltd., Stocksfield, England 1980, 12.

2.   Rahner & Vorgrimler, 'Religion,' *Concise Theological Dictionary*, 2nd edition, Burns & Oates, London 1983, 437. The broad understanding of such terms as 'belief', 'faith', 'religion', which pertains throughout this paper, can be, to a large extent, supported from the writing of many contemporary theologians, primarily Karl Rahner. [Cf. art. 'Faith,' *Encyclopaedia of Theology*, (ed.) Karl Rahner, First published 1975, Burns & Oates Ltd., London. Cf. also 'Christianity and the Non-Christian Religions,' *Theological Investigations* , 5, 115-34; 'Christology within an Evolutionary View of the World', Ibid., D.L.T., London, 1966,157-92] .

3. David Tracy, *The Analogical Imagination: Christian Theology and the Culture of Pluralism*, SCM Press Ltd., London 1981, 110.
4. Max Paddison, 'Adorno's Aesthetic Theory', *Music Analysis*, 6:3 (1987), 366.
5. Jean Christensen, 'The Spiritual and The Material in Schoenberg's Thinking', *Music and Letters*, 65 (1984), 340.
6. ibid., 340-341.
7. David Tracy, op. cit.
8. George Steiner, *Real Presences*, Faber and Faber Ltd, London 1989, 218.
9. Quoted in B.M. Maciejewski, *Twelve Polish Composers*, Allegro Press, London 1976, 53-54.
10. Charles Seeger, *Studies in Musicology 1935-1975*, University of California Press 1977, 48.
11. Nicholas Cook, *A Guide to Musical Analysis*, J.M. Dent, London 1987, 1.
12. Steiner, op. cit. , 217.
13. Henry Holt & Co., New York 1944, 28
14. ibid.
15. Leonard B. Meyer, *Emotion and Meaning in Music*, University of Chicago Press 1956, 1.
16. Quoted in Deryck Cooke, *The Language of Music*, Oxford University Press, London 1959, 273.
17. Michael McMullin, 'Musical Analysis and Appreciation: A Critique of "Pure Music" ', *Music Review*, 45 (1984), 47-48.
18. Cf. Paddison, art. cit. , 368, 362 for a fuller account of these points.
19. Paddison, art, cit. , 358.
20. ibid. , 363.
21. Paddison, art. cit. , 371.
22. Steiner, op. cit. , 218.
23. McMullin, art. cit. , 51.
24. Paddison, art. cit. , 368-369.
25. Quoted in Adorno, *Philosophy of Modern Music*, translated by Anne G. Mitchell and Wesley Bloomster, The Seabury Press, New York 1973, 3.
26. Quoted in Seeger, op. cit. , 55-56.
27. Leslie Taylor, *The Evening Herald* Review, 6.3.1984.
28. Charles Acton, *The Irish Times* Review, 3.3.1984.
29. Gabriel Marcel, *The Philosophy of Existence*, Philosophical Library Inc. London 1948, 1969 ed. , 31.
30. *Gustav Mahler, An Introduction to his Music*, Faber Music Ltd., London. First published 1980. Second Edition 1988, 57.
31. Steiner, op. cit. , 226.
32. John Steinbeck, *Burning Bright*, Pan Books Ltd. , London 1954, 155.

Where Hope And History Rhyme: The Poetry of Seamus Heaney

John Devitt

In the final moments of this lecture I hope to justify my title, with the stealthy addition of a suggestive note of interrogation. Hope and history refuse to rhyme obediently, though the desire to bring them into harmonious conjunction is persistent and not negligible. If only the reality of history would take the form the hopeful imagination desires! In this mood we may posit a moment in the past when the tense opposition which disturbs us profoundly was resolved in some unitary state of being and call it Byzantium, or the age of the Antonines, or the *Saturnia regna*. Equally, if we are temperamentally more suited to a prospective view, we might anticipate a future dispensation and strive to realise it, conscious of all that defeats our hope but unwilling or unable to abandon it. Perhaps it is so with all forms of prayer: the attempt to pray may be as close as we can get to the real thing.

More modestly, this lecture might have been entitled "Some Strategies for Reading Heaney", and you may prefer to receive it under some such rubric. I find that Heaney's work, the prose as well as the verse, keeps company in my mind with that of other masters, in ways that you may find at least fitfully illuminating, though I anticipate a degree of dismay at the very thought. It was a shock for me to discover that the most passionate and seemingly spontaneous poet of antiquity was described as a matter of course by his earliest readers as *doctus Catullus*, 'the learned Catullus'. To insist at the outset that Heaney is not only prodigiously gifted but almost outrageously learned may shock those who have registered his emotional force and compiled a personal anthology of his most deeply moving poems, many of which write themselves on the fleshy tablets of the heart. But Heaney is alive to the works of his predecessors and alert to that of his contemporaries, be they insular, European or American; to ignore this element in his work is to impoverish our reading of it. Anything less naive than a poem by Seamus Heaney would be difficult to conceive.

My aim, then, is to draw attention to the strangeness, the intensity, the contrariness and sheer perversity of Heaney's best poems. The enterprise may be premature and therefore doomed. For this is the age of publicity and no writer or reader can escape the consequences of this disagreeable fact. We all know Heaney well, at least the public persona, from poetry readings, television interviews, radio programmes and the like. These must be good for sales, but it is not certain that they promote solitary reading. The illusion of intimacy and knowledge generated by the image is too pleasing and sedative to put at risk by engaging in the intolerable wrestle with words and meanings, to borrow Eliot's description[1] of the writer's dilemma and apply it to the reader's. Especially when the image is irresistibly attractive, composed, serene, intelligent, affable, a trifle circumspect, maybe, but undoubtedly sincere. Should we go on to read the poems, we encounter the same persona on a number of occasions, more particularly in the low-voltage conversation pieces which can be found in the second half of *North*.

The poems I want to focus on, for the simple and sufficient reason that I relish them most, are a very different matter: deeply troubled, agitated by dynamic scruples of doubt and guilt, hesitant, uncertain, compelled often to tell against themselves, sometimes lurid, at other times grotesque. I have in mind poems like "Undine", "Punishment", "Strange Fruit", "Casualty", most of the sequence "Station Island", the final sonnet in "Clearances", the title poem and many others in the magnificent recent collection *Seeing Things*. The poems I am indicating here are voiced for speakers who are variously exhilarated, alarmed and appalled by what their words say and do. As well they might be. We cannot account for these poems by surmising and then assiduously describing a unified sensibility from which they issue. The term 'sensibility' is altogether too limp, the strategy too mechanical, to do justice to their chameleon, quicksilver and unpredictable quality. Sensibility is a serviceable notion in the case of quite distinguished minor poets where it may indicate a certain kind of susceptibility, a predisposition to respond to certain experiences in certain ways, or even a degree of nervous intensity. We do not distort the works of, say Edward Thomas or Richard Wilbur, to name two very different poets whose work I admire, by treating of them under the rubric of sensibility. But Heaney's development can hardly be described in terms of a noun which is largely passive and redolent of something rather precious.

We might take a hint from Wallace Stevens' famous lecture, "The Noble Rider and the Sound of Words". There Stevens speaks of the violence within which answers the violence without: "It is the imagination pressing back against the pressure of reality."[2] The emphasis on violence is surprising, even allowing for the barbarity of the times; the lecture in question was delivered in Princeton in 1942. One thinks routinely of Stevens as the most fastidious of phrase-makers, the most self-reflexive of modern poets, indissolubly wedded to a lovely, ambiguous music; in short, the man of letters least likely to engage in the melodramatics of crisis-rhetoric. It is true that he is elsewhere content to use the term 'sensibility', but the meaning he attaches to it is modified by the passage just quoted, and even more sharply qualified by the one which follows. "We are confronting, therefore, a set of events not only beyond our power to tranquillize them in the mind, beyond our power to reduce them and metamorphose them, but events that stir the emotions to violence, that engage us in what is direct and immediate and real, and events that involve the concepts and sanctions that are the order of our lives and may involve our very lives; and these events are occurring persistently with increasing omen, in what we may call our presence."[3] This is hardly crisis-rhetoric. The deliberate syntactical parallelisms, the repetitions of key terms, the insistent use of the conjunction 'and' to emphasise the discreteness of terms in a sequence, the refusal to concede to mind an easy victory over what assails it simply by taking thought, all persuade us that Stevens is not solicitous of any effect, beyond being perfectly understood. This remarkable sentence has a life beyond its context and we can register that life by substituting the word 'imagination' for the word 'mind'. The argument can be advanced by citing a stanza from the last poem in Yeats' great suite "Meditations in Time of Civil War".

'Vengeance upon the murderers' the cry goes up,
'Vengeance for Jacques Molay'. In cloud-pale rags, or in lace,
The rage-driven, rage-tormented, and rage-hungry troop,

Trooper belabouring trooper, biting at arm or at face,
Plunges towards nothing, arms and fingers spreading wide
For the embrace of nothing; and I, my wits astray
Because of all that senseless tumult, all but cried
For vengeance on the murderers of Jacques Molay.[4]

It would only be a moment's work to adduce observations or anecdotes of violence from "Meditations in Time of Civil War", or from other poems by Yeats.[5] But the stanza in question is not a piece of reportage: it dramatises a violence which comes from the depths and does so with all the terrible and undeniable clarity of nightmare, and is barely mastered in the utterance. This takes us further even that Stevens gave us warrant. It is not the external violence of a brutal civil war which threatens to humiliate the operative powers of the mind; it is the demonic energy of the mind or imagination which threatens to overwhelm poet and reader. "Meditations in Time of Civil War" is a great poem, *not* because it is the work of a decent and humane witness moved to register a protest at the horrors of the time, but because it gives licence to the demon within that noonday decencies repudiate or simply denounce. In fact, the poem escapes altogether from the gravitational field of its title: it is not meditative, but intensely and dangerously dramatic.

On other occasions, Yeats compels us to register the destructive power of the imagination in lines like the following which are instinct with unholy joy.

We the great gazebo built,
They convicted us of guilt;
Bid me strike a match and blow.[6]
("In Memory of Eva Gore-Booth and Con Markieviez.")

To round off this excursion, I cite the octet of the great sonnet "Meru", where the violence of the mind is generalised powerfully and seen at work throughout human history.

Civilisation is hooped together, brought
Under a rule, under the semblance of peace
By manifold illusions; but man's life is thought,
And he, despite his terror, cannot cease

110

Ravening through century after century,
Ravening, raging, and uprooting that he may come
Into the desolation of reality:
Egypt and Greece good-bye, and good-bye, Rome! [7]

I invoked Stevens and Yeats in order to reinstate the old idea of the imagination, one with which the Greeks were familiar as a glance at the tenth book of Plato's *Republic* will show.[8] Contemporary discourse favours a more sedate approach, preferring to qualify imagination with terms like 'moral' or 'creative'. But in phrases like 'the creative imagination' or 'the moral imagination' the adjectives neuter the noun and surround it with a halo of easy approbation. I am prepared to go along with this bland deception, if it helps to keep literature and the arts on the syllabus. But the energy and attack, the demoniacal power and intensity, the utter freedom and mischievousness of great imaginative literature expose the poverty of that prim parlance. It would be foolish to pretend that Heaney has an energy equivalent to that of Yeats, or the poetic resources to harness it. He has not got the ferocious zest, nor the imperious syntax, nor the control of elaborate stanza forms which Yeats was able to command in his great period. Nowhere does Heaney attempt the high style, as Yeats does repeatedly and without ever falling flat on his face. Nor, in spite of his huge popularity, has he got Yeats' sense of a public role, one that might be disputed or doubted but could still be asserted on occasion with complete conviction. Indeed, some at least of Heaney's demons are rather shamefaced in comparison with Yeats's: a lurking eroticism, often indistinguishable from voyeurism; a fascination with violence which he longs to confront but dare not, for perfectly understandable reasons. But in the more recent work there is increasing evidence of a willingness to live dangerously, to take delight in the free play of the mind, as well as a relish of disobedience and a shedding of inhibitions. Imagination in Yeats exercises its power and counts the cost; in Heaney it is still testing its freedom and enjoying the sensation. A few lines from "Markings" will help to confirm the point; Heaney is replaying one of those distant but well-remembered magical evenings in which children kick football on an improvised pitch only notionally demarcated, on into the evening, past sunset, endlessly.

> It was quick and constant, a game that never need
> Be played out. Some limit had been passed,
> There was fleetness, furtherance, untiredness
> In time that was extra, unforeseen and free. [9]

'Played out' is an ambiguity to savour: the colloquial sense hints at the exhaustion of the ludic impulse, but this notion is promptly made untenable by the more formal sense of a game there is simply no need ever to finish or play out. The play on words renders active the very possibility the poem celebrates. The same process is at work in the phrase 'time that was extra' where the notion of 'extra time' in a game of football yields to the idea of being in some other dimension than that measured by the clock or the sun.

I hope that what I said a moment ago won't be construed as churlish, or as an excessively limiting judgement on Heaney. It shouldn't; Yeats is, after all, the major English language poet since the death of Wordsworth. But it *is* appropriate to invoke Yeats, for Heaney is the first poet strong enough to open himself to Yeats' influence without being submerged, to echo him without appearing ridiculous. There is also a salient chronological point. Heaney is fifty-three, at which age Yeats had yet to publish those magisterial collections which put his greatness beyond dispute. Furthermore, as Heaney's oeuvre expands and complicates itself, we find ourselves attending more and more to internal echoes, observing the redeployment of earlier themes, motifs and images with a curious incremental growth of meaning and suggestion. This interplay is at work within the individual collections as well as between them. Thus, *Seeing Things* opens with a translation of that celebrated passage in Vergil where Aeneas plucks the golden bough which will be his passport to the Underworld; there he will meet and commune with his father Archises whom he carried on his back from the burning city of Troy. The closing lines of 'Man and Boy' (in the same collection) deliberately recall that act of singular *pietas* in what the syntax converts into an oddly moving role reversal, with Heaney as the father figure:

> he will piggyback me,
> At a great height, light-headed and thin-boned
> Like a witless elder rescued from the fire.[10]

Not any old fire this, but the fire of Troy. A less subtle but no less telling instance of this interplay occurs between section VIII of the sequence "Station Island" and the elegy on the death of Colum McCartney, "The Strand at Lough Beg", which appeared in *Field Work*. The ghost of McCartney speaks in the idiom of rebuke in "Station Island", and expresses Heaney's own misgivings about the lyric sweetness of the earlier elegy.

> 'You confused evasion and artistic tact.
> The Protestant who shot me through the head
> I accuse directly, but indirectly, you
> who now atone perhaps upon this bed
> for the way you whitewashed ugliness and drew
> the lovely blinds of the Purgatorio
> and saccharined my death with morning dew.'[11]

I would remark that the elegy is not utterly discredited by this deadly critical onslaught. "The Strand at Lough Beg" answered in conventional terms a particular need; its tenderness and pathetic fallacy are admittedly inadequate to the victim; they minister rather to a moment of bewilderment and pain in the Heaney cousin who survived. A third instance of this interplay shows Heaney as a professional writer rescuing some vivid lines from perhaps the least satisfactory poem in the "Station Island" sequence and turning them to unsuspected account. In the penultimate stanza of Section III we find these lines:

> I thought of walking round
> and round a space utterly empty,
> utterly a source, like the idea of sound ...[12]

The last phrase is banal but the mind moves in silent speculation across the earlier lines, perhaps remembering Eriugena's meditations on nothingness in the *Periphyseon* or Bishop Berkeley's conviction that we Irish persist in finding something and nothing near neighbours.[13] In the final sonnet in "Clearances", the centrepiece of *The Haw Lantern*, Heaney presses those lines into service again and extracts from them a music and meaning only dimly heard when they first presented themselves.

> I thought of walking round and round a space
> Utterly empty, utterly a source

Where the decked chestnut tree had lost its place
In our front hedge above the wallflowers
The white chips jumped and jumped and skited high
I heard the hatchet's differentiated
Accurate cut, the crack, the sigh
And collapse of what luxuriated
Through the shocked tips and wreckage of it all.
Deep planted and long gone, my coeval
Chestnut from a jam jar in a hole,
Its heft and hush become a bright nowhere,
A soul ramifying and forever
Silent, beyond silence listened for.[14]

What you see in this poem is a remarkable quickening of the imagination. In an autobiographical passage in the essay on Kavanagh which is printed in *The Government of the Tongue* Heaney supplies the originating image of the tree planted at his birth and subsequently, after his family had moved, cut down; its absence was subsequently felt as a higher form of presence.[15] Eriugena and Berkeley are certainly present in the sonnet as sponsors at the birth of a conscious soul. You can hear in the sonnet, too, the precision of the imagination: the sound of the axe, the cracking of the weakened trunk and the slow whoosh of the leafy branches falling through the air are perfectly audible. But 'ramifying' is nothing less than a stroke of genius, for Heaney is enlisting the almost forgotten word *"ramus"* (Latin, a branch) which is deliciously appropriate here.

I do not want to claim that this process of development is an infallible indicator of poetic greatness. Hardy, for instance, does not develop in this way; you would be hard put to distinguish between an early poem and a late poem of his on the basis of any kind of growth. Much the same is true of Robert Frost and Emily Dickinson. Nor can we say, with a sideways glance at Heaney's prose, that all great poets develop their own explicit poetics. Yeats and Eliot did, and in the process made their own work more available by creating an understanding audience for it. Indeed, they did more: they provided a basis for understanding poets whose work differed in important respects from their own. I think Heaney's criticism has the same sort of generosity; in *The Place of Writing*, for instance, his readings of Longley, Mahon and Kinsella are simply dazzling, yet there is no sense in which he patronises them by dissolving the radical differences between his own work and theirs.[16]

But I want to turn now to the elegy "Casualty"; indeed most of what I have been saying so far is a prelude to the reading of this remarkable poem. In *Field Work*, "Casualty" is preceded by two other elegies to named victims of the Northern violence: "The Strand at Lough Beg" which, as we have seen, commemorates Colum McCartney, and "A Postcard from North Antrim" which commemorates Sean Armstrong. The victim in "Casualty" is rendered with incomparable subtlety and vividness, but is unnamed. It is here that Heaney, for the first time I think, engages seriously with Yeats; the poem could hardly have been written without "The Fisherman" to inform it. There are several deliberate echoes of other poems by Yeats. Thus, the lines 'I would manage by some trick/To switch the talk to eels' recall "Her Praise" where Yeats would 'Manage the talk until her name came round'.[17] Rather more daring is Heaney's rewriting of one of the most impressive images in "The Statues"; "Casualty" speaks of moving, under the influence of a rhythmical necessity, 'Into your proper haunt'; while Yeats insisted with an aristocratic hauteur that

> We Irish, born into that ancient sect
> But thrown upon this filthy modern tide
> And by its formless spawning fury wrecked
> Climb to our proper dark, that we may trace
> The lineaments of a plummet-measured face.[18]

The resemblances, however, serve only to heighten the differences which are a matter of tone, idiom, syntax and attitude.

Very much the same could be said of the connection between "Casualty" and "The Fisherman", even where it amounts to a kind of dependance. The central figures in both poems are fishermen; but Yeats' fisherman is a confessedly ideal figure ('a man who is but a dream'[19]), while Heaney's is a dead acquaintance. As Augustine Martin noted, Heaney's fisherman is evoked through the precisely observed gestures he makes in ordering various

115

drinks, in very much the same way as a novelist might establish character by the use of significant detail.[20] This is a technique which Yeats rarely employs, except, perhaps, in evoking Mabel Beardsley in "To a Dying Lady"; it would be ludicrous in a poem of powerful and generalised insult like "The Fisherman". Both "Casualty" and "The Fisherman" are exercised by questions about the nature of poetry, and the kind of relationship which exists between the poet and his society. Yeats adopts a characteristically extreme position by rejecting the only audience available and opting instead for a lonelier course and a more severe discipline: 'I shall have written him one/Poem maybe as cold/And passionate as the dawn.'[21] Heaney's relations with his fisherman are far more intimate; indeed each seems aware of the other to the extent that they mirror each other and are implicated in each other. The relation is not sentimentalized: in life Heaney thought the dead man 'Sure-footed but too sly',[22] and his failure to meet the poet's eye confirms as much. But the poem compels us to see them as far more like than unlike. The poet is politic and evasive, as slyly observant as the man he observes: 'But my tentative art/ His turned back watches too...'[23] Furthermore, the fishing expedition on Lough Neagh in the cold sunshine of the dawn, in which both are involved, is at once an occasion for poetry and a metaphor for the poetic process. The cold severity of the dawn is reminiscent of Yeats, but the voice is the voice of Heaney.

> I tasted freedom with him.
> To get out early, haul
> Steadily off the bottom,
> Dispraise the catch, and smile
> As you find a rhythm
> Working you, slow mile by mile
> Into your proper haunt
> Somewhere, well out, beyond...[24]

Yet we recall the phrase 'my tentative art' with its sense of incapacity and uncertainty. The last lines in the poem admit that the dead man's presence is a literary fiction, that poetry cannot restore the dead to life. And the central question about the victim reflects an angular light on the poet who frames it:

How culpable was he
That last night when he broke
Our tribe's complicity?[25]

Evasion ends here, in a frank admission: but to admit complicity, as Heaney does, is already to move beyond it. This does not seem like an easy paradox in the poem, for it is immediately followed by a bitter, vindictive speech from the dead victim in which Heaney's question is fielded and returned with interest.

For all its indebtedness to Yeats, "Casualty" is finally obedient only to its own logic. Any conceivable paraphrase would imply a poem at once crabbed and involuted, but that is not my sense of it at all. What I *would* remark is the increasing rapidity and daring of its transitions, a process which is deliberately at odds with the prescribed elegiac tone. The first of the poem's three sections is the most conventional, slow and measured, detailed and literal. In the second section the funeral of the victims of Bloody Sunday is pictured as a procession of 'blossoms on slow water' but it immediately becomes a strange birth when it is visualised as the unrolling of a swaddling band. The victim's murder is described in ambiguous terms: the light from the bomb illuminates 'His cornered outfaced stare/Blinding in the flash.'[26] 'Blinding' means 'going blind' and refers to the victim; but it also refers to the imaginative response of the poet and of the reader, who are not blinded by the flash but blinded by the victim's fate, which is therefore brighter than the flash. In the final paragraph of the second section the fisherman *becomes* a fish drawn by the lure of the pub who defies the curfew only to be trapped in 'The blurred mesh and murmur'.[27] In the third section, the dawdling engine of the hearse *becomes* the engine of the boat as poet and victim move over the waters of the lough in a vivid present tense within a single syntactical unit which contains no enabling or facilitating conjunction.

They [the mourners who walk in the victim's funeral]
They move in equal pace
With the habitual
Slow consolation
Of a dawdling engine,
The line lifted, hand

Over fist, cold sunshine
On the water, the land
Banked under fog...[28]

You will have noticed that the mourners here have *become* the engine by virtue of the dual syntax of the opening, unpunctuated phrases. But the most startling feature of these lines is the swiftness of the transition to the waters of the lough which is only translated into the past tense when it has already been experienced as a present reality. The ambiguity of 'line' (a fishing line, a line of verse) anticipates the way the rhythm of the two fishermen becomes the informing rhythm of a poem, the poem we are actually reading. Even the subtlest critic could only pant after these becomings and transitions. Osip Mandelstam in "Conversations about Dante" provides a beautiful figure for this kind of poetic activity. 'Imagine an airplane', he recommends, 'which in full flight constructs and launches another machine'.[29] Mandelstam takes an earlier stab at meaning when he visualises a river crowded with Chinese junks, all moving in different directions; the poetic intelligence athletically crosses the river from junk to junk, improvising a pontoon as it goes.[30] Heaney's elegy defies the gravity of its occasion without betraying the humanity of the victim it celebrates. It has obvious affinities with those poems in *Seeing Things* which also push out 'somewhere, well out, beyond...' In fact "Casualty", without ceasing to be an elegy, displays the same energy and inventiveness which characterise the latest book, and identifies the territory into which it will move.

It is futile to seek out a theory of language which will account for Heaney's practice. 'Theory' presupposes a vantage point of utter superiority from which a privileged view of the whole field is possible. No such position is available, for we are always enmeshed in words. In a brief but brilliant meditation on language from within its inveterately metaphoric processes, Heaney arrived at a memorable paradox. 'A human being pondering the nature of language is not unlike a snowman pondering the nature of snow, for the snowman's instruments of cognition are no less snowy than the human being's are wordy.'[31] Language redeemed from blather not only enables us to identify ourselves and our purpose, but introduces us to that life beyond life, life raised to a higher power, so to speak, of which words would speak, if they were let.

> Words of the fragrant portal, dimly starred
> And of ourselves and of our origins
> In ghostlier demarcations, cleaner sounds.[32]

The words of a poem are Janus-like, radically ambiguous. To the casual glance they reveal prosaic sense, but they have also a shyer eloquence which only discloses itself reluctantly. Heaney relishes the mischievousness of words which 'stand smiling at the audience's way of reading them and winking back at the poet's way of using them'.[33] To see him as a passionate etymologist or linguistic archaeologist who specialises in excavating the meaning of Irish placenames or in restoring almost forgotten Anglo-Saxon monosyllables, is partial and limiting. His alertness to the secret life of language is always a question of sound values and of the magical, evocative power of words. Hence his devotion to Eliot's description of the auditory imagination which he quoted in his Cheltenham lecture of October 1986: 'the feeling of syllable and rhythm, penetrating far below the levels of thought and feeling, invigorating every word: sinking to the most primitive and forgotten, returning to an origin and bringing something back...fusing the most ancient and civilized mentalities'.[34] This is a richer and more helpful notion than Eliot's equally celebrated aside on the practice of certain Elizabethan and Jacobean writers: 'Their words have often a network of tentacular roots down to the deepest terrors and desires.'[35] But the truth is we need both of Eliot's formulations, as well as Heaney's own, if we are to come to terms with the poetry of *North* and of *Seeing Things*. Nevertheless, we persist in wanting poems to be as legible as other texts, to be as obedient to our anxious desire for meaning as discursive prose; such is our readerly impatience with complexity. We are schooled in our academies, and acquire at least a degree of proficiency, in those techniques of reading which are plausible, certifiable and transferable. But a poem is a performance in language in which at every point things are happening simultaneously. Hence the notorious resistance to paraphrase with which poems scandalously affront mere intellect. This is true even of those poems, like Larkin's "An

Arundel Tomb", which consist, apparently, of description followed by clinching statement, and of poems, like Yeats's "Easter 1916", which seem to be no more than elaborate commentaries on the historical events which occasioned or provoked them. The last line of "An Arundel Tomb" offers a statement ('What will remain of us is love') which may be bleak but is also consoling; the syntax of the stanza in which it is incised with appropriately lapidary economy prevents the reader from taking it for granted.

> Time has transfigured them into
> Untruth. The stone fidelity
> They hardly meant has come to be
> Their final blazon, and to prove
> Our almost-instinct almost true:
> What will survive of us is love.[36]

In his recent book *Minotaur*, the poet and critic Tom Paulin reminds us of the circumstances attending the first publication of "Easter 1916" which Yeats hesitated to publish until Terence McSwiney's hunger strike had begun to affect British and Irish opinion. Excited by this four-year moratorium on publication, Paulin proposes to read the poem univocally as Yeats' hunger-strike poem. "Easter 1916" becomes almost indistinguishable from a pamphlet or a piece of journalism. Its publication in the *New Statesman*, Paulin notes, may have influenced leading members of the British Labour Party. 'That party had established a commission to inquire into the Anglo-Irish War in the autumn of 1920, and Yeats' poem might be regarded as a piece of evidence submitted to the commission'.[37] There is, however, no compelling reason to do so; readers do not forfeit their rights because an interesting footnote has expanded uncontrollably.

The figure a poem makes on the page with its unjustified lines, or in the cave of the ear with its curious resonances, demands and rewards a kind of attention which is quite different to that we accord discursive prose or ordinary conversation. Furthermore, poetry is not so much an abstract noun as a collective one, indicating a repertoire of formal possibilities some of them as yet unrealised and discovered only in the writing. Here we touch on the question of influence, already glanced at in the treatment of "Casualty". If time permitted we could expand on the influence Kavanagh has exerted on Heaney, or move into less well-charted territory by considering the even more pervasive influence of Robert Frost. It is Frost's narrative voice I hear in "Station Island", particularly in the great and moving seventh section. But Heaney's exploitation of the sonnet form owes at least as much to the Frost of "The Silken Tent" as to Kavanagh's slightly dishevelled "The Hospital". A more surprising case is "Well Water", an unrhymed sonnet which is deliberately cheated of its fourteenth line.

> What a girl called 'the dailiness of life'
> (Adding an errand to your errand. Saying,
> 'Since you're up...' Making you a means to
> A means to a means to) is well water
> Pumped from an old well at the bottom of the world.
> The pump you pump the water from is rusty
> And hard to move and absurd, a squirrel-wheel
> A sick squirrel turns slowly, through the sunny
> Inexorable hours. And yet sometimes
> The wheel turns of its own weight, the rusty
> Pump pumps over your sweating face the clear
> Water, cold, so cold! you cup your hands
> And gulp from them the dailiness of life.

One can see in "Well Water" a bridge between the Heaney of *Death of a Naturalist* (1966) and the Heaney of *Seeing Things* (1991). The preoccupation with the cotidian ('the dailiness of life'), the fascination with the dynamics and hydraulics of the well, the risky recourse to colloquial banalities, are all suggestive of the workaday pastoral poetry Heaney produced in the sixties. On the other hand, the sprightliness of the diction (the sudden and repeated conversion of the noun 'pump' into a verb), the openness to the suffering of the sick squirrel, and, most striking of all, the celebration of the miraculous energy of the wheel which turns, or seems to, by its own weight, anticipate the "lightenings" which *Seeing Things* so often enacts. In "Wheels within Wheels", for instance. In fact, "Well Water" is not by Kavanagh or Frost or, indeed, Heaney; it is a beautiful late poem by Randall Jarrell. It can stand as a reminder of how the auditory imagination of one poet can be called to, and answered, by the work of another.

In October 1990 Heaney's play *The Cure at Troy*, a version of the *Philoctetes* of Sophocles, received its first production at the Guildhall in Derry and subsequently toured the country. The publication of the text by Faber coincided with the Guildhall opening. In 1991 the BBC broadcast a radio production by Pam Brighton with Stephen Rea in the title role. The play, however, has excited surprisingly little comment, though the themes it rehearses are intimately connected with the concerns of Heaney's recent poetry and criticism. His interest in the myth and its dramatic possibilities may have been quickened by an essay in Edmund Wilson's *The Wound and the Bow* which offers an allegorical account of the Sophocles play. You will remember that Philoctetes is a Greek captain in the Trojan War who is abandoned by his comrades on an uninhabited island because of a disgusting, suppurating wound in his foot; so terrible are his screams of agony when the pain bites home that it is impossible for the priests to attend to their rituals. The Greek attitude to Philoctetes changes some years later when a captive Trojan soothsayer pronounces an unambiguous prophecy: Troy can be taken, and the long siege ended, only when the bow and arrows of Philoctetes, magical gifts of the dying god Hercules to the man who lit his funeral pyre, are brought to bear against it. In the *deus-ex-machina* ending of the Greek play, Hercules intervenes in person to influence Philoctetes who buries his hatred of the sons of Atreus in his decision to rejoin his former comrades.

In Wilson's reading of this fascinating story, Philoctetes becomes a type of the artist, at once gifted and cursed, alienated and outcast, but finally indispensable. He is a pariah, an impious distraction, yet he is also a sacred figure, like the blinded Oedipus, endowed with superhuman power and insight. Wilson translates a passage from André Gide's *Philoctéte* in which the eponymous hero celebrates the freedom that his protracted sufferings have brought in terms that irresistibly suggest a highly self-conscious poet. 'I came to understand that words inevitably become more beautiful from the moment they are no longer put together in response to the demands of others.'[38] In Gide's version Wilson found the hero to be 'at once a moralist and an artist, whose genius becomes purer and deeper in ratio to his isolation and outlawry'.[39] But all of this is implicit in the original myth and Sophocles's handling of it. Wilson characterizes the imagination of the Greek dramatist in terms that are relevant here: 'He has balance and logic, of course; those qualities that the classicists admire; but these qualities only count because they master so much savagery and madness.'[40] The emphatic quality of the final clause may recall the passages from Wallace Stevens and Yeats which I quoted earlier. Finally, Wilson has an interesting comment on the role of Neoptolemus in Sophocles. Initially the tool of the wily politician Odysseus, Neoptolemus recovers his integrity when he refuses to continue deceiving Philoctetes and, in effect, makes an appeal to the latter's better nature. 'Yet in taking the risk to his cause which is involved in the recognition of his common humanity with the sick man, in refusing to break his word, he dissolves Philoctetes' stubbornness, and this cures him and sets him free, and saves the campaign as well.'[41]

Heaney may have found in *The Wound and the Bow* a luminous and congenial reading of a neglected play with a suggestive mythic basis. He may have been encouraged to venture on a personal version by Wilson's observation that the myth has not excited the modern imagination, as well as by his vivid demonstration of its richness. Alternatively, he might have been alerted to its power by Denis Donoghue's reflection on it in the Reith Lectures of 1983.[42] Or he may simply have come on the play in the course of his own omnivorous reading. It is no matter. I have dwelt at length on Wilson's treatment, and quoted extensively from it, because it is the most likely source, though not the only possible one. Heaney found the myth congenial because it answered the same concerns that he found himself addressing in his version of the medieval Irish text *Buile Suibhne* on which he worked intermittently for ten years or so before producing his translation *Sweeney Astray* in 1983. The figure of Sweeney haunted the poet who relished the way his own name rhymed with that of the demented, driven Irish king; Sweeney even enjoys a weird kind of posthumous existence, liberated from his original context, in the remarkable sequence of poems which constitute the final third of the volume *Station Island*. In the Introduction to his translation, Heaney proposes Sweeney as an allegorical figure with a dual significance: on the one hand an instance of the tension between Christianity and the Celtic paganism it has never quite supplanted; on

123

the other a moving exemplar of the perennial poetic dilemma. Heaney remarks of the latter reading of the old text: 'insofar as Sweeney is also a figure of the artist, displaced, guilty, assuaging himself by his utterance, it is possible to read the work as an aspect of the quarrel between free creative imagination and the constraints of religious, political and domestic obligation'.[43] It is scarcely surprising, then, that the poet who gave us a version of the anonymous *Buile Suibhne* along these lines should also be tempted by the *Philoctetes* of Sophocles and that in the guise of translator he should produce some of his most vivid writings.

In *The Cure at Troy* Philoctetes is heard before he is seen; the chorus glosses his cries of agony for the benefit of Neoptolemus.

> This is not some shepherd in a book
> With his Pan pipes and his shepherd's crook.
> This is a danger-man.
> That shouting's desperate and it's violent.
> He sounds provoked.[44]

This is as much as to say that Philoctetes is no conventional pastoral poet from whom only routine, picturesque gestures can be expected: he is possessed, demoniacal, destructive. Some of the most striking passages in the play elaborate on the utter loneliness and isolation he experiences on Lemnos, 'a home where I was never at home'.[45] When Philoctetes finally confronts Odysseus he speaks in painful, passionate prose of the desolation to which he is habituated but not reconciled. 'Odysseus, you have taken everything I ever had and was. The best years of my life, my means of self-defence, my freedom, the use of my two hands. Everything that made me my own self, you've stripped away…'[46] Most memorable of all is the speech Philoctetes delivers when the great bow has been spirited away from him and he celebrates the gift he has lost, even though it made him, once again, a victim of the Greeks.

> I loved the feel of it,
> Its grip and give, and the grain
> That was seasoned with my sweat.
> When I held it, I had a hold
> On the crossbeam of the world.

> I was the wind and the trees
> And the pillar of Hercules.[47]

It is clear that Heaney has invested Philoctetes with the aura of poet in a quite explicit and deliberate way. But the opening speech of the Chorus is also concerned with the poetic dilemma, the sense of occupying a difficult borderline between two irreconcilable views, that of the distant gods and that of human beings.

> And that's the borderline that poetry
> Operates on too, always in between
> What you would like to happen and what will –
> Whether you like it or not.[48]

Interestingly, as one might expect in the case of a true poet, poetry takes precedence over divinity.

>   Poetry
> Allowed the god to speak. It was the voice
> Of reality and justice.[49]

(The final phrase is another deliberate borrowing from Yeats). But the *The Cure at Troy*, like *Sweeney Astray*, contains other interesting elements apart from its concern with the extreme though exemplary figure of Philoctetes. What leaks into the play in the opening speech of the Chorus is the sense that we cannot always live in the consciousness of the wrongs inscribed by history in the particular circumstances in which we have our individual and collective being. Heaney is identifying a malaise which has been called the laager mentality.

> People so deep into
> Their own self-pity self-pity buoys them up.
> People so staunch and true, they're fixated,
> Shining with self-regard like polished stones,
> And their whole life spent admiring themselves
> For their own long-suffering.

> Licking their wounds
> And flashing them around like decorations
> I hate it, I always hated it, and I am
> A part of it myself.[50]

It is, of course, easier to discourse learnedly on the aetiology of a disease than it is to effect a cure. The passage I have just quoted renders in the first place the Ulster Unionist position, though it also allows us to think in terms of the Nationalist position as well, North and South. To be identified with one's wound, to cherish the long years of neglect, to be at one with a well-founded historical narrative which imposes its forms on the present and future, to wear righteousness with complete conviction, may solve the problem of identity, after a fashion, but it creates and maintains the conditions of perpetual mistrust and worse. And worse means war. The extraordinary thing about *The Cure at Troy* is not only that Philoctetes serves as a kind of surrogate for the poet in his anxious meditation on his dilemma as an artist; he is also, simultaneously, Heaney's anti-self, a figure from 'the other side' seen with the clarity of a tragic vision, but not without sympathy and not without hope. This understanding of Philoctetes is promoted by severely negative descriptions such as Odysseus gives Neoptolemus to justify a policy of deviousness, or the subsequent standardised account of Philoctetes which Neoptolemus gives the Chorus:

Festering inside and out.
Contrary, hard and proud.[51]

(In the radio production, presumably with Heaney's approval, 'twisted' was substituted for 'hard'.) Philoctetes himself verifies what is said about him:

I managed to come through
But I never healed.
My whole life has been
Just one long cruel parody.[52]

As the play moves towards its crisis the stricken Philoctetes admits 'All I've left is a wound' only to be immediately rebuked by the Chorus: 'Your wound is what you feed on, Philoctetes.'[53] But the political dimension of the allegory is made most explicit when Neoptolemus echoes the absolutism and intransigence of the familiar Unionist fundamentalism in a memorable question.

Things are different now. I ask again:
Are you going to stay here saying no for ever
Or do you come in with us?[54]

And almost immediately Neoptolemus goes on to undermine the

notion that there is anything admirable in maintaining the integrity of a quarrel which proves so murderous and self-damaging.

> You aren't
> Bearing up, you are bearing down. Anybody
> That ever tries to help you just gets savaged.
> You're a wounded man in terrible need of healing
> But when your friends try, all you do is snarl
> Like some animal protecting cubs.[55]

Hearteningly, when the god Hercules speaks through the Chorus by a process of ventriloquism, as Apollo did through the Oracle, Philoctetes finds that he can move from his entrenched position, that he can cope with his own misgivings, and make a new commitment.

> But I can't believe I'm going. My head's light at the thought of a different ground and a different sky. I'll never get over Limnos; this island's going to be the keel under me and the ballast inside me ... I feel like the sixth sense of the world. I feel I'm a part of what was always meant to happen, and is happening now at last.[56]

These are exhilarating words, but with a striking honesty Heaney allows a scruple of doubt to qualify the moment. The final speech in the play is given to a somewhat sceptical Chorus which is no more than 'half-ready to believe' what is enacted in the play's final movement, and knows that love is a 'half-true rhyme' in the world to which it and the audience must return. [57]

This reading of *The Cure of Troy* throws a new light on those tender and delicate lyrics, "The Other Side" and "An Ulster Twilight", in which Heaney dramatizes without condescension or sentimentality his own relations with Northern Unionists. The lyrics render cultural and religious differences manifest in speech and manners, and are rich in political implications. "An Ulster Twilight", particularly, for its title echoes ironically that marvellous collection of short stories by Daniel Corkery whose critical works refuse to recognise the reality of Northern Unionism as a force in Irish politics and literature. Indeed, in his ideologically committed *Synge and Anglo-Irish Literature*, Corkery pronounces a virtual anathema on the Irish Protestant strain in its literary and cultural manifestations. Heaney is instructed by experience and imagination; Corkery lacked the former and effectively silenced the latter in the euphoria of political dogmatism disguised as criticism.

The Cure at Troy has another kind of interest for readers of Heaney. It touches several times on motifs which are more fully developed in the more or less contemporary poems. Odysseus's invocation of Hermes, for instance, the god 'that guides the go-betweens and dealers', suggests an implied divinity behind the apparently realistic observation of cattle dealers in "Everything Flows". When Neoptolemus hesitates to take the proferred bow from Philoctetes ('I want to take it but I don't want to/Go beyond the bounds of what is allowed'),[58] he voices the inhibition that Heaney overcomes in poem after poem in the volume *Seeing Things*. Indeed the ambiguity of that title is underlined in Neoptolemus's injunction to Philoctetes: 'Stop just licking your wounds. Start seeing things.'[59] For the imperative is not simply to see things as they are, the first construction we put on these words, but also to see in a more visionary way the as yet unrealised possibilities of a situation which closely resembles stalemate. One could add to the list, but perhaps enough has been said to suggest that *The Cure at Troy* belongs in the field of force created by Heaney's verse and prose and alters our sense of its dynamic. Nevertheless, it is important to note that the very things which make the play interesting and helpful to the critic of Heaney do not guarantee its validity as drama; in the theatre *The Cure at Troy* is less rewarding than in the study.

In his recent pamphlet *Whatever You Say, Say Nothing; Why Seamus Heaney is No. 1*, Desmond Fennell deplores the lack of Irish criticism of Heaney's work and promises to supply what is needed. Sadly, he fails to offer any detailed criticism of the poems; on the rare occasions when he gives us Heaney's own words, it is almost invariably the prose and not the verse which he quotes. The pamphlet is preoccupied with the question of how poetic reputations are made and consolidated, a subject on which Fennell is consistently interesting and often illuminating. My *present* concern, however, is with his characterization of Heaney's poetry.

According to Fennell, Heaney's verse lacks music and is, therefore, not memorable. His imagination is conventional, inhibited
and thoroughly predictable. 'He must confine himself to using
language, nervously and carefully, so as to avoid doing harm -
keeping to safe themes and modes of address, and doing good
only in this negative, protective fashion.'[60] The poetry is thin on
content, communicating 'no structured worldview'.[61] Most damn-
ing of all, Heaney writes to delight the academic critic and not to
reach and move the ordinary reader; his poetic theory and practice have been corrupted by mandarins like Helen Vendler.
Although I am grateful for the clarity of Fennell's exposition, I do
not feel obliged to register assent where Heaney is concerned. Indeed, I have doubts about the validity of his general thesis that
poetry is being strangled by the academies – *ach sin scéal eile*. My
real quarrel with Fennell is on other grounds. His sense of what
constitutes great poetry is not in general mine; even where our
views coincide, our readings differ. No doubt these differences
are partly matters of temperament and taste about which little can
usefully be said.

But something more is involved. It is not enough to say that one
reader relishes what another deplores: a poet's continuous experimentation with his language. I am persuaded that the increasing
interest and authority of Heaney's work is due as much to his
heightened sensitivity to language as to any observable moral or
psychological growth; in fact, these supposedly different elements cannot be distinguished with confidence in the finished
poems. The heavy emphasis in the pamphlet on caution and can-
niness, on effective silence, is also misplaced, for Heaney is a poet
who knows full well the murderous potential of words. The grad-
ual shedding of inhibitions, on which I have dilated at length,
passes without any acknowledgement from Fennell. Furthermore, in claiming and exercising his imaginative freedom, Heaney has made himself intensely vulnerable, especially in "Station
Island" where he seems to be sharpening his critics' weapons.
Besides, in critiquing his inheritance, he has risked the accusation
of impiety, while at the same time opening his poetry to new impulses and influences. Even in the early books, he has shown an
appetite for the great subjects of love and loss, of suffering and

death, of childhood and change, themes which he has personally inflected in ways that are surely memorable. The penultimate Audenesque chorus in *The Cure at Troy* shows him in the unfamiliar light of prophet, a role few of his contemporaries would dare to assume.

> History says, Don't hope
> On this side of the grave.
> But then, once in a lifetime
> The longed-for tidal wave
> Of justice can rise up,
> And hope and history rhyme.
>
> So hope for a great sea-change
> On the far side of revenge.
> Believe that a further shore
> Is reachable from here.
> Believe in miracles
> And cures and healing wells.[62]

Heaney has both the courage and the technique to descend into the abyss of the self where anarchy simmers. Whether the demons who stir the pot belong to a comic or tragic masquerade is only ascertainable when they have been named and given scope in a poem. "Fosterling", in its admission of fantasy, suggests a grave comic dance, an insouciant demon given to the mischievous use of dialect ('Of *glar* and *glit* and floods at *dailigone*') as well as to delight in the occasional, unreasonable benedictions of ordinary experience.

> Me waiting until I was nearly fifty
> To credit marvels. Like the tree-clock of tin cans
> The tinkers made. So long for air to brighten,
> Time to be dazzled and the heart to lighten. [63]

But Heaney's most recent poem, "Weighing In", embraces a rougher and more demotic idiom; it might be construed as an answer to his critics and a promissory note to the reader.

> Two sides to every question, obviously...
> But every now and then, putting the boot in
> Is what it must come down to, and without
> Any self-exculpation or self-pity.[64]

Notes

1. *Four Quartets* (London: Fabar and Faber, 1959), 26
2. Walace Stevens, *The Necessary Angel* (London: Faber and Faber, 1984), 36
3. ibid., 22
4. W. B. Yeats, Collected Poems, ed. Augustine Martin (London: Arena, 1990), 212
5. For a particularly vivid instance, see "Reprisals", ibid., 180-181
6. ibid., 242
7. ibid., 302
8. *The Republic* trans. H. D. P. Lee (Harmondsworth: Penguin Books, 1970) 383-386
9. *Seeing Things* (London: Faber and Faber, 1991) 8
10. ibid., 68
11. *Station Island* (London: Faber and Faber, 1984), 83
12. ibid., 68
13. I cannot recall where in Berkeley I found this memorable phrase.
14. *The Haw Lantern* (London: Faber and Faber, 1987), 32
15. *The Government of the Tongue* (London: Faber and Faber, 1987) 32
16. *The Place of Writing* (Atlanta: The Scholars' Press, 1989), especially 48-51 and 57-63
17. Yeats, *Collected Poems*, 148
18. ibid., 350
19. ibid., 147
20. Augustine Martin, "The Apocalypse of Clay: Technique and Vision in *The Great Hunger*", in *Patrick Kavanagh: Man and Poet* ed. Peter Kavanagh (Newbridge: The Goldsmith Press, 1987), 286
21. Yeats, *Collected Poems*, 147
22. *Field Work* (London: Faber and Faber, 1979) 23
23. ibid., 22
24. ibid., 24
25. ibid., 23
26. ibid.
27. ibid.
28. ibid.
29. Osip Mandelstam, *The Collected Critical Prose and Letters* trans. Jane Gary Harris and Constance Link (London: Collins Harvill, 1991) 414
30. ibid., 398
31. "Words Alone", Heaney's lecture to the Ninth World Congress on Reading, was published in a special supplement to *An Múinteoir*

Náisiúnta (Vol 26, No 3; Autumn 1982)

32. These are the last lines of Wallace Stevens's "The Idea of Order at Key West", with which Heaney concluded his lecture "Words Alone".

33. *Preoccupations* (London: Faber and Faber, 1980), 54

34. *The Government of the Tongue,* 148

35. T. S. Eliot, *Collected Essays* (London: Faber and Faber, 1972) 155

36. Philip Larkin, *Collected Poems* ed. Anthony Twaite (London: The Marvell Press and Faber and Faber, 1988) 112

37. Tom Paulin, *Minotaur: Poetry and the Nation State* (London: Faber and Faber, 1992) 150

38. Edmund Wilson, *The Wound and the Bow* (London: Methuen, 1964), 259

39. ibid.

40. ibid., 263

41. ibid., 264

42. Denis Donoghue, *The Arts without Mystery* (London: The BBC, 1983) 13

43. Introduction, *Sweeney Astray* (Derry:The Field Day Theatre Company, 1983) VIII

44. *The Cure at Troy* (London: Faber and Faber, 1990), 14-15

45. ibid., 29

46. ibid., 56

47. ibid., 60

48. ibid., 2

49. ibid.

50. ibid., 1-2

51. ibid., 12

52. ibid., 18

53. ibid., 61

54. ibid., 69

55. ibid., 72

56. ibid., 80

57. ibid., 81

58. ibid., 36

59. ibid., 74

60. Desmond Fennell, *Whatever You Say, Say Nothing: Whay Seamus Heaney is No. 1* (Dublin: ELO Publications, 1991)

61. ibid., 14

62. *The Cure at Troy,* 77

63. *Seeing Things,* 50

64. *The Times Literary Supplement,* 17 January 1992, 28

The New Agenda of Unbelief and Faith

Michael Paul Gallagher SJ

Some months ago in Rome I was present at an international vow ceremony for sisters, a liturgy that was exceptionally well done, imaginative, prayerful, quietly emotional, and humanly joyful – with African style dancing and Korean style singing. In the midst of it all, I realized how relatively easy it is to believe when the flow is right and the disposition is in tune. Then later that day I found myself on a bus that stopped in Piazza Venezia; it happened that an evangelist with a loud-hailer took the opportunity to shout into the bus that 'you are all sinners in need of a Saviour'. I could hardly disagree with the content of his preaching but the tone made me cringe, and the contrast of the two occasions highlights a theme that will be in the background of this lecture – that it is the language of faith that is in crisis, not usually faith itself in its credal content. Or more positively, faith is an inside-job, so to speak, at least in terms of lived credibility today.

In short, that liturgy summarizes the privileged places where faith finds its existential truth, and that loudhailer symbolizes no doubt a well-intentioned effort of evangelization, but one that seems sadly lacking in relationship, in community, or in anything of pre-evangelization. On the title page of E. M. Forster's novel, *Howard's End*, he wrote as an epigraph the words 'Only connect'. That 'only' is ambiguous, in that it could mean 'simply' or 'if only'. But either way his intuition – that in modern times the building of bridges is crucial, because so much seems fragmented – seems still of pastoral relevance. The liturgy connected. The evangelist did not. All this is just a parable from my own experience that can serve as a backdrop for our reflections here. It is only a variation on the old wisdom connecting worship and faith – *lex orandi, lex credendi*.

I want to tackle two questions here, one about changes in unbelief and the other about emerging faith languages. What has happened to the unbelief agenda since 1965? I choose that date as the moment when for the first time in history a church council pronounced on atheism, and in a positive spirit. It is also the year of the foundation of the Secretariat for Non-believers, renamed as the Pontifical Council for Dialogue with Non-believers, where in fact I work. Therefore in view of so many cultural and even political changes since the Sixties, what are the now typical tones of unbelief? The second question can be put like this: How does this different accent of unbelief and context of the Nineties change the pastoral responses needed?

PART 1: CHANGES AND TONES

Clearly, the cultural setting for faith is very different from that of the Sixties. But the basic option for dialogue with non-believers has remained – even though it also has inevitably changed in focus. A recent and public example of this openness to dialogue came in some remarks of Pope John II about Mikhail Gorbachov. The ex-President of the Soviet Union had published and article (in March 1992) in which he spoke of a 'spiritual understanding between us' and how recent changes 'in Eastern Europe would not have been possible without the presence of this Pope'. Commenting on this essay, the Pope himself described Gorbachov as 'a man of principles, spiritually very rich' and added: 'he does not call himself a believer, but with me, I remember, he spoke of the great importance which he attributed to prayer, to the inner dimension.'

Even the coincidence that each described the other as 'spiritual' is an indicator of a major shift of wavelength. It would have been impossible for one of the Communist leaders or one of the Popes of the first half of this century to use such language about one another. Equally it is a symbol of a shift within theological reflection on unbelief - that it is increasingly seen in non-doctrinal terms as an existential issue involving the spiritual horizon of each person and indeed of each culture.

Since the sixties, the fall of Soviet Communism as an atheist system in power is a major event but far from the only important development. The whole issue of non-belief has become less linked with pure ideas and seen as much more connected with cultures. Few people live by ideas. Most people, whether believers or non-believers, are more influenced by the images that surround them in their societies and that shape the horizon of their hopes. In this changing context, theological discourse has gradually come to avoid the term 'atheism' and to speak rafter of 'unbelief' or 'non-belief'. This shift in terminology represents a different agenda – not an 'ism' but rather a whole complex of influences in contemporary 'mindsets and heartsets' as Peter Steele, an Australian priest-poet, has put it.

In other words, the typical mood has moved from a definite and sometimes militant denial of God to a more vague distance from religious faith. Some commentators describe this as the transition from the 'modern', with its trust in reason and technology, to the 'post-modern', with its scepticism about large humanist claims and its corresponding mood of unease over meanings and values. If the word 'atheism' tended to suggest a concrete decision, or an ideology that rejects God, the term 'unbelief' evokes less clarity and more confusion and doubt. Religious faith is not so much denied as sensed to be unreal. The 'only connect' does not easily happen and God seems absent form consciousness rather than repudiated. A non-specific religious indifference, sometimes allied to a non-dogmatic agnosticism or a non-angry distance from church, seems to be the commonest family of unbelief now. It is usually interpreted as a by-product of secularized lifestyles and of 'thin' and even externalist levels of religious belonging even among many of the baptised today. Seldom is it a form of thought-out negation of the existence of God; its tone is more one of unaggressive puzzlement and an unbridged gap of credibility in experience.

But if hard-line atheism has become rare, lack of faith or loss of faith is still a crucial challenge for theology and for the Church. This truth and this urgency can be found in two quite independent statements made by theologians in the course of 1991. The first is from the French Dominican writer Jean-Pierre Jossua and the second from a Spanish-Catalan Jesuit, Josep Vives.

> The number one problem which theologians have to confront is that of unbelief, whether argued or lived, and of an indifference and absence of desire towards what to me is most alive and precious: the gospel, the figure of Jesus, the nearness of God.[1]

> If the old forms of atheism and agnosticism are now out of date, it is clear that one cannot yet proclaim the reflourishing of theism. What more truly characterizes the present moment is that 'God is missing but not missed'. This is a genuinely new situation, which never existed before in the world. [2]

We used to speak of anonymous Christians. Now it might be right to speak of anonymous unbelievers: many are so far from militancy or from questions of faith as not to notice the absence of a religious horizon in their lives. From another point of view they could be seen as victims of an 'anonymous idolatry', in that the images that surround them kidnap their hearts into superficial patterns of life. Or again, some of those described as unbelievers might be more accurately called 'pre-believers' or 'post-believers': some have never known the 'inside' of faith in a genuinely personal way; others have become uprooted from childhood patterns without ever experiencing church as a living community.

Three Circles of Change

After this more general evocation of tonal changes, it may be helpful to name some of the so-called 'mega-movements' in cultural horizon over these decades. For simplicity they can be envisaged as three concentric circles – of thought systems, of social assumptions and of spiritual attitudes. In each case we are dealing with a 'post' situation, in the sense that a previously dominant model seems to have suffered a sudden and even unexpected decline.

In terms of *thought systems* the most obvious novelty is the post-communist surprise. Many people will have seen images of toppled statues of Lenin and others, but now after the excitement, there is a real question: what or who will occupy, at least symbolically, those empty pedestals? A likely candidate is an inhuman economy and a different materialism. Thus from the point of view of unbelief, the downfall of Soviet Communism as a system led to an initial euphoria but then to a sense of spiritual vulnerability, perhaps especially in view of the pastoral unpreparedness of many churches in those newly liberated countries.

Other faces of this change can be named as post-ideology or post-utopia, and these trends seem to be present not only in the eastern bloc but throughout the world. There is a different tentativeness now about large claims or hopes. If the justice agenda within the

Church seems to have become shy in recent times, perhaps it is only shadowed by disappointment on the global level but emerging into strength within local and from-below communities of patient commitment.

Atheism itself, as already mentioned, is less and less used as word. In the forties Henri de Lubac published a famous book entitled *The Drama of Atheistic Humanism*: it remains a seminal text but each key term of its title is strangely out of tune with contemporary sensibility. There is more confusion than conflict or drama, and both systems of thought linked in his title are under clouds of suspicion – as being overweening and dogmatic. There is a distrust of militant 'isms' of any kind and of answers that seem too neat and definite. Once again, as will be seen later, this fading of militancy opens the agenda to new possibilities.

As to social assumptions, twenty years ago there was much writing about irreversible secularization which now reads as naïve and excessively pessimistic. Religion has refused to disappear quickly, and instead there is much commentary about the re-sacralization and about a public profile for faith. In his Reith Lectures for 1990, Rabbi Jonathan Sacks made a strong case for the unexpected resilience of faith and argued whereas the backwash of the Enlightenment had a devastating impact on the political and individual dimensions of religion, 'community is the missing third term in our social ecology' and the essential place 'where we discover who we are and why.'[3] What he sees with a Jewish traditional eye is also being verified in the burgeoning of so many community groupings within Catholicism: they seem to stem from secularization but in a sense to represent a post-secularization language of faith. (Since moving to Rome, I have come to learn that Italy is the home of many movements within the Church and to witness how impressive some of them are; my own experience has drawn me to the Sant'Edigio Community where several thousand young lay Catholics in Rome alone unite a commitment to communal prayer with a series of initiatives for the poorer and more marginalized people of the city. But this is to anticipate: a later section here will describe some of the new faith languages brought to birth by these changes.)

Turning to the *spiritual climate* of today, there are many aspects that were not forseen in the Sixties and not envisaged by the Second Vatican Council. As James Fowler has written recently, 'because the alternatives have defaulted', we are 'in the midst of a shift in cultural consciousness of major proportions', where people turn again to 'religion, mysticism and spirituality'. [4]

Although terms like post-atheism, or post-materialism, or post-modernism seem tainted with jargon, they nevertheless point to major shifts of tone that influence the possibility of faith. Many commentators form Andre Malraux to Harvey Cox have commented that the turn of the century would be more religious. Yes, but in what sense? The current situations seems fraught with ambiguity: among the ways in which, as is often said, religion is making a 'return', are several that seem deceptive to say the least: they range from a frightened and frightening fundamentalism to a more glossy but vague fashion of New Age spirituality.

The so-called First World is showing signs of disenchantment with mere materialism – even while it seems to invade and flourish in the ex-communist situation. Many commentators, as different as Gilles Lipovetsky in France or Francis Fukuyama in the United States, have noted a new quest for the quality of life beyond the outer satisfactions and securities. With the end of global hostility comes a new dissatisfaction in the First World: entrenched comfort and spiritual emptiness are the warders in the prison of individualism. *Brave New World* is vindicated as the liberal world discovers the cramping of creativity in its lack of goals other than the narcissistic ladder of self-comfort.

Narcissus returns
From the point of view of faith or spirituality, the unbelief agenda can shrink in this context from the older rejection of God to either the exclusion of God through distractions, or more subtly, to a shrunken God made in the image and likeness of a self-concerned and self-satisfying culture. Religion can lose an essential Christian transcendence and become a factor in meeting 'my' needs, a nourishing of a new sense of spiritual wholeness or well-being. Certainly I have needs, and my wholeness and wellbeing is an authentic goal, but not by shirking the cost of the gospel and the reality of revelation. The rich world has a powerful capacity for

selecting its favourite parts of scripture and suppressing what does not fit: if so, the much vaunted return to religion – in its liberal and non-fundamentalist guise – could simply be another off-shoot of gnosticism. That most ancient and perennial of spiritual temptations prefers the self-superior security of 'feeling good' to the concrete challenge of the Incarnation and the conversions required to serve and heal this wounded world. As Jean Guitton perceptively commented, the depths of God and the depths of our own being are not the same thing: 'faith gives us the first, gnosticism the second.'[5]

Parallel to what 'post-modernism' summarizes on an intellectual level, these 'New Age' tendencies have come to shape spiritual assumptions within contemporary culture: inward looking, forgetful of conversion or social conscience, immune to any need for salvation except of consciousness, cultivating a superior hedonism of self-exploring, to say nothing of the weirder theorizing associated with it. But it is easy to highlight the dangers in all this: it is a more difficult job of pastoral imagination to weigh the new tones and desires, to seize the day and discern the good earth of now.

Faces of Post-Modernism
Even in so-called post-modernism, which is often looked on as a new nihilism disdainful of any religious dimension, it is not clear that this is the whole story. 'Post-modern' has become an intellectually fashionable term with many meanings. One widely accepted implication is that the so-called 'modern' project valued rational clarity, and had a huge confidence in the human capacity to dominate the world with wisdom. It shared and developed the Enlightenment trust in political technologies and in dismissive positions such as atheism. But the nausea of Sartre gives way to mere boredom in the post-modern. Many structures collapse into incredibility, rather like the collapse of the communist party. Post-modern summarizes a dull unease and impotence before big questions rather than any 'drama of atheistic humanism'. Thought becomes shy and deliberately 'weak'. Great projects are viewed as overweening or too 'total'. Large claims or 'meta-narratives' come under a similar cloud of suspicion. People are surrounded by the

immediacy of communications – so that it was possible to watch a missile 'live' during the Gulf war. Instead of old uniformities, the tendency is to relish differences. Instead of explanatory history we are invited to be content with partial and changing stories. We are told to live more naked and more quietly anguished. Narcissus comes back into flavour, as a shield of the fragile self. Subjectivization and selectivity rule in religious matters as in the global market place.

Initially such a description hardly seems a hopeful scene for faith and yet on reflection not all is so bleak. It helps to pinpoint what is more a sensibility than a system, and indeed this is typical of contemporary culture in general and of unbelief in particular – to be increasingly undefinable in the neat language of any system. From the religious point of view there are two rather different readings of this situation. One would stress the boom of esoteric' approaches that seems to come automatically whenever 'aesthetics takes the place of ethics', or when tyranny of feeling replaces a tyranny of reason.[6] But a more optimistic reading is also possible. Leaving aside the rage-for-disorder in some 'post-modernism', at least one theologian has discerned an invitation to a sober humility of faith claims within today's world. After the collapse of excessive 'modern' certitudes, the way is open for a religious faith that would be more experiential, more rooted in narrative, in culture, in dialogue as well as more fruitful in commitments of service.[7] In line with this, the second part of this presentation will argue that parallel to the new agenda of non-aggressive unbelief, a different agenda of faith is both called for and actually emerging in practice.

To sum up this first and descriptive section, the post-modern situation in religion seems both more open and more ambiguous than before. What seems clear is that the culture surrounding the decision of faith has shifted radically since the sixties and the believer is now much more likely to be unsupported through the surrounding silence than assaulted by overt hostility. Where previously there was conflict with parents about 'opting out', now there can be conflict with peers, or at least incomprehension, over a young person 'opting in to' faith. And yet precisely that 'opting in' is crucial as a road to maturity of faith for today. The courage to be different does not come easily, and is well nigh impossible without community aliveness and community supports. Unbelief is now more a question of life-style than of mind-set. It is nebulous rather than concrete. It takes the form of alternative idols for the heart rather than arguments against God or church. It prefers a vaguely spiritual attitude of the self to any firm decisions or social solidarities or church belonging. It involves a paralysis on the threshold of commitment rather than a total dismissiveness of the religious dimension.

Thus there is a new freshness together with a new fragility. Although indifference and apathy *seem* enthroned, perhaps they show only the disappointed surface of our post-modernity. They could merely be the masks of a shy hunger that awaits its language. It is time then to ask about that possible new language of faith: because all this cultural analysis has the ultimate purpose of identifying a suitable pastoral and spiritual theology for now.

PART II: CONVERGENCES OF HOPE

Listening to the pastoral scene internationally in recent years, certain positive lights emerge and converge. While many people may remain passive victims of this new unbelief, more than a few are finding different expressions of faith.It is honest to recognize the shadows and to name the new underminings. But it is better still to notice how, under the pressures of these shifting cultural situations, Christian faith is in many places finding new confidence about how to live the gospel now. That confidence is expressed on many levels, from the repeated calls of the Pope for a 'new evangelization' to the burgeoning of youth ministry and the diversity of movements where many lay people find spaces of faith growth.

A new tone and confidence is also exemplified within fundamental theology and within apologetics in particular, where the old rationalism is seen to be counterproductive and – to simplify a vast field – the agenda has changed from arguing-the-existence-of-god to discerning the human experiences that point towards faith. In this respect I am struck by the following description from Cardinal Lustiger:

The problem of faith in God is not first of all that of knowing whether there is an unknown object one can conveniently call God and whose probable or certain existence can be demonstrated with more or less security ... The problem of faith is to accept that human persons, to discover God, are compelled to situate themselves differently with respect to themselves, with respect to the world, and therefore with respect to him whom they do not know. Abraham was a deist ... revelation is precisely this: God himself is manifest as totally different form any idea that we can have about him. [8]

In this light, modern pastoral and apologetic approaches overlap in insisting that a key preparation for evangelization lies in a different spiritual stance of readiness. If you stand outside yourself, looking for an object-God, you will find a flimsy and impersonal First Cause. But if you listen honestly to your hunger and heart, you will at least have the reverence that could recognize a God of relationship and of surprising revelation. Or to cite Marcel Legaut, a distinguished lay thinker who died at an advanced age within the last year, and who always stressed that to pass from externalist or even deist 'belief' to 'faith in God' requires a presence to oneself and a journey of spiritual interiority:

To start talking to people today about God can court sterility from the outset. To do justice to the subject, you need a previous exchange on the level of humanity, marked by honesty and depth, about what people really live, and even more about what they have truly experienced in privileged moments of the past.[9]

Although they might not be in full theological accord with one another, Legaut's emphasis on fostering the wavelength of faith through getting in touch with human depth finds a notable parallel in Hans Urs von Balthasar, speaking of what makes the perception of God possible:

We can understand this best from the astonished realization we experience in privileged moments and encounters ... (which) elicit ... wonder. [10]

Wonder: first of three conversions
In this light, and even at the risk of interpreting von Balthasar in a way that might not be fully in tune with his own vision, I would

suggest that in pastoral practice are three essential freedoms on the road from unbelief to faith today. Moreover, I want to argue that these freedoms usually come in a certain order: doors of self-wonder precede options of love which in turn leave a person ripe for revelation and faith. In other words, echoing both von Balthasar and Kierkegaard, one can point to three conversions – aesthetic, ethical and religious. In each instance there is a break with the surface assumptions and oppressions of the surrounding culture.

This first conversion is one of disposition – as in the liberation from disillusionment to 'heart burning' dramatized on the road to Emmaus. Many a person lives imprisoned in 'un-wonder' even about his or her own self, and some different level of self-experience is needed to awaken the dulled imagination to hope. 'The heart's wonder' as is exclaimed in *The Playboy of the Western World*, a drama that also cruelly exposes how this wonder can be starved or failed in the pettiness of society. Similarly, if the dominant rhythms today can block key experiences of transcendence, a certain pre-evangelization is needed to liberate a different listening. Drawing on St. Paul, one knows that faith comes from hearing (Rom 10: 17), but one has to ask in practice where people are on the Areopagus of today (cf Acts 17). More particularly, where is that hearing blocked and what roads of imagination need to be found to arrive at fruitful hearing?

The God of many a so-called unbeliever can be a strange sub-Christian mixture of deist distance and of demanding dictator. If so, the God of Christian revelation needs to be encountered beyond such deserts of conceptualism or of routine images. As a first step, quite simply God must become attractive, but exhortations or eloquent sermonizing about the marvellous nature of revelation will never overcome the accumulations of alienation or non-attractiveness on the level of experience. Only some alternative experience heals a previously wounded experience.

In a striking way modern theology has discovered the paradigm of art as a model for what used to be called the preambles of faith. For all their divergences, it is one of the points that links von Balthasar and Karl Rahner. In Rahner's view there is a preparation which a person 'must undergo to be or become a Christian, which turns out to be a receptive capacity for the poetic word' and he sees this whole wavelength as able to 'reach the heart, the centre' where mystery becomes incarnate.[11] In another essay he described the theological relevance of great literature as leading a person

> into the immeasurable depths upon which his existence is founded...he is compelled by such writing to face up to the hidden depths which a man can find within himself. [12]

There are less specialist ways of opening this receptivity through wonder - not everybody is reached by poetry or literature. The key issue is that for many people doors need opening before the hearing-that-leads-to-faith can be fruitful. But the parallel between the receiving of art and the receiving of revelation hinges on an 'unblocking' of inadequacies and resistances in order that the 'poem may give itself': this is a key 'analogy for authentic listening to the Gospel'. [13]

I have been arguing that in pastoral practice there is often a malnutrition of wonder, affecting believers and unbelievers alike. How can this lack be made good? Answers can range form something as simple but special as a heart-to-heart conversation, or the liturgy mentioned at the outset to the level of awareness awoken by art or by love or even by suffering. Whenever honesty of feeling becomes possible or wherever a person is able to imagine life in new ways, then self-horizons expand beyond their usual cramped quarters and equally a more authentic image of God becomes glimpsable.

To close this section on the disposition of wonder, let me cite a typically insightful claim of Sebastian Moore. He strongly rejects the commonplace assumption by 'the believer as well as the non-believer' that God is discovered through human emptiness or lack and that a sense of human richness renders faith redundant:

> The exact opposite is the case. A sense of human worthlessness makes God unbelievable; a sense of human greatness is the threshold of belief. The threshold of belief is that special sense of human greatness which is had in the experience of our larger, intersubjective life. [14]

A Conversion of Choices

When a person has half a chance to listen with awakening surprise to their own spiritual depths, then in my experience two further horizons naturally open up – the drama of goals and the threshold of revelation itself. This paper has put most of its emphasis on the need for an initial expansion of the agenda of wonder. The two remaining growth areas can be treated more briefly.

At least for some socially critical unbelievers, religious faith is perceived as irresponsibility, a regression to infantile attitudes, as a half-life of private safety rather than as a costly adventure within history. For them it is vital to know Christian faith as a promise of fullness, which certainly involves a costly passover from hedonism to self-giving. But this has to be seen as a non-cramping liberation of hopes and values – something other than Nietzsche's 'sick contradiction of life'.

For the less militant and – as outlined earlier – more typical half-believer of today, the situation is somewhat different. For them the surprise of knowing something of their own hungers and depths expands usually into some question about how-am-I-to-live. Perhaps this questioning in its turn is born from getting in touch with a healthy dissatisfaction over how her or his life has been lived so far. But if the horizon of wonder prevails, then these negatives can be fruitfully faced.

It can be akin to that moment in Luke's gospel (chapter 5) when Peter discovers his sinful unworthiness: when surrounded by the fullness of the net, it is the right moment to recognize sin in a spirit of fruitful sorrow in relationship rather than of self-burdening guilt. So too, once in touch with wonder, a person can own the shadows with honesty and reach towards light to be lived.

At its simplest whenever the imagination is liberated for wonder of some kind, the question of embracing a direction for one's life enters almost automatically. Ultimately it is a decision between living for love or living without goals. Even though this choice may at first seem a purely ethical-existential affair, it is never that alone. The crucial relation between love-options and faith-finding is rooted in the Bible in such passages as Isaiah's promise that if you struggle for justice, then your cry will be answered by God saying 'I am here' (Is 58: 9). Or there is the famous gospel saying that whoever does the truth comes into the light (Jn 3: 21). All this suggests an epistemology of faith that overturns rational expectations of working something out and verifying it: faith is more a form of love-truth than of reason-truth.[15] This seems of special pastoral relevance now in reaching out to unbelievers. But it is an ancient insight, expressed with transparent simplicity by William of St Thierry in the twelfth century: 'You do not believe because you do not love; you do not love because you do not believe'. Or in the striking words of Carlyle Marney, 'There is no growth that is Christian without the nerve to submit to the correcting of my images of the self.' [17] There is grit in the conversion to love.

The Surprises of Revelation

As the final statement of the Bishop's Synod of Europe expressed it, 'The heart of evangelization is "God loves you. Christ came for you."' This is the goal of the journey. To put it too early could risk a crudity akin to that loudhailer evangelist. Pastorally, there is a crucial John-the-Baptist ministry of preparation of another hearing – for hearing a Word that is known to be from God.

The French theologian Jean-Luc Marion has written extensively of the crucial shift from idol to icon as casting light on this different receptivity for God and for faith: the idol-god is a prison or echo-chamber of subjectivity, allowing me hear only a version of my own desires but the icon looks at me so that I am no longer at the centre.[18] There are many versions of this temptation to miss the shock or differentness of faith and to rest content with the old territory of self-shaped religion. It was a blockage known by St. Paul and evoked by him as a religion of lonely law and of frustrating self-effort – until his paradoxical release through being captured by Christ (Phil. 3: 6-12). On another level it can be the fate of many who were brought up within the Church but who never had the chance of developing from passive belonging into personal believing.

The core of this third conversion can be described in many ways – as seen in all the theologies of revelation and of faith. I propose the simplest of formulations: faith is a 'yes' to a 'yes'. It is a recognition that God has already and indeed always reached out to me/us in love. The Yes of God is the core of revelation and its climax in Christ. It is a Yes of total understanding ('I have been fully understood' – 1 Cor. 13:12). It is a yes of promise and partnership. The other yes is our response, hesitant, groping, unsure, slow, and yet emerging, however unsteadily, into the security of the steady Yes of God.

The whole thrust to this essay has been that in a time of unbelief, and in the shadow of the particular tone of unbelief that pervades today, that encounter of yes with yes needs delicate pastoral preparation. Evangelization goes further than aesthetics and ethics, and yet in the yes of faith to the Yes of revelation these two dimensions are not jettisoned like booster rockets. Indeed the shifting agenda of unbelief in our culture is inviting theology to rediscover something of its more poetic and Patristic wavelength – where spirituality was never separated from doctrine. The contemporary revaluing of the aesthetic in theology is already a significant move in this direction and – as argued here – can have a pastoral relevance that has not been fully appreciated.

It would be equally wrong to leave the impression that aesthetic wonder is 'only' of pastoral relevance – as liberating unbelievers from anti-dogmatic slumbers. The vision that is faith is a gift, 'independent of the upward striving of my consciousness' and a gift which in turn transforms the sense of both wonder and of good. In Robert Doran' s words,

> Affective space is opened, and one becomes free to assume responsibility for what previously one could not negotiate. A movement form above downwards in consciousness can begin, a movement rooted in and guided by a gift that is not of one's own making.[19]

Resting in Goodness and in Love, one can revisit the roads that brought one to this recognition, only to see that the gift was guiding all the way. 'Affective space' was there both at the outset and at the end, and it has been the hinge of this essay.

Conclusion

In the first part of this paper I tried to describe a multi-faceted shift in the agenda of unbelief and then in the second part I have sought to suggest a parallel shift needed in the agenda of faith as pastorally presented. It involves a move from the concepts of culture, from doctrine to disposition, from apologetics about the 'existence' of God to a spiritual-cum-pastoral theology that ponders how faith can be prepared and nourished today. From wherever round the world faith is flourishing, the evidence seems clear and convergent. In this culture it is more obvious than before that some new *experience* of faith is the most fruitful road to Christian conversion, and that to arrive at an experience of the primacy of revelation often needs a prior phase of awakening to hungers and hopes.

What builds up that experience is as old as the *Acts of the Apostles*: some convergence of genuine community, initiation into prayer, and the challenge of concrete service of others, especially of the wounded of the world. But there are new notes within the chord of spirituality now. An older atheism of some thirty years ago was responded to by a theology of God as dark mystery, ineffable, even radically absent. The newer unbelief may call for a contrary image of God as radically present, hidden in the ordinary, in the grace-guided narrative of each person and people.

To go back to the images of the opening, the last thing the un- believer needs is a fundamentalist and humanly insensitive language of faith. Instead, in this culture beyond 'isms', faith needs a convergence of gifts such as embodied in that liturgy: wonder, decision, prayer, community, and a call to hear with Christ the cry of humanity now.

Notes

1. Jossua, 'Le Congrès 1990 de Concilium', *Revue des Sciences Religieuses*, 1991, p. 27.
2. Vives, 'Dios en el crepusculo del siglo XX', *Razón y Fe*, Mayo 1991, p. 468.
3. Jonathan Sacks, *The Persistence of Faith: Religion, Morality & Society in a Secular Age*, London, 1991, pp. 90, 14.
4. James W. Fowler, *Weaving the New Creation: Stages of Faith and the Public Church*, 1991, p. 13.
5. Jean Guitton, *Great Heresies and Church Councils* , 1965, p. 74.
6. Luis Gonzalez-Carvajal, 'Ideas y creencias del hombre postmoder- no', *Razón y Fe*, Marzo 1992, pp. 259, 265.
7. Julio Colomer, 'Postmodernidad, fe cristiana y vida religiosa', *Sal Terrae*, Mayo 1991, pp. 413-420.

8. Jean-Marie Lustiger, *Dare to Believe*, New York, 1986, p. 117.

9. Marcel Legaut, *Un homme de foi et son Eglise* , Paris, 1988, p. 16.

10. Hans Urs von Balthasar, *Theo-Drama*, Vol. II, *Dramatis Personae: Man and God*,1990, p. 21.

11. Karl Rahner, *Theological Investigations*, Vol. IV, 'Poetry and the Christian', pp. 357-361.

12. *Theological Investigations* , Vol.VIII, 'The Task of the Writer in Relation to Christian Living', p. 120.

13. Jean-Marie Martin, 'Les eaux usees de l'Occident', *Christus*, No.153, Janvier 1992, p. 60.

14. Sebastian Moore, *Let this Mind be in You* , 1985, p. 25

15. See my own book, *Where is your God?* , 1991, pp.112-116 .

16. William of St. Thierry, *The Mirror of Faith*, Kalamazoo, 1979, p. 18.

17. Cited by James Fowler, *Weaving the New Creation: Stages of Faith and the Public Church*, 1991,p. 49

18. Jean-Luc Marion, *L'Idole et la distance* , 1977, pp. 23-26.

19. Robert M. Doran, *Theology and the Dialectics of History* , 1990, p. 243.

Glimpsing the Divine
Metaphor and Religious Thinking

Andrew G.McGrady

Introduction

The aims of the teacher of Religion are many; they include the goal of assisting pupils to develop their capacity for religious thinking. In general terms this can be regarded as being concerned with the cognitive aspects of articulating and interpreting the religious dimension of human experience. At the heart of such experience is a sense of wonder and awe, of presence and absence, of immanence and transcendence, of drawing near to a loving presence and of keeping a fearful distance from the sacred. The tone of religious thinking is one of exploration and search. Like the blind men in the classical parable of the elephant, we can only partially and inadequately know that which is beyond. We see in a mirror dimly rather than seeing clearly, we know only in part rather than in full. Ours is an on-going struggle to glimpse the Divine.

Defining religious thinking in more than a general way is in fact quite problematic and begs many questions. Is there such a thing as religious thinking as a distinctive activity or is religion simply the content to which normal thought processes are applied, that is, is religious thinking simply thinking about religion? How does religious knowing relate to such thinking and what is the balance and interrelationship between the affective and cognitive aspects of such knowing? How does religious thinking relate to theological thinking, that is to a systematic and propositional reflection within the context of a particular religious tradition? How does religious thinking relate to the religious use of language? How does religious thinking relate to other forms of thinking such as scientific thinking or the contemplative perceptions provided by music, poetry, literature and art?

1. PREVIOUS RESEARCH DEFINING RELIGIOUS THINKING IN PIAGETIAN OPERATIONAL TERMS

Previous research has tended to define religious thinking in terms of Piaget's theory of operational development. For Piaget cognitive development is the result of the construction of progressively more complex mental structures which characterize various stages as follows:

Sensori-motor stage (from birth to 2 years),
Pre-operational stage (from 2 - 7 years),
Concrete operational stage (7 - 13 / 14 years)
Formal operational stage (13 / 14 onwards)

An operation is an internalized action enabling an individual to test out an idea in thought, and predict its outcome, before acting. During concrete operations logical thought is possible but is limited to the immediate, observable features of a situation, and while several features can be recognised, these are not integrated in a unified or constistent manner. Further, the implications of a line of reasoning may not be recognised. These limitations are overcome with the emergence of formal operations which are characterised by the use of propositions drawing on the capabilities to think symbolically, abstractly and hypothetically without the impediment of observable instances. A situation is interpreted in the wider context of related situations. The implications of a line of thought are recognised, and several propositions can be related together in a consistent manner.

The bench-mark study into religious thinking using a Piagetian approach was the research of Ronald Goldman (1962, 1964, 1965)[1], carried out during the late 1950s as part of a series of studies at Birmingham University into the applicability of the Piagetian paradigm to a range of curriculum areas. Goldman interviewed 200 subjects, (both male and female), aged 6 to 15 years in English State schools, (Roman Catholic and Jewish subjects were excluded). His individual interview was largely based upon simplified versions of three biblical stories, the Burning Bush, the Crossing of the Red Sea, and the Temptations of Jesus. Goldman identified three stages in the development of religious thinking interspersed by two transition periods. The stages followed the classical Piagetian pattern moving from intuitive thinking, to concrete religious thinking, and to abstract formal religious thinking. The last two stages can be illustrated from the story of the Temptations of Jesus by a consideration of responses to the question, "if Jesus was hungry why didn't he turn the stone into bread" interpreted in the light of follow-up questions such as "how would he do it"? Goldman classified as indicative of concrete operations responses to these questions which either appealed to a magical power that Jesus possessed but which he wouldn't use for the devil, or which could not consistently relate Jesus' refusal to turn a stone into bread with his action of turning water into wine at Cana. He classified as exhibiting formal operational thought any response which was an orderly systematic proposition, such as that it was a test to show if Jesus was worthy to be the son of God, or that if he turned the stone into bread Jesus would be using his powers for trivial things, or for his own good, rather than for the kingdom of God.

Goldman (1965) outlined the curriculum implications of the research, emphasizing that since the religious thinking of the pupil exhibits a developmental pattern then the religious education curriculum should reflect a psychological and child-centred sequence rather than a theological, doctrinal sequence. Specifically Goldman argued that most biblical material used in the curicula of the period was unsuitable before the onset of abstract religious thinking at about 13 years mental age, and that a thematic, life-centred approach was educationally acceptable as an alternative and would facilitate readiness for religious thinking at around 13 years mental age.

Later research, such as a large-scale study by Peatling (1973),[2] confirmed Goldman's view that religious thinking can be investigated using a Piagetian paradigm and that development follows the clear pattern of stages already identified with respect to other areas. The research of Elkind (1961, 1962, 1963)[3] examining the emergence of the child's religious identity, and of Long, Elkind an Spilka (1967)[4] into concepts of prayer, are of particular importance since such investigations were a part of wider research carried out by prominent general Piagetian scholars. Further the stage theories in the related areas of moral judgment, faith development, and religious judgment, proposed by Kohlberg (1958)[5], Fowler (1981)[6], and Oser (1980)[7] lend credence to a stage related developmental sequence in related areas.

While such research has been valuable in establishing a field of inquiry, some problems arise. The curriculum recommendations that are based upon Goldman's research, particularly those relating to the balance between experiential and systematic doctrinal approaches, were over-generalised and were used politically to provide academic respectability for changes that teachers of Religion wished to make anyway. More importantly, research can only reflect the concerns of its day and the educational, sociological, biblical and theological assumptions underlying the teaching of Religion have changed radically over the past thirty years. For most teachers a developmental, pupil-centred approach no longer needs to be justified. Note also the concern for the dialogue between experience and tradition reflected in praxis-centred approaches, the emergence of a theology of story and its implications for approaches to the scriptures, the growing sensitivity concerning the nature and limitations of the religious use of language, and the distancing of the enterprise of teaching religion from the notion of indoctrination. Such concerns of themselves demand a re-examination of the dichotomies underlying Goldman's work.

Difficulties in defining Religious Thinking solely in Piagetian terms
A number of difficulties arise with equating religious thinking solely with operational thinking. These can be illustrated by a brief review of some of the criticisms of Goldman's research. The three stories used by Goldman, the Burning Bush, the Crossing of the Red Sea, and the Temptations of Jesus, are all to a greater or lesser extent, miracle stories which many adults have great difficulty interpreting successfully and which are remote from the experience of children. Goldman reported that eight possible stories were piloted; the three finally chosen were those which most clearly discriminated between the Piagetian forms of logical reasoning. The representativeness of the material used in the research as a basis for making generalised statements concerning religious thinking, can therefore be immediately questioned. Further there

has been constant criticism of the simplified versions of the three biblical narratives used by Goldman.[9] The religious significance of the two old testament stories especially was minimised by a series of additions, omissions and changes of emphasis which highlighted the tension between a biblical and scientific world-view.[10][11]

It is usually assumed that Goldman established that the Piagetian stages of intuitive, concrete and formal, abstract thinking were applicable to religious thinking. In fact he presumed that these capabilities were applicable and examined a limited selection of biblical dilemmas that were suitable to such investigation. While his findings provide a useful indication as to how the individual at various stages of her development reconciles biblical and scientific world-views, especially when confronted with the miraculous,[12] his research cannot be regarded as having exhausted the definition of religious thinking.

A broader definition of religious thinking is therefore needed. This must clearly articulate the relationship between operational development and religious thinking, and define religious thinking in a way that highlights that which is distinctive about religious knowing. The beginnings of such a broader definition are to be found in the work of Fritz Oser. During the 1980s Oser examined the development of religious judgment and compared this with the research of Kohlberg (1958, 1980)[13] and Fowler (1981) into the development of moral judgment and faith development, both of whose stage theories are clearly influenced by the development of Piagetian operational thought. Oser usefully proposed a dynamic interactive paradigm of cognitive structure, distinguishing between a common core of logical operations which underlie all thought and influence thinking in any area of discourse, and the distinctive structures which underlie a specific area of discourse, and which therefore also influence moral judgment, religious judgment and faith development (which Oser defines as *world view*). Such a stance allows a redefinition of the relationship between the development of religious thinking and Piagetian stage development. Applying Oser's model, operational religious thinking can be seen as the application of the common cognitive core operations to the interpretation of religious content, with particular relevance for the reconciliation between the biblical and the scientific. Thus, rather than talking of stages of religious thinking development, it may be more accurate to refer to the effect of the underlying stages of operational development upon skills relating to moral judgement, faith development, religious judgment and religious thinking. If religious concepts and dilemmas are seen as the content to which the processes of operational thought are applied, it can be acknowledged that the child at a pre-operational stage of thinking will be happy to resolve a problem (such as the interpretation of miracles), by appeal to magic, while the older adolescent at a formal stage of thought will seek to resolve the problem by examining a range of hypotheses relating to the interaction between culture and the explanation of extraordinary phenomena. Such approaches are clearly not available to the pre-operational child.

2.   METAPHORICAL RELIGIOUS THINKING

At a general level operational capabilities can be seen to influence religious thinking in a way that is similar to all thinking – that is the ability to think concretely or abstractly, and to shift from egocentric and subjective perspective to an objective perspective. These capabilities are particularly relevant for the ability to reflect systematically and propositionally upon religious experience, an ability which underlies the 'science' of theological discourse, and the ability to resolve the conflicts that arise when biblical and religious world views compete with scientific world views. The range of capabilities constituting religious thinking cannot however be reduced to these valid operational skills. Recent investigation of the nature of religious language has highlighted its analogical status and the development of metaphors into extended interpretative systems or models. A broader definition of the nature of religious thinking must therefore take account of the ability to interact with metaphor as part of such thinking and to structure thought within models. [14]

A metaphor may be embedded within a word, sentence, paragraph or a short passage. It may be expressed verbally, textually or visually. It involves the conscious, intentional, contextual displacement of a concept in order to think of one thing in terms usually associated with another. Each of these features will be briefly considered.

• Metaphorical thinking involves the transfer of meaning from one area of discourse to another, an activity which is genuinely cognitive. A metaphor is a *displaced concept* which formulates new meaning by shifting an existing concept from its native context, where its meaning is primarily generated, to a displaced context where it did not initially apply. This process of the displacement of concepts is on-going and never-ending; new concepts come through the shift of old ones to new situations. [15]

• Metaphor is a type of *comparison* (along with some literal statements, similes and analogies). It invites the individual to think of one thing in terms of another. There are two broad types of metaphoric comparison: that of similarity, (A is B), and that of proportionality (A is to B as C is to D). Richards (1936),[16] describes the metaphoric process as follows. One term, the *topic* is illuminated in terms of another element, the *vehicle*. While the topic and the vehicle are drawn from different domains, in a given context they prove comparable. The basis on which the comparison is founded is the *ground*, which is usually implicit. The dissimilarity between the topic and the vehicle, determines the metaphoric *tension*. Thus in the metaphoric statement, "God is a rock", "God" is the topic, "the rock" is the vehicle, and the implicit ground is "firmness", "steadfastness", and "timelessness". The tension between the two terms arises from comparing the spiritual and the physical domain.

• The status of a concept as a metaphor depends upon its use in a particular *context*.[17] A metaphor lives so long as it causes an idea to appear in improbable contexts, the word suggesting one reference, the context another. When an idea becomes as familiar in its new context as it was in the old, the metaphor dies, that is it ceases to be recognised as a metaphor, and its power of disclosure declines.

• The understanding of a concept as metaphoric depends upon cooperation between the author of the metaphor and the receiver of the metaphor. Through context, or other device, the author signals the *intention* to be understood metaphorically. Such communication assumes also that the receiver of the metaphor has sufficient understanding of the concept in its native state, and is willing to actively engage with the metaphor.

• Resonant metaphors can be developed into models. A *model* can be regarded as a sustained, systematic metaphor. For Black (1962) "every metaphor is the tip of a submerged model." Models are dominant metaphors, which gain wide appeal and become major ways of structuring and ordering experience. Several other contemporary philosophers and theologians (such as Kuhn 1970, Ramsey 1973, Barbour 1974, McFague 1983, and Soskice 1985), have stressed that such models are at the heart not only of theological enquiry, but also of scientific discourse. Science, like the humanities and literature, is an affair of the imagination that takes place within a paradigm and a set of assumptions which guide its questions and provide a context for its answers.

The available literature on metaphors and models can be summarized as follows...

1. Metaphors and models are constructed either by the individual or inherited from the wider parent community. Their construction and interpretation requires insight.

2. The relationship between a metaphor or model and the modelled entity is one of analogy; a similarity of feature and or structure is postulated between the object or process modelled and the metaphors that constitute the model.

3. Despite this postulated similarity the phenomenon used as the source of the model, and the modelled entity are distinct entities. Similarity does not equate with identity. Awareness of the status of a metaphor as metaphor and a model as model is a necessary corrective to the model being regarded as a full statement as to the way things are.

4. It is possible to construct a range of alternative metaphors and models of the same entity or process. Metaphors and models are not exclusive and some may be more adequate than others.

5. The use of several metaphors and models to conceptualize a single entity requires such analogies to be interrelated.

6. Metaphors and models use the 'known' to make the 'unknown' accessible. They enable exploration leading to explanation.

7. This increased accessibility is the result of simplifying that which is complex.

8. Metaphors and models are subject ultimately to some test of their validity. In science a model enables the construction of testible hypotheses and predictions, permitting control over the phenomenon modelled in a situation in which control was previously not possible. In religious discourse, on the other hand, a model is validated by its explanatory power, by its status as a classic that has stood the test of time, by its consistency with other models, and by its relation with personal and communal experience.

Both the individual thinker and the wider community use models as the culture within which thought and discussion can occur. The notion of 'God the father' provides an interesting example of an externally presented metaphor interacting with the cognitive and affective schema of the individual. This is the dominant metaphor of Christian theology being an analogy permitting certain statements about God to be made, such as God is a person who enters into relationships with men and women, God is the source of life, and God has a relationship of care and love with each individual. The metaphor also functions as a model, being used to make disclosures not only about God but also about related concerns. Thus if God is 'father', humankind can be conceptualised as the 'children of God', Jesus Christ as 'the son of God', Christians as 'brothers and sisters' of each other, and the church as the 'mother of believers'. The metaphor is therefore extended beyond a way of conceptualising the divine and becomes as well a way of conceptualising the relationship between many entities associated with the divine. This model of God as 'father' is constantly presented to the child by Christian society and interacts with the individual's personal schema. (Freudian analysis of the emergence of the 'God' concept considers that the child has already used her relationship with her father as a way of establishing the identity of the divine).[22] Continuing appreciation of the model of God as 'father' by the individual is dependent upon the recognition of the metaphorical status of the analogy. McFague (1983) argues strongly that the failure to recognise the status of 'God as father' as a metaphor results in the individual identifying the attributes of God solely with the attributes of the human male and rejecting the potential of the female dimension of human experience as a source of analogy for the divine.

Six Capabilities of Metaphorical Religious Thinking
The core metaphorical components of religious thinking can be
regarded as consisting of six linked processes:

Recognition
Comprehension
Production
Elaboration
Interrelation
Validation

These processes can be illustrated by an example taken from the
research reported later in this paper. The material under discussion was two parabolic statements of Jesus, the saying concerning
riches which concludes the story of the rich young man ("it is
harder for a rich person to enter the kingdom of heaven than for a
camel to pass through the eye of a needle"), and the parable of the
treasure hidden in a field (figure 1). Interpreted literally these two
items are contradictory; their interpretation demands the adoption of a metaphorical mind set.

Figure 1
Two Extracts from the Gospel of Matthew

Jesus said to his disciples, "It is much harder for a rich person to enter the Kingdom of God than for a camel to go through the eye of a needle".

(Mt 19: 23-24, GNB)

Jesus said, "The Kingdom of heaven is like this. A man happens to find a treasure hidden in a field. He covers it up again, and is so happy that he goes and sells everything he has, and then he goes back and buys that field".

(Mt 13:44, GNB)

Recognition is the ability to identify the presence of a metaphor. A
non-recognised metaphor can be regarded as a 'dead' metaphor,
incapable of generating insight, McFague (1983). Recognition
involves *contextual recoil*, that is, the rejection of a literal interpretation of an idea within a given context, and the adoption of an
analogical mind set which acknowledges that a concept has been

displaced and engages with the comparison explicitly made or implicitly suggested. In terms of the above texts this requires the recognition that the camel is a metaphor for a rich person and that passing through the eye of the needle is a metaphor for entering the kingdom of God, or that finding the hidden treasure is being compared to finding the kingdom of God.

Metaphoric *comprehension* relates to understanding the comparison that is being suggested. This involves the process of *translation*, that is the articulation of the relevant elements of the analogy by identification of the criterial attributes of the 'native' concept and their use within the displaced context. The ground between the vehicle and the topic must be mapped in a way which permits of a plausible set of comparisons. Such translation must sustain metaphoric *tension* to prevent the establishment of identity relationships. This requires control of the transfer of the attributes of the native concept into the displaced state. Such comprehension can be seen in responses to the hidden treasure parable which highlight the central concept of renunciation in terms of a proportionate structure (i.e. selling everything is to buying the field in which the treasure is hidden, as renunciation is to gaining the kingdom of heaven). This can be seen in the following translation "once you have found heaven, that is more important than anything else; you would give up everything else just to be there" (female, sixth year, 17 years). Inadequate translation is evident in literal interpretations such as "he didn't behave very well, he should have left (the treasure) there, it doesn't belong to him" (male, first year, 13 years), or the kingdom of heaven "is a big place full of treasure," (also a male, first year, 13 years).

A metaphor can be either inherited from the wider community or generated by the individual. Metaphoric *production* is the ability to generate metaphors that are personally novel. This involves the reorganisation of existing ideas from a new perspective, and often occurs within a problem solving context in which the production of a metaphor functions in a way similar to a hypothesis. In seeking to understand that which previously could not be grasped or expressed the individual constructs a metaphor. An example of such metaphoric production can be seen in the response of a female pupil who considered God to be a "pop superstar and we are his fans; he is great, he is brilliant; he is brilliant on stage, the stage being the world", (female, third year, 15 years).

Elaboration is the ability to actively use a metaphor by extending and sustaining its interpretative range. By such extension metaphors become cognitive models. Significant metaphors require a radical adjustment of many facets of our assumptions and beliefs. At the heart of metaphoric elaboration is the *extension* of the metaphor into a wider interpretative framework by further specification, discrimination, or exploration of the common ground between the vehicle and the topic. This frequently requires *contextualization* by which a received metaphor is situated within a wider cultural or religious context or applied to interpret specific life experiences or dilemmas. Such elaboration always involves a *critical awareness* of the strengths and weaknesses of a particular metaphor resulting from the analogical tendency to simplify that which is complex. Thus, while in order to say anything about God we must use metaphors, in order to say anything appropriate about God we must qualify such metaphors. Interestingly, in the sample studied the above parables were rarely elaborated to interpret significant human experiences such as the meaning of suffering. The following response clearly indicates an absence of elaboration "the man who owned the field would suffer because his treasure had been taken" (male, first year, 12 years).

The ability to use harmoniously a number of metaphors to think about a single topic constitutes *interrelation*. No one metaphor will be adequate, we need a great number of metaphors to explore the mystery of the Divine. Interrelation involves three processes: *co-ordinate interfacing*, that is the extrapolation of the common ground between adjacent metaphors and models, such as 'shepherd' or 'guide' or 'light'; *hierarchical interfacing*, that is the identification of core superordinate metaphors and subordinate dependent or derived metaphors or models, such as 'parent ' and 'father'; and *compensation*, that is the adjusting for a weakness in one metaphor or model by reference to another metaphor or model, such as 'father' and 'mother' or 'king' and 'servant'. Such interrelation is central to the interpretation of the above two parabolic statements of Jesus. If interpreted literally, the parable of the hidden treasure contradicts Jesus' teaching illustrated by the camel and the eye of the needle. Interrelation involves resolving conflict by appeal to metaphoric status, or by extrapolation of their common metaphoric ground. This is successfully illustrated by the following response: "it is probably not about the man getting rich; it is probably symbolic ... It depends what the treasure is. The treasure could be happiness, or it could be money. I'd say it must be happiness, otherwise the two (stories) don't match" (male, third year, 15 years). Interrelation is absent in a literal interpretation stressing that the man who found the treasure would become really rich and therefore find it hard to get into heaven.

The final capability of metaphoric *validation* involves awareness of the status, accuracy, or attractiveness of a metaphor to interpret personal, social or communal religious experience. It can be of three types. *Affective justification* appeals to feelings. Metaphors are regarded as having high inspirational or motivational value making the material vivid, interesting, pleasant or attractive. *Substitutive justification* appeals to the availability of a non-metaphoric translation. Metaphors are regarded as useful, but expendable, making complex ideas simple and easy to understand, or allowing chunks of information to be conveniently transfered.[23] *Incremental justification* appeals to the power of the metaphoric device to disclose a realm of meaning which could not be disclosed in a non-metaphoric form, although it could, at least in part, be translated into an equivalent metaphoric form.

The processes of recognition, comprehension and production can be regarded as basic processes by which a metaphor is either constructed by the individual or meaningfully received from the wider tradition. Elaboration is a bridging process by which a simple metaphor is developed to provide a framework for a complex interpretative system – a model. The final processes of interrelation and validation might be termed 'advanced' and generally dependent upon prior recognition, comprehension and production.

3. INVESTIGATING METAPHORICAL RELIGIOUS THINKING AND ITS RELATIONSHIP TO OPERATIONAL RELIGIOUS THINKING.

Between 1987 and 1989 research was undertaken with Irish Roman Catholic secondary school pupils to locate instances of the six capabilities of metaphorical religious thinking and to examine the relationship between fluency on these capabilities and the developmental stage of the operational component of religious thinking. In part this involved a replication of previous work as well as the construction of new test instruments. Subjects were 117 students from a Dublin Community School randomly selected to form a sample stratified according to sex and grade level. Subjects were selected from first, third and sixth year with mean ages of 12.86, 14.78 and 16.74 years respectively (the school followed a five year pre-Leaving Certificate cycle). All subjects received a battery of multiple choice tests including a paper and pencil version of Goldman's test, known as *Thinking About the Bible*[24] (TAB, Peatling 1973), used to establish the subjects' stage of operational development, and the *Religious Commitment Inventory* (RCI), a specially constructed device used to gather information concerning the subjects' present commitment to the religious denomination into which they were baptised, belief in God, frequency of formal worship, frequency of personal prayer, and frequency of personal bible reading. Before the individual interviews all pupils in the classes from which the research subjects were randomly selected were given two lessons on identifying a series of non-religious metaphors taken from junior cycle English course texts and from the lyrics of the songs of the pop group U2. Subjects were then randomly assigned into one of the three groups to receive one of three individual interview devices.

The 58 subjects who constituted the largest group were administered individual interviews based upon a specially constructed device – the *Metaphor and Model Test of Religious Thinking* (MMTRT), designed to elicit responses on the six capabilities of metaphorical religious thinking. The test consisted of seven sections. Section one required subjects to complete and explain four *common religious metaphors* drawn from biblical and liturgical sources, for example Jesus as the Lamb of God. Section two required both recognition and comprehension of four probably *unfamiliar religious metaphors*: the potter and the clay (Jer 18:6, Is 29:16 and Rom 8:15), the hub of the wheel (Hindu scriptures); the canoe on the sea of life (a prayer from the New Hebrides), and the needle and the thread (a prayer of a convert from Islam to Christianity). Section three required recognition, com-prehension, and interrelation of two *parabolic statements* of Jesus, the camel and the eye of the needle, part of Jesus' teaching concerning riches, (Mt.19:24), and the parable of the treasure hidden in the field, (Mt.13:44).[25] The interrelation of these parabolic statements sought to initiate a state of cognitive conflict in which the inconsistencies inherent within a literal interpretation encouraged the subject to search for a metaphoric resolution. Section four examined *parental metaphors of the Divine* inviting subjects to explore images of God as father and as a woman feeding her child. Section five discussed the subject's *personal metaphors of the Divine* and required subjects to interrelate these with other metaphors presented during the interview. Section six explored three *important religious questions*, the meaning of life, the meaning of suffering, and belief in an after-life. Subjects were required to select one metaphor from among those discussed previously and to elaborate upon it in terms of its usefulness in approaching the three questions. Finally section seven invited the subject to consider why metaphors are used as part of religious discourse. The test provided a base of fifty questions over the seven sections. The earlier sections were expected to initiate a conversation utilizing the capabilities of metaphoric recognition, comprehension and production. Later sections built on these to allow for the possibility of metaphoric elaboration, interrelation and validation.

Since the *Metaphor and Model Test of Religious Thinking* excluded an investigation of miracle stories, Goldman's research into the story of the Temptation of Jesus was also replicated. A second group of subjects were administered the relevant part of the Goldman interview following the procedure outlined in his original research. This group functioned as a control group for a third group of subjects who received a modified form of the test, known as *Jesus at Thirty* (JAT), which included questions relating to both metaphorical and operational concerns.[26][27] (The extract from St Luke's gospel used as the basis of the JAT interview is presented in figure 2). The subjects' recognition and comprehension of several metaphors central to the story was explored, (the most important of which being, "the devil said to Jesus 'if you are God's son order this stone to turn into bread'", and "Jesus replied 'man cannot live on bread alone'"). The operational concerns of the original Goldman device were also discussed using his interview questions relating to the possible tension between a scientific and miraculous world-view. (The key questions here were, "If he was hungry, why didn't Jesus turn the stone into bread?" and "Could Jesus have turned the stone into bread if he had wanted to? How?").

Figure 2
The text of Luke 3 used in the JAT Interviews

When Jesus was about thirty years of age he went to the River Jordan and was baptised by John the Baptist. In his gospel St.Luke tells us what happened to Jesus afterwards.

After all the people had been baptized, Jesus also was baptised. While he was praying, heaven was opened, and the Holy Spirit came down upon him in bodily form like a dove. A voice came from heaven, 'You are my own dear Son. I am pleased with you.' Jesus returned from the Jordan full of the Holy Spirit and was led by the Spirit into the desert, where he was tempted by the Devil for forty days. In all that time he ate nothing, so that he was hungry when it was over. The Devil said to him, 'If you are God's Son, order this stone to turn into bread'. But Jesus answered, 'The scripture says, "Man cannot live on bread alone."' Then the devil took him up and showed him in a second all the kingdoms of the world. 'I will give you all this power and all this wealth', the Devil told him. 'It has all been handed over to me, and I can give it to anyone I choose. All this will be yours, then, if you worship me.' Jesus answered, 'The scripture says, "Worship the Lord your God and serve only him!"' Then the Devil took him to Jerusalem and set him on the highest point of the Temple, and said to him, 'If you are God's Son, throw yourself down from here. For the Scripture says, "God will order his angels to take care of you". It also says, "They will hold you up with their hands so that not even your feet will be hurt on the stones"'. But Jesus answered, 'The scripture says, "Do not put the Lord your God to the test."' When the Devil finished tempting Jesus in every way, he left him for a while. Then Jesus returned to Galilee, and the power of the Holy Spirit was with him. The news about him spread throughout all that territory. He taught in the synagogues and was praised by everyone.

Prior to use the MMTRT and JAT devices were piloted and modified. Typed transcripts of the final research interviews were submitted to a panel of judges for scoring. In scoring the notion of fluency was adopted as an index of the degree of sophistication in the use of each metaphorical capability. According to Gaden (1985), a capability is exercised fluently when a performance is "effective and broadly correct, showing an immediate facility in the execution of its elementary operations, procedures or movements, and an integration of these elements in a way expressive of a distinctively personal engagement ...together with a degree of sensitivity and flexibility with regard to the demands and circumstances of the particular case ".[29] In scoring the *Metaphor and Model Test of Religious Thinking* interviews, the following convention was adopted: score 2 = fluency exhibited; score 1 = partial fluency exhibited; score 0 = absence of fluency exhibited.

4.   RESEARCH RESULTS

This short paper does not allow for a presentation of all the findings of the research project. The individual interviews provided a rich collection of examples of the metaphoric thinking of post-primary school pupils which cannot be reported here.

Results relating to the Capabilities of Metaphorical Religious Thinking.
Incidents of each of the capabilities of metaphorical thinking were evident in the religious discourse of the sample of the MMTRT subjects (see figure 3). The levels of fluency clearly differed between capabilities (see table 1). Across the sample performance was best at the recognition level for which the overall mean was 1.4646 (sd = 1.4872). Comprehension scores were lower with an overall mean of 1.0067 (sd = 1.0091). Scores for interrelation and production were similar (means = 0.8384, 0.8100, sd = 0.8276, 0.7880). The lowest level of fluency was obtained for metaphoric elaboration (mean = 0.5322, sd = 0.4967). Inter-judge consistency on the scoring of the interview transcripts was too low for metaphoric validation items to allow for a statistical analysis to be undertaken with confidence. The considerably higher level of fluency for recognition items should be treated with caution and may be distorted by the pre-research lessons on identifying non-religious

metaphors and by the act of testing itself which, of necessity, highlighted an attentional set to search for metaphors.

Figure 3
Fluency of Five Metaphorical Capabilities (MMTRT)

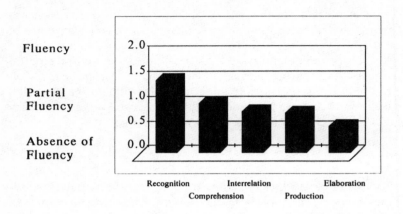

The pattern of development towards fluency during the period of post-primary schooling also differed between capabilities. Metaphoric recognition scores, as indicated by the MMTRT interviews, were high across the post-primary school grades, and approached fluency by 6th year.[30] Metaphoric comprehension scores were lower than those for recognition but increased uniformly with successive grade level. Partial metaphoric comprehension of a range of religious material was firmly established by third year.[31] Metaphoric production scores were very low and showed little variation between grades.[32] There was an almost total absence of metaphoric elaboration in the lower post-primary school grades, and only a movement towards very hesitant elaboration in later grades.[33] A similar pattern was evident for metaphoric interrelation for which performance on the MMTRT indicated a lack of fluency in the early grades and hesitant use in later grades. [34]

Table 1
MRT Capabilities
Total Scores on the MMTRT
(N = 58)

	Mean*	Standard Deviation	s e. Mean
Recognition	1.4646	1.4872	0.0419
Comprehension	1.0067	1.0091	0.0541
Interrelation	0.8384	0.8276	0.0822
Production	0.8100	0.7880	0.1060
Elaboration	0.5322	0.4967	0.0667

* Score of 2 = Fluency; 1 = Partial Fluency; 0 = Absence of Fluency

The above general picture can be briefly illustrated by a few specific examples.

• While most subjects had no difficulty in recognising some common religious sayings as metaphors, comprehension of these items was very low. For example only 3.45% of subjects could provide a fluent translation of the metaphor of Jesus as the 'lamb of God', while 77.6% of the subjects were unable to provide any translation of the image of the Holy Spirit appearing as tongues of fire at Pentecost.

• Comprehension of probably unfamiliar metaphors was in fact superior to that of common metaphors. Thus 32.7% of subjects exhibited fluent translation of the metaphor of God as a potter moulding the clay, the frequency of subjects exhibiting fluency moving from 10% in first year to 30% in third year to 61% in sixth year.

• Concerning the two parabolic statements of Jesus examined in the interview, while 70.7% of all subjects were able to recognise fluently that Jesus was using a metaphor when he compared the rich person wishing to enter the kingdom of heaven with a camel trying to get through the eye of a needle, only 24.1% of subjects fluently recognised the metaphoric status of the parable of the treasure hidden in a field. Comprehension scores also differed between the items with 84.5% of all subjects being able to give a partial or fluent translation of the camel metaphor and only 44.8% being able to give a partial or fluent translation of the hidden treasure parable. Further when asked to interrelate the two items 79.3% of subjects were unable to do so. The most common difficulty that arose was due to a literal interpretation of the hidden treasure parable by which the person in the story was regarded as either having stolen the treasure or having obtained it slyly, or by finding the treasure had become rich. Each of these actions were seen as making it impossible for the person to enter the kingdom of heaven.

• With respect to parental metaphors of the divine while 72.4% of all subjects recognised the image of God as father as a metaphor, only 47% were able to offer a fluent translation of it. While recognition and comprehension scores for the 'father' metaphor were very similar across grades, the pattern for the metaphor of God as a woman with her child was radically different. Thus while only 5% of first year subjects exhibited a fluent recognition of this metaphor by third and sixth year this increased to 60% and 55.6% respectively. Similarly fluent comprehension of the metaphor increased from 10% in first year to 45% in third year to 50% in sixth year. However the ability to fluently interrelate these metaphors remained low at 15.6% across the sample with little variation between grades. The most common stance adopted was one classified as exhibiting partial fluency of interrelation, namely that God was in fact a man but could be compared to a woman in the same way that God could be compared to a potter or a shepherd.

• Scores for metaphoric elaboration with respect to significant questions, such as the meaning of suffering or the afterlife, were low. For example 63.2% of the sample were unable to select or propose a metaphor that would allow insight into the experience of suffering. Fluent elaboration concerning this question was only evidenced by 7% of the sample, there being little variation across grades. The potter metaphor was often selected for this purpose, as was the case in the response of a subject who explored the suffering of a handicapped child as follows: "(God) develops you the way you are going to be, you can't change it. You can't change a pot when it is heated up in the kiln, you can't remodel it", (male, sixth year, 17 years). Other subjects referred to suffering as being the breaking of a pot.

• Finally while a statistical analysis of metaphoric validation items was not possible, (due to low levels of inter-judge agreement on the classification of responses), many instances of such thinking were identified. Affective justification was surprisingly rare across the sample. It was partially exhibited in first year, for example "metaphors are a nice way of talking about God" (13 years, male), and by a sixth year subject (17 years, male), who felt that while we could talk about God without using metaphors they are nice for young children. Substitutive justification was more common and was often linked with the power of metaphor to simplify, for instance "a metaphor can make the smallest thing that you wouldn't understand into something that is very easy to understand" (15 years, 3rd year, female). Evidence of incremental justification was also found. While this was most clearly articulated in sixth year it was also frequently observed in third year, for example: "because God is a mystery, (metaphors are) a comparison of different ideas that helps us to understand God in a better way" (14 years, female), or "there is no definition of what God is, you have to compare him to other things" (15 years, male), or "there is no word that could explain what God is like ... so you have to use metaphors" (15 years, male). Some of the criteria identified by subjects as making a metaphor effective included ease of translation, sensitivity to the ultimate otherness and superiority of God, realism and credibility, compactness, consistency, and fit with personal experience.

Results relating to the relationship between
Metaphorical and Operational religious thinking
We must first briefly consider the development of operational religious thinking (ORT) itself. For subjects who received the MMTRT interviews this was measured by the test device *Thinking about the Bible* (modified from Peatling 1973). There was a clear shift from dominant concrete operations to dominant formal operations between the first and third years of post-primary school (table 2). This shift between stages was highly statistically significant (Chisquare = 8.76, df = 2, p = 0.013). The results pro-

vide strong evidence of an early entry into formal operational religious thinking following a relatively short intermediate stage, a position similar to that reported by Goldman (1962).

The research results indicated that the relationship between metaphorical fluency and operational stage was far more differentiated than that suggested by previous research. Concerning the broad range of material presented in the *Metaphor and Model Test of Religious Thinking* three levels of relationship between these two dimensions of religious thinking were identified. Level 1 reflected a medium degree of association between the stage of ORT and the fluency of MRT. This was evident for metaphorical comprehension for which the correlation with ORT stage was $r = 0.451$ ($R^2 = 0.2034$). The influence of ORT stage was however at its greatest during the movement from pre-operational to concrete operational thinking, and was less important during the movement from concrete to formal operations. The difference in the fluency of metaphoric comprehension, when grouped according to the stage of ORT, was highly significant (one way ANOVA: $F=3.55$; df 5,52; $p=0.008$). However it should be noted that even here metaphoric comprehension was firmly established during the stage of concrete operations, and, although fluency improved with formal operations, formal operations could not be regarded as a necessary pre-requisite for the metaphoric comprehension of MMTRT items. Level 2 reflected a low degree of association between the stage of ORT and the fluency of MRT. This was evident for both metaphoric recognition and metaphoric interrelation for which the correlation with ORT stage was $r = 0.319$ ($R^2 = 0.1018$), and $r = 0.360$ ($R^2 = 0.1296$), respectively. In both instances the relationship between ORT stage and MRT capability was greater during the movement from pre-operational to concrete operational thinking, and weaker during the movement from concrete to formal operations. Variations in the fluency of recognition, when grouped according to stage of ORT, approached significance (one way ANOVA: $F=2.76$; df 2,55; $p = 0.072$), as did that for interrelation (one way ANOVA: $F=2.03$; df 5,27; $p=0.106$). Level 3 reflected an absence of association between the stage of ORT and the fluency of MRT. This was evident for both metaphoric production and metaphoric elaboration for which the correlation with ORT stage was

Table 2
Development of Operational Religious Thinking
as Measured by Modified TAB

	Concrete (-) *	Intermediate	Formal
First Year	12 60.00%	5 25.00%	3 15.00%
Third Year	5 25.00%	4 20.00%	11 55.00%
Sixth Year	3 16.67%	5 27.78%	10 55.56%

* Concrete (-) included responses at the pre-operational, intermediate to concrete, and concrete operational stages.

r = 0.064 (R^2= 0.0041) and r = 0.079 (R^2= 0.0062), respectively. The small variations in fluency between stage of ORT groupings were not significant, (one way ANOVA: F=0.280; df 5,52; p = 0.924, and F=1.90; df 5,52; p = 0.111 respectively). These findings were therefore at variance with the suggestion of previous research (such as Goldman 1962, Beechick 1974, and Cometa and Eson 1978), that formal operational thinking is a prerequisite for metaphorical thinking.

Table 3
Jesus at Thirty
Metaphorical Comprehension of the 'by bread alone' metaphor
grouped by Operational Stage (n=29)

	Absence of Fluency	Partial Fluency	Fluency
Concrete Operations n=6	6 100.00%	0 0.00%	0 0.00%
Intermediate n=11	6 54.55%	5 45.45%	0 0.00%
Formal Operations n=8	2 25.00%	3 37.50%	3 37.50%
Advanced Formal Operations n=4	0 0.00%	0 0.00%	4 100.00%

As depicted in table 3, a radically different position concerning the relationship between operational and metaphorical thinking emerged from the use of the *Jesus at Thirty* (JAT) interviews investigating the story of the Temptations of Jesus, (Goldman 1962, story C).[37] This can be illustrated by considering the subjects' responses to the "man does not live by bread alone" metaphor. While all subjects who were classified as being at a stage of concrete operations exhibited a total absence of fluent comprehension of the metaphor, this declined to 55% of subjects at an intermediate stage, 25% of subjects as classified as being at a stage of formal operations, and zero percent of subjects classified as being at a stage of advanced formal operations. Conversely 75% of subjects at a stage of formal operations exhibited partial fluency or fluency, while 100% of subjects at an advanced stage of formal operations exhibited fluent comprehension. This variation in fluency across operational stage was highly significant (Chisquare $=12.07$, df 3, p $= 0.007$). A similar pattern emerged for recognition items. A high positive correlation ($r = 0.663$, $R^2 = 0.4400$), was obtained between the stage of operational development and the fluency of metaphoric recognition, and a very high positive correlation was found between ORT stage and the fluency of metaphoric comprehension ($r = 0.769$, $R^2 = 0.5914$). These results tend to support the finding of Goldman (1962) that for miracle stories there is a very close relationship between metaphorical thinking and formal operational thought.

Resolving the conflict between these results requires the proposal that there may be three phases in the application of Metaphorical Religious Thinking to biblical material. *Phase 1*: the application of MRT to short statements (such as 'God is the potter, we are the clay', or the 'camel through the eye of a needle' metaphor), which are based upon displaced metaphoric concepts that are within the experience of the individual. *Phase 2*: the application of MRT to the interpretation of extended metaphors (models), including simple parables, such as the notion of renunciation in the 'treasure in the field' parable. *Phase 3*: the application of metaphorical thinking as a broad, generalised paradigm extending the range of valid interpretative possibilities that can be appealed to generally and specifically when conflict arises with a scientific world-view.

This final phase includes the possibility of seeing miracle stories as symbolic or the Genesis creation accounts as mythic. While formal operational thought does not seem to be a pre-requisite for phase 1, or aspects of phase 2, it seems that it may need to be firmly established for phase 3.

Results relating to the relationship between
Religious Thinking and Religious Commitment
The data gathered by the *Religious Commitment Inventory* (RCI), enabled an examination of the relationship between the capabilities of metaphoric religious thinking and several indices of religious commitment such as the level of belief in God, and the frequency of participation in formal acts of worship, and of personal prayer, and of personal bible reading. (Such indices of religiosity are of course common and conventional. No data was gathered concerning other possible indices of religious commitment such as participation in social action for justice). In passing it is worth noting that while there was an overall decline in each of these indices over the post-primary school period, this decline was uneven. There was a rapid decline between first year and third year coinciding with the emergence of formal operational thinking. Thereafter the decline slowed considerably during the period of senior cycle study. For example 92.5% of first year subjects expressed a firm belief in the existence of God, by third year this had declined rapidly to 76.9%, while the decline to sixth year was slight, to 75%. Again, while 87.5% of first year subjects attended Mass at least once a week, by third year this had declined rapidly to 48.7% while the decline to sixth year was slight, 47.22%. While 40% of first year subjects never read the bible personally, by third year this had declined sharply to 69.2% and stabilised thereafter to 64% in sixth year. These findings suggest that the final year of junior cycle study is a critical period in terms of the religious stance adopted by the individual.

Perhaps the most surprising finding of the research project was that the analysis of data relating to both metaphoric and operational religious thinking clearly indicated that scores declined as indices of religious belief and practice increased. When tabulated against various indices of religious commitment, mean scores for both metaphorical religious thinking and operational religious thinking were frequently lower for those groups which scored higher on the indices of religiosity.

Table 4 depicts the negative correlations between religious commitment and fluency on the MRT capabilities. Metaphoric recognition, comprehension and elaboration correlated negatively with each of the indices of religious commitment examined, while production and elaboration correlated negatively with many of them. For example metaphoric comprehension scores when grouped according to three levels of belief in God, indicated a strong decline with increasing belief. Thus a lower level of belief was accompanied by a movement towards fluency of metaphoric comprehension, while a higher level of belief was firmly associated with partial fluency. These trends approached, or reached, significance, (p = 0.069). A similar pattern was evident for formal worship, (p = 0.072), and frequency of personal prayer, (p = 0.043). To consider another example, frequency of personal bible reading had a high negative correlation with three of the MRT capabilities. This was most clearly seen when the frequency of bible reading was grouped according to three levels, low, medium and high. The correlation between personal bible reading and metaphoric recognition was r=-0.500, that for metaphoric comprehension was r = -0.422, and that for metaphoric elaboration was r = -0.376. These were the highest negative correlations between the MRT capabilities and any index of religiosity. [38]

How can these two findings concerning the relationship between metaphorical religious thinking and operational thinking on the one hand, and between religious commitment and religious thinking on the other hand, be interpreted? It may be that the expectation of the secondary school pupil is limited to applying metaphoric thinking to short sayings especially when these include contextual clues such as 'like' or 'as'. The pupil's expectations concerning the applicability of metaphoric thinking does not extend to miracle stories especially when these induce an apparent conflict between a biblical world-view and scientific thinking. The pattern observed by the present investigator closely resem bles that dis-

Table 4

Correlations between the MRT capabilities and
Five Indices of Religious Commitment.

	Recognition	Comprehension	Production	Elaboration	Interelation
Belief in God	- 0.101	- 0.302	- 0.088	0.088	- 0.238
Importance Religion	- 0.150	- 0.280	0.008	0.025	- 0.274
Formal Worship	- 0.368	- 0.294	0.060	- 0.002	- 0.142
Personal Prayer	- 0.215	- 0.366	- 0.007	- 0.189	- 0.249
Personal Bible Reading	- 0.500	- 0.422	0.080	- 0.376	- 0.104

cussed by Poole (1990 p.365) by which the rift between religious and scientific thinking is strongly articulated by the "end of the third year of secondary schooling, when some science teaching has been experienced and a more rigourous operational mode of thinking develops" . With the onset of formal operations the individual is provided with a range of critical and analytic tools not previously available, and the religious ideas of childhood may wither under their scrutiny. Only later, as formal operations become firmly established, and the relativity of scientific thinking is grasped, is the apparent conflict between the scientific and the biblical-religious examined in a way that is open to the symbolic and the metaphoric.

5. IMPLICATIONS FOR THE TEACHING OF RELIGION

The research reported here was initial and exploratory seeking to broaden the possible perspectives from which religious thinking could be examined. Care should always be exercised in generalising from such initial research, especially with a relatively small sample of 117 subjects, to the classroom teaching of Religion. Replication studies which use paper and pencil tests with larger samples are clearly needed before recommendations can be made with confidence. However five broad implications of the above study for the teaching of Religion can be initially suggested.

The need to teach pupils to think religiously.
The very low levels of fluency with respect to elaboration and production suggest that metaphorical thinking is largely neglected by religious education which tends to approach religious metaphor as occasional subject-content rather than as a defining cognitive process. Teachers should be encouraged to facilitate the development of the religious thinking of their pupils and to do so in a way that takes account of the distinctive metaphorical nature of religious language. In a real sense teachers of Religion are teachers of a language. Central to such facilitation is the promotion of responses that articulate the mystery of human experience partially and fleetingly via metaphors and models. There is an urgent need to free the metaphoric to become a creative element in the imaginative exploration of the limits of human experience which

underlie religious belief. Metaphoric thinking allows the depth experiences of human existence, such as the meaning of suffering and death, or the experience of the active presence of a personal God, to be approached in a spirit of exploration and openness.

Possible approaches to develop such metaphorical skills include the translation of classical received metaphors into contemporary or personal forms, and exploration through art and gesture as well as through verbal or textual modes of articulation. Metaphorical thinking can of course be developed in other areas than the teaching of Religion. The study of literature and art feed the metaphoric imagination. Further within the area of media studies an examination of the role of visual analogy in advertising is of particular importance since many of the images and symbols traditionally associated with religion are being used to promote various products. Contemporary advertising is both directly and indirectly subverting the religious imagination.

Implications for the approach to biblical material
Goldman's suggestion that the use of biblical material be restricted before the onset of formal operations was not supported by the present study, which indicated that pupils were able to think metaphorically before the onset of formal operations (although a particular problem with interpreting miracle narratives parabolically was confirmed). It may be that rather than enhancing readiness for the examination of biblical material, formal operations may actually inhibit the pupil's appreciation by limiting the realm of that which is perceived as valid. Mitchell (1986, p.48)[40] describes the reductionist tendency during early formal thought as follows.

> When children reach the age at which their spiritual capacities begin to develop, there occurs a split between thinking and feeling which affects their capacity to deal with ultimate questions. Thinking is confined to facts which are scientifically demonstrable and are to be expressed in flat, literal language, capable of precise definition.

Such a tendency may underlie the significant negative correlations between bible reading and the fluency of metaphorical capabilities that emerged in the present study, which suggest a large degree of literalism or fundamentalism on the part of pupils with higher levels of religious commitment, and a rejection of the validity and relevance of biblical material by many other pupils. Thus rather than waiting in hope for the emergence of formal operations so that pupils can think religiously, it may instead be necessary to strengthen the pupils metaphorical capabilities to withstand the reductionist aspects of early formal operations.

There is clearly a need for a continuing and sustained emphasis on imaginative and experiential approaches to biblical material that enhance the pupils awareness of the symbolic and metaphorical dimensions of the narratives examined and which explicitly develop skills of interpretation. It seems that such a focus may be of particular urgency during the final grades of primary, and the initial grades of post-primary, schooling in order to prepare the pupil's religious imagination for the onslaught of formal operations. It may also be important that literal interpretations are avoided which will have to be untaught at a later phase. Unteaching such literal interpretations implicitly suggests to pupils that an appeal to the metaphoric or symbolic is an escape route when a literal interpretation can no longer be sustained in the face of adult, logical or empirical inquiry, and runs the associated risk that such an appeal may being regarded as diminishing rather than enhancing an idea - the "it's only a metaphor" syndrome. This is a poor substitute for highlighting the uniqueness and validity of metaphorical thought forms from the very start of the educational process and enriching the pupils' religious imagination by approaching the classical biblical narratives in a manner which cherishes their use of analogy, image, symbol and myth as ways of articulating the deeper realities underlying human experience.

Metaphoric Religious Thinking needs a comparative environment
Our concern however must be wider than the Judaeo-Christian scriptures. The study of comparative religion is a methodological as well as a content issue for the teaching of Religion. Without such an environment it is difficult to see how the skills of metaphoric thinking can be fully developed. Various religious traditions address similar fundamental human questions and use overlapping metaphors to illuminate and articulate various aspects of the ultimately inexpressible mystery of existence. The

availability of a comparative stance enables the standing outside of discrete ideas and the dialogue with other possible paradigms. Such a comparative environment involves an introduction to the metaphors and models that the major world religions, differing traditions within a major world religion such as Christianity itself, and non-theistic belief systems, use in approaching distinctively religious questions and dilemmas. While an individual religious tradition is defined by its classical, cherished metaphors and models, a comparative environment need not seek to undermine the strength of these metaphors, but rather to maximise their potential, by encouraging their recognition as metaphors, and stimulating the respect of the pupil for the fruits of the exercise of the religious imagination over the centuries as expressed in the other great religious traditions of humanity.

The need to liberate dead or dormant metaphors
There is also a need to liberate many classical received metaphors so as to permit them to achieve their potential as heuristic devices invigorating the religious imagination. The research indicated little comprehension of common religious metaphors (such as God as 'shepherd' or Jesus as 'the lamb of God'). Further, it is interesting to note that these metaphors were rarely used by subjects for metaphoric elaboration in approaching important religious dilemmas. The potential of the classical metaphors within the Christian tradition needs to be unlocked so that they can cease being regarded as literal statements and exercise their true function as vehicles of disclosure. Of particular concern is the metaphor of the fatherhood of God. This powerful metaphor was frequently interpreted as an identity statement providing evidence of the maleness of God. There were a number of reasons for this including confusion between God and Jesus (who was obviously male), and over-familiarity with the analogy. This metaphor too needs to be liberated to achieve its potential. This is best done by reference to other parental metaphors especially that of God as 'mother' or 'parent', and to other metaphors of intimacy which image God as 'spouse', 'lover' or 'friend'.

Religious Thinking and Scientific Thinking
The research results strongly suggest that the relationship be-

tween religious and scientific thinking needs to be addressed by the teacher of Religion especially during the critical period surrounding the emergence of formal operational thought towards the end of the post-primary junior cycle. This is a complex problem since the tension is not only evident within the educational enterprise but is also a powerful force within wider culture. The limitations of the scientific method need to be considered and the role of the imagination in scientific theory highlighted. Kuhn's description of the role of paradigm in the construction of scientific theory and the phenomenon of paradigm shift offer an important perspective.[41] Further the metaphoric status of common scientific concepts such as a 'black hole' or the 'birth of a star', or the contradictory analogies underling the physics of light, are worthy of consideration. The differing roles of scientific and religious discourse need to be explored. Thus while scientific discourse seeks to separate and analysis in terms of cause and effect, religious discourse seeks to unify and synthesize in terms of ultimate personal meanings.[42] If the split between religious and scientific thinking is to be prevented or minimised then the imagination of pupils must be carefully nourished by engagement with images and symbols encountered in liturgy, prayer, drama, poetry and fiction, music and the visual arts. At the same time such devices must be presented as vehicles of exploration which enable us to glimpse the mystery of the encounter between the divine and the human which lies at the heart of our most significant experience.

Notes

1. Goldman, R.J. (1962) *Some aspects of Religious Thinking in Childhood and Adolescence*, unpublished PhD dissertation, University of Birmingham; (1964) *Religious Thinking from Childhood to Adolescence*. Routledge and Kegan Paul, London; (1965) *Readiness for Religion*, Routledge and Kegan Paul.

2. Peatling, J.H. (1973) *The incidence of concrete and abstract religious thinking in the Interpretation of three Bible stories by pupils enroled in grades four through twelve in selected schools in the United States of America*, unpublished Ph.D dissertation, University of New York.

3. Elkind, D. (1961) 'The child's conception of his religious denomination: (1) The Jewish Child,' *Journal of Genetic Psychology*, 99, 209-225; (1962) 'The child's conception of his religious denomination: (2) The Catholic Child', *Journal of Genetic Psychology*, 101, 185-193; (1963) 'The child's conception of his religious denomination: (3) The Protestant Child', *Journal of Genetic Psychology*, 103, 291-304; (1965) 'The child's conception of his religious identity', *Lumen Vitae*, 19, 635 - 646.

4. Long D., Elkind D., and Spilka B. (1967) 'The Child's Conception of Prayer', *Journal for the Scientific Study of Religion*, 6, 101-109.

5. Kohlberg, L. (1958) *The Development of Modes of Moral Thinking in the years 10-16*, Ph.D. Dissertation, University of Chicago.

6. Fowler, J. (1981) *Stages of Faith: the Psychology of Human Development and the Quest for Meaning*, Harper and Row, San Francisco.

7. Oser, F. (1980) *Stages of Religious Judgment*, in Brusselmans, C., (ed) *Towards Moral and Religious Maturity*, Part 2, pages 277-315, Silver Burdett Company, NJ.

8. The evidence supporting this position is outlined by Andrews, M.M. (1981), *The use of Metaphors as Models in Religious Discourse, with special reference to implications for Syllabuses in Religious Education*, M.Phil. dissertation, University of Aston in Birmingham.

9. See Howkins, K. (1966) *Religious Thinking and Religious Education - a critique of the research and conclusions of Dr.R.Goldman*, Tyndale Press; and Murphy, R.J. (1975) *The development of Religious Thinking in Children, a Review*, paper presented at the first Lancaster Colloquium on the Psychology of Religion.

10. See McGrady, A.G. (1983) 'Teaching the Bible, Research from a Piagetian Perspective', *British Journal of Religious Education*, 5, 126-133.

11. Thus for instance the story of the *Call of Moses* is reduced simply to his sudden encounter with a burning bush with little reference to God's concern for the Hebrews, and later the Red Sea is presented as parting immediately Moses raises his arms.

12. The question must be asked as to how suitable a Piagetian paradigm

is for the examination of miracle narratives? Piaget's work was carried out largely in the realm of practical science situations in which either the investigator or the subject was able to manipulate physical entities, such as the size and shape of various fluids or quantities of plasticine. Only the responses to five questions of the thirty eight core questions used by Goldman in his interviews proved suitable for operational analysis and provided evidence that religious thinking followed the classical Piagetian pattern, this being especially clear when mental age was used as a metric. Three of these five questions related to the apparent manipulation of physical realities involving the conservation of substance. These were, "how would you explain the bush burning, but not being burned"; "how would you explain the dividing of the waters of the Red Sea"; and "why wouldn't Jesus turn the stones into bread". Are the parallels between the biblical narratives and classical Piagetian experiments sufficiently close to apply a Piagetian model? Can transformation of substances such as plasticine or water be equated with the kind of intended transformation of a stone into bread, or the reported transformation of the waters of the Red Sea into a dry river bed? Surely no adequate answer is available in terms of the normal laws of conservation or causality. The research subject must either appeal to direct divine intervention to set aside those laws, or else search for an alternative framework in which the physical reality of the event is either minimised or denied. It is understandable that many a child would appeal to magic as a source of an explanation.

13. Kohlberg, L. (1980), 'Dialog: L.Kohlberg talks to L.Kuhmerker about Moral Development and the Measurement of Moral Judgment', in Kuhmerker, Mentkowski and Erickson (eds.) *Evaluating Moral Development*, Character Research Press, New York.

14. Goldman, R.J. (1964) recognized that the language of the bible is "almost entirely based upon analogy and metaphor, inferring from other non-religious experience the nature of the divine and supporting such concepts upon previously acquired concepts". He noted that religious thinking is dependent upon understanding the original experience upon which the analogy or metaphor is based. However he did not systematically explore metaphor, and there is no notion of model in his work, despite his classification of at least one of the biblical stories he used as 'parabolic'.

15. Schon, D. (1963) *The Displacement of Concepts*, Humanities Press, New York, p.53

16. Richards, I.A. (1936, revised 1973) *The Philosophy of Rhetoric*, Oxford University Press.

17. Black, M. (1962) [*Models and Metaphors, Studies in Language*, Ithaca, Cornell University Press], uses the terms *frame* and *focus* instead of Richard's terms of *topic* and *vehicle*. His classical example of a metaphor is: "the poor are the negroes of Europe", (1962 p.27/28). In this, as in any metaphor, two kinds of language use can be identified; the *frame* (e.g. "the poor") is literal and straightforward; the *focus* (e.g."negroes") is recognisably non-literal in the context of the metaphor. It is this particular context that indicates "negroes" is a non-literal focus. In other cases it could be the non-literal frame.

18. Black, M. (1979) 'More about Metaphor, in Ortony, A. (ed.) *Metaphor and Thought*, Cambridge University Press, p.31

19. The literature on the role of models in science and religion is now quite extensive, including the following key sources. Kuhn, T. (1962) *The Structure of Scientific Revolutions*, (1970 revision), University of Chicago Press; Ramsey, I.T. (1973) *Models for Divine Activity*, SCM Press; Barbour, I.G. (1974) *Myths, Models and Paradigms*, Harper and Row; McFague, S. (1983) *Metaphorical Theology, Models of God in Religious Language*, SCM Press, London; Soskice, J.M. (1985) *Metaphor and Religious Language*, Clarendon Press, Oxford.

20. Black 1962 p.243

21. McFague 1983 p.90

22. Freud, S. (1913) [*Totem and Taboo: Resemblances between the Psychic Lives of Savages and Neurotics*, Penguin Books Ltd], p.147, states that "the psychoanalysis of individual human beings teaches us with quite special insistence that the god of each of them is formed in the likeness of his father, that his personal relationship to God depends on his relation to his father in the flesh and oscillates and changes along with that relation, and that at bottom, God is nothing other than an exalted father'. Commenting on Freud, in the light of her own later extensive research, Rizzuto, A.M. (1980) 'The Psychological Foundation of Belief in God', in Brusselmans, C. (ed.) *Towards Moral and Religious Maturity*, Silver Burdett Company, N.J.Rizzuto (1979), p.7-10, states that "the mature person recovers the God of his childhood in later years at every corner of life, birth, marriage and death. God may have to be repressed again, or dug out of the unconscious and re-evaluated". No child arrives at the 'house of God' without his 'pet' God under his arm.

23. Substitution theory acknowledges only one instance in which metaphor briefly serves a genuine cognitive function, namely as a species of catachresis, that is, the use of a word in some new sense in order to remedy a gap in vocabulary. However such a new sense quickly becomes part of the literal domain.

24. The modifications to Peatling's original instrument were based upon the empirical findings reported in McGrady A.G.(1990), *The Development of Religious Thinking: a comparison of Metaphoric and Operational Paradigms*, unpublished Ph.D thesis, The University of Birmingham. They included the use of an authorised version of the biblical narratives to replace the simplified Goldman version; the limiting of subject responses to the single category of 'most agree'; and the use of an alternative scoring system.

25. Crossan, J.D. (1973), [*In Parables: the Challenge to the Historical Jesus*, Harper and Row], considers this to be one of the three key parables that provide a basis for understanding the whole of Jesus' message. Three themes are evident within it, advent, reversal and action. It invites a range of possible metaphoric stances, from seeing it as a single elaborated metaphor, to treating it as a number of related metaphors.

26. Goldman recognises the story of the Temptations of Jesus as being "in parabolic form", (Goldman 1962 p.27, 38). As a result of his research he concludes that the limits of concretist thinking are so restricting, and the possibilities of misunderstanding at a literal level are so great, that the story is unsuitable for use before 14 years of age. Goldman occasionally uses metaphoric interpretations as examples of advanced formal religious thinking. While such interpretations are certainly metaphoric, Goldman restricts them to the stage of formal operations and rejects the possibility of analogical structures during concrete operations. He provides no sustained theoretical justification for this stance, (Goldman 1962 p.277-278)

27. *Jesus at Thirty*, (JAT), differed from Goldman's original version by using an authorised version of the text, (Good News Bible), and by drawing upon more of the gospel text to establish the wider context of the story in which the metaphorical thrust of some of the elements was more evident. Despite the inclusion of a wider section of the gospel narrative the interview schedule was based only upon that part of the story included in the Goldman 1962 schedule.

28. Lk 3:21-22, 4:1-15.

29. Gaden, Thomas G (1985), *On the Participant's identification with his activity and the value of specialization in Post-Primary Education*, unpublished PhD thesis, National University of Ireland, p.70.

30. This increase in fluency across grades was significant, ($p = 0.045$), and exhibited a low positive correlation, ($r = 0.30$).

31. The increase in fluency across grades was highly significant, ($p=0.0001$). The association between grade level and fluency of metaphoric comprehension exhibited a medium positive correlation, ($r = 0.534$).

32. There was an absence of correlation between grade level and metaphoric production, (r = -0.014). Males however scored higher than females for metaphoric production, a difference which approached significance, (p = 0.127).

33. The small increase towards partial fluency was not however significant, (p =0.301), and the correlation between grade and metaphoric elaboration was very low, (r=0.19).

34. Once again the small increase between grades was not significant, (p=0.222), and the correlation between grade level and interrelation was low, (r=0.262).

35. Beechick, R.A. (1974) *Children's Understanding of Parables: a Developmental Study*, Ed.D. Dissertation, Arizona State University.

36. Cometa, M.S. and Eson, M.E. (1978) 'Logical Operations and Metaphor Interpretations – a Piagetian Model', *Child Development*, 49, 649-659.

37. Comparison with the control group who received the original form of the interview used by Goldman indicated that the test device *Jesus at Thirty* was a comparable indicator of operational religious thinking. No significant differences were found between the ORT scores of both groups.

38. The decline in recognition scores with increased frequency of personal bible reading was highly significant, (p=0.001), as was that for comprehension, (p=0.007) while that for elaboration approached significance, (p = 0.013).

39. Poole, M.W. (1990) 'Science and religion in the classroom', in Francis, L. and Thatcher, A. (eds.) *Christian Perspectives for Education*, Gracewing, Fowler-Wright Books, p.365

40. Mitchell, B. (1986) 'Being Religiously Educated', in Leonard, G. and Yates, J. (eds.) *Faith for the Future*, National Society, Church House Publishing.

41. As an alternative to the assumption that science deals with reality in an objective and direct manner, Kuhn (1962) proposes that it interacts with the world through an on-going process of paradigm construction and paradigm shift. As succeeding paradigms replace former ones in the continuous process of scientific revolution so the facts assumed in earlier paradigms are shown to be wrong even if they had been apparently verified empirically. Facts are not neutral, they are paradigm dependant, and paradigms are subject to change. A paradigm is a cluster of broad conceptual and methodological presuppositions that mould the assumptions of the scientific community as to what kind of entities nature does and does not contain, and which suggests methods of inquiry suitable for studying them.

Those whose research is based on shared paradigms are committed to the same rules and standards for scientific practice. A shift in a paradigm is a reconstruction of a field from new fundamentals that change many of the field's most elementary theoretical generalisations, methods and applications. To change one's paradigm is to view the world in a different way.

42. Phenix, P. (1964) [*Realms of Meaning*, McGraw-Hill], identifies six realms of meaning which can be briefly described as follows. *Empirics* is the realm of hypothetical inquiry where facts are experimentally determined by propositional logical thought. *Esthetics* relates to artistic activity and the meanings arrived at by contemplation, empathy, and the search for harmony. *Synnoetics* is the realm of self-knowledge and the meanings that arise through relationships. *Ethics* is the content of personal behaviour, decision and choice, involving the struggle to distinguish right from wrong. The realm of *Symbolics* relates to the creative imagination as expressed in silence, word, movement, music, ritual, metaphor, symbol and analogy. Finally the content of the *Synoptics* is that of integrative knowing which unites the other realms into a unified structure. Religion is part of this synoptic realm.

The Media and the Church

Donal Harrington

There is much to be said for initiating a serious dialogue between the media and the Catholic church in Ireland. It is frequently remarked (not just by church people) that the church receives a bad press, though this is true of some papers and programmes more than others. It is further felt that this reflects a desire to dethrone the church from its position in Irish society. Thus there is a suspicion within the church of persecution and partiality on the part of the media. This in turn is reflected in a fear of interviews, a fear of being misrepresented and being put in a bad light.

Journalists in the press and electronic media have another perspective. While the image of dethroning may capture the purpose of some, others would speak differently. They would find church officials unwilling to play the game according to the same rules as everybody else. They sense an ivory tower mentality, superiority and condescension. Where church people might speak of prejudice among media people, the latter might point to dogmatism and a lack of democracy within the church.

Someone said that most problems are problems of communication, and there is certainly a problem of communication here. Quite apart from the rights and wrongs, there is a wide gap between perspectives and a failure of mutual sympathy and trust. The thrust of the reflections that follow is not one of taking sides, but rather of assembling issues and articulating a challenge to both sides. In other words, the focus is not just on how church and media relate to one another, but on how each relates to the ethical ideal of communication. It will be suggested that when church and media desist from questioning one another and engage in self-questioning instead, some significant points of intersection and possibilities for dialogue come to light.

Unfortunately, such a critical approach falls foul of the danger of generalising. So it may be worth stating that this essay is not unmindful of the very creative contributions being made by both church and media to the quality of Irish society today. In much of what follows we are speaking of the church and the media as systems and structures – any sweeping categorisation of all representatives or practitioners is the last thing intended.

Questions to the Church
A first question to the church concerns its perception of recent cultural shifts in Irish society. Here, surveys of religious practice in the church can come across as strangely optimistic. Cardinal Daly, for instance, in a homily for World Communications Day said:

> Ireland has a degree of religious practice which is unique in the Western world. The statistics of religious practice have remained remarkably consistent over the last two decades of rapid and unprecedented social and economic change in Ireland... there is little real evidence to support claims of the sort of radical secularisation which many theorists predicted and which many commentators still assume. [1]

This is hard to understand. One would have thought that Irish culture has in fact changed dramatically, that Ireland is now a pluralist society, that it is no longer 'Catholic Ireland'. Of course Catholicism is far and away the predominant religion; and of course the majority of baptised Catholics are still 'practising'. But things have changed. There is now a substantial and growing population who do not 'practise' or even subscribe to catholicism, as well as a significant population for whom religion plays no part in their life or their view of life.

The quotation is only one isolated comment, but it nevertheless invites the question, how well does the church recognise the new situation of pluralism and secularism that has come about? Of course, the word 'pluralism', like the words 'tolerance' and 'liberalism' which also recur in this analysis, is more ambivalent than is often supposed in debate. In the present context, the nub of the issue is whether and to what extent a particular group in society presumes that everything should continue to be seen in its terms and from its perspective.

For the new situation raises a new agenda, namely, how is Ireland to be run, now that it is no longer to be run along Catholic lines? Perhaps it is this issue, of finding a coherent base that can encompass the new plurality, which lends confusion and frustration and ambiguity to many of our current debates, including the ongoing debate between church and media. But to what degree does the church recognise and accept this new agenda which the new situation imposes? Given the context, it would seem reasonable to expect that recognition and acceptance would not be easy.

In his recent autobiographical reflection *More Kicks than Pence*, the journalist Michael O'Toole speaks of the timidity until recently of Irish journalism:

> From the foundation of the state until well into the 1960s Irish journalism suffered from the general paralysis that afflicted Irish society. There was an almost complete failure on the part of newspapers to apply decent critical analysis to practically any aspect of Irish life... The reporting, more often than not, was on the terms and under the control of the authority figures – which is the real reason why ageing politicians, prelates and sundry potentates pine for the days of the old-style journalism.[2]

In the uniform world of Catholic Ireland, critical journalism wouldn't really have fitted in. Something like loyalty to the community would have been a better description of the role of journalism then. Perhaps it is anachronistic to expect that anything other than what O'Toole describes should have been the case.

But in a society (brought about in part by the media themselves) where there is a plurality of value systems, the situation is notably different. There is less and less sympathy with the image of a vertical line of command working down from the spiritual authority through the temporal authority. For who is to be regarded as the spiritual (or moral) authority now? In a pluralist society, what bestows greater ultimacy or significance on what a church – or any other critical institution – has to say?

This leads into a second question for the church: given this situation, how is the church to locate itself in Irish society? On the same day that it reported Cardinal Daly's homily, the *Irish Times* in its editorial said that journalists would 'respond eagerly to a more communicative Hierarchy and to a church which was willing to stand its ground in the marketplace of ideas'. But, it went on, the church declines to engage in public debate: 'its definition of communication is monologue rather than dialogue'.[3] Implicitly, this is saying that the Irish church is still living in the world O'Toole described, monolithic and not pluralist, and that it therefore prefers the caution and control of monologue to the risk and openness of dialogue. Therefore, one has to ask; does the church still hope that the media will give it preferential and deferential treatment?

In this context, one must scrutinise the comments of the recent instruction from the Pontifical Council for Social Communications. It states that 'The media can be used to proclaim the Gospel or to reduce it to silence in human hearts', and it speaks of the power of the media 'either to reinforce or override the traditional reference points of religion, culture, and family'.[4] While these comments recognise the power of the media to 'influence how people understand the meaning of life itself', they also seem to suggest that it is part of the role of the media to proclaim the gospel. This in turn implies an identification of the gospel with 'the meaning of life itself' and with 'the principles of the moral order' that will hardly be accepted without question in a pluralist society.

The problem here may be that the document's attention to what the media can do for evangelisation could obscure the point that the duties of the secular media towards the church are essentially no different from the kind of responsibility the media has to any other group or institution in society.[5] Andy Pollak captures the problem and the challenge well:

> The Irish Church has been a comfortable... majority Church for too long to be good at fighting its corner and presenting its message attractively. This is one area where pluralism has been shown to have real benefits in forcing Churches to compete for people's attention.[6]

We would ask, though, how much benefit has there yet been? It would seem more accurate to say that this is a time of transition, that the church is still coming to grips (as is most everybody else) with what it means to live in a secular, pluralist, post-Christian society, and that it still retains many vestiges of the monolithic worldview of the past.

A third question arises when one considers also the church's problem of credibility in the perception of Irish society. There is a growing sense that the official church is not credible when it speaks on a range of issues. When it speaks of sexuality, marriage, and fertility, what many hear is celibacy, maleness and dogmatism. When it speaks of justice, many people note that questions of power and wealth and privilege and authority are problems within the church as well as outside. Many people are coming to the conclusion that there is no particular reason to be listening to this group speak on ethical issues over any other group.

Here, the church has to question itself before it questions journalism and the media. For our purposes, this self-questioning relates to the theme of communication. The church must ask: what is the state and quality of communication within the church itself? How does it itself measure up, and how has it measured up, in terms of healthy public opinion, open, lively and respectful debate, a minimum of censorship and control? Who has and who does not have a voice when it comes to communication within the church?

Gabriel Daly wrote recently on this question of the quality of communication within the church itself:

> The real danger of enforced conformity... is the building up of a climate of mental dishonesty where one thing is said in private and quite another in public... The greatest casualty in all this is free and open communication together with respect for legitimate diversity within unity... Healthy communication does not depend on total agreement about ideas or ideals. It does depend on willingness to listen sympathetically to convictions and viewpoints which one may not happen to share but which one has no right to smother. [7]

This would prompt us to scrutinise the idea of truth implicit in church practice. On the one hand, there may be operative an understanding of truth as something that is predetermined and prepackaged. On the other, this 'truth' may be seen to be in the possession of certain 'authorities'. If such understandings do underlie communication within the church, one must wonder what kind or quality of communication there can then be.

Perhaps most significantly, one is prompted to ask about the relationship between truth and experience implied in this. If truth is prior to and independent of people's experience, then is the corresponding model of communication that which is symbolised by the pulpits one finds in older churches – that of authority-based, one-way communication? If this is the case, with what persuasiveness can church representatives comment about truth and communication in Irish journalism?

Obviously, the problem of credibility has to be seen in the context of cultural shifts that have been taking place in society, and which are often unfavourable to the flourishing of a religious mindset. By this is meant that the decreasing credibility of the church in the public perception is to be explained also in terms of factors other than that of the witness given by the church itself – for instance the manner in which the energies and potential of liberal capitalism are forming our culture. Nevertheless, it remains true to say that the church itself is to some extent responsible for the problem. This is meant in the spirit in which *Gaudium et Spes*, when analysing the causes of modern atheism, included among them the failure of Christian witness:

> But believers themselves often share some responsibility for this situation... To the extent that they are careless about their instruction in the faith, or present its teaching falsely, or even fail in their religious, moral or social life, they must be said to conceal rather than to reveal the true nature of God and of religion.[8]

This spirit of self-criticism is an essential quality of being a Christian. However, to say that it is the Christian attitude is not to say that it is always the attitude of Christians. Often out of fear, people in the church may think more in terms of survival, of winning out or holding out, rather than looking into their hearts. It may not be unreasonable to suggest that this dynamic may be at play in the church in Ireland at the moment. While the cherishing of traditional perceptions may indicate the value of those perceptions, it may also reflect an unease with new contexts which threaten them or invite their reconsideration.

Questions to Media/Journalism

When it comes to the self-questioning that would be desirable among media and journalists, the territory is perhaps more unchartered than in the case of the church, in that a critical discussion of the role and function of the media in Irish society has hardly begun. Indeed, one journalist spoke of 'two of the deadly sins of the Irish media – its reluctance to look objectively on its own activities and its almost total inability to report objectively on the media industry.'[9]

A first set of questions concerns the competitive dimension of the work of the media. It would be unwise to underestimate the level of competition for readership or audiences that is at work between newspapers, between radio stations, between television stations, and even between different programmes within a particular station. Nor should one underestimate the pressure which such competition places on Irish journalists.

Here, as elsewhere in society, competition can make at the same time both for an increase in quality and for a lowering of professional and ethical standards. Accuracy of information can lose out to speed of communication. There is the temptation to appeal to less admirable human tendencies in order to win over audiences. In the desire for a story, the end can become the sole justification of the means. Privacy may be invaded in the enthusiasm for a scoop. Grief may be trivialised in the effort to hold audiences. When basic criteria are about keeping customers, there is the tendency to pander to majority taste, and thereby to neglect minority voices and concerns.

More seriously perhaps, competition reveals the commercial aspect of media and journalism. One can see press, television, radio either as public services or as commercial interests, as cultural realities or as market realities. While both roles persist, more and more the former is giving way to the latter – media is increasingly about selling rather than serving.

A major part of this commercial reality is the extent to which journalism is in the power of advertisers. Are newspapers going to carry much in the line of news items critical of their major advertisers – with the advertisement possibly on the same page? Again, if a newspaper relies on advertisements appealing to a middle-class audience, will one expect much of a bias of interest in its columns in favour of the poor or the unemployed? One notes in this context the comments in the Pontifical Council's instruction, concerning the commercialisation and privatisation of broadcasting:

> Profit, not service, tends to become the most important measure of success. Profit motives and advertisers' interests exert undue influence on media content: popularity is preferred over quality, and the lowest common denominator prevails. [10]

In the light of such considerations, how sanguine can one be about the assertion of Ben Bradlee (of Watergate and *Washington Post* fame), that in the newspaper world excellence and profits can go hand in hand?[11] What we are suggesting is that journalism cannot be understood adequately unless it is seen in the context of the system of which it is a function. Because of this, much of the criticism of journalism along the above lines might more accurately be cast as a criticism of that underlying system. Advertence to this context in turn makes it difficult to understand Vincent Browne's reference to those who 'control and dominate the media – primarily writers, journalists and editors'.[12] Does he believe that writers, journalists and editors control the media?

A second line of questioning concerns the element of bias in media and journalism. This is not unrelated to the last question because, if journalism is to be seen in its commercial context, then the controlling interests are going to be reflected in editorial policy and political viewpoint. But there are also a number of other aspects to the element of bias.

The very choice of what to report is one such. This is most obvious in the case of the sensational press, but it is more widespread than that. The BBC news guide states that 'The BBC has no editorial opinions of its own. It has an obligation not to take sides; a duty to reflect all main views on a given issue.'[13] This comes across as false innocence. Even the choice of what to report and what to headline, out of the vast amount of material that comes in from correspondents and news agencies, is itself a bias. So the question arises; what do the media pay attention to and what do they neglect or ignore?

Cardinal Daly suggested in his homily that what the media attend to is the 'liberal agenda' and that they ignore the poverty in the world. Vincent Browne agreed.[14] But in their post-Maastricht reflections, Browne and John Waters gave more devastating responses to the question.[15] According to both, the Irish media failed to challenge or to question the 'yes' chorus during the Maastricht debate, and this was because of what Browne called 'an economic and cultural bias, which afflicts the media in a profound and disconcerting way'.

According to Waters, journalists belong to the affluent sector of society, so that their views tend to be those of the establishment – and the addition of their media voice renders the establishment view almost unassailable. In this they reflect 'the drift of Irish society away from aspirations of a collective nature in the direction of a more consumerist, individual-centred model of society.' Browne suggests an exercise: imagine that the poorest one-third of the population had comparable political backing, public relations, access to the media; would the debate about and the perception of Maastricht have been different?

So, the question of bias subsumes large issues regarding agendas, assumptions, influences. But there are further aspects to the question of bias. In newspapers, the impression can be that opinion is confined to the editorial, and that all the rest is factual information. But in reality, both in print and on television, factual research and moral comment run into each other. Further, the extent to which the whole argumentation is emotive may be far more than we realise.

For instance, a short report on some matter contains a certain amount of facts and figures, but not enough to enable an independent judgment; what in fact is being communicated is the emotional *blik* of the writer or editor – and the reader lacks the data whereby to withstand. On some occasions, opinions can appear in the form of facts; or one side of a story may be emphasised; or emotive rather than neutral words may be employed. Sometimes the matter is serious enough to justify one asking: are some presentations at root a management or manipulation of the emotions? when does legitimate bias shade over into emotional manipulation?

197

The factor of bias raises a question about the relationship between the media and truth. Are the media (not just the journalists, but also the controlling interests, be they owners, advertisers or politicians) uncovering reality or inventing reality for us? Are they presenting the truth, or are they shaping and creating it? Are the media mirroring the values of society or are they actually forming those values? Or – another possibility – are they rather mirroring back to their readers their readers' own prejudices?

A further aspect of the question of bias concerns how it manifests itself in the treatment of the church by the media. As we have already noted, journalists express frustration at the reluctance of church people to participate 'in the marketplace'; at their preference of monologue to dialogue; at their engaging only on their own terms. And one must have a certain sympathy with this; if church people do not participate and their voice is not heard, then the appearance of bias is accentuated.

At the same time there is some justification for the hesitation of church personnel to participate (particularly on radio and television) – and this returns the question to the media. For instance, it may happen that a recorded interview with a church leader is edited, distorting the spirit and substance of what he wished to communicate. Again, it may happen that church figures are subjected to an arrogant and aggressive journalism that belittles or caricatures their standpoint.

One realises that there may be others besides church people who feel aggrieved on such counts. But when these things happen, they leave one wondering what is the bottom line of the journalist when it comes to the church. Obviously one can overgeneralise here, but it is interesting to note what Irish journalists themselves say. Andy Pollak observed that the consensus among Dublin print journalists is certainly liberal; that editors and journalists are increasingly drawn from the urban middle-class; that they share both the 'concern with material prosperity and individual freedoms' and the 'mild anti-clericalism' of that class.[16] Vincent Browne commented that journalists hold views which are not representative of the majority of Irish people; that they are more liberal than the average; that the practice of religion is lower among them than in society as a whole.[17]

Such uniformity may be more true of the national than the local media, but it accounts for some of the fear and suspicion among church representatives. Even so, Michael O'Toole can say that 'Many priests and prelates who should know better like to spread the notion that there is some sort of plot against the Roman Catholic church in the Irish media', and conclude that 'There is no plot.' There is only what he sees as the inevitable tension between the liberal world of journalism and a still too authoritarian church.[18]

Many in the church would require more convincing on this. While one presumes that the mainstream of journalism simply wants the church in the marketplace on the same terms as everybody else, there would seem to be another thread also to the picture, not so visible and not so positive, which lends some intelligibility to the fear of the media that exists within the church. This is the kind of anxiety that dialogue may ease.

A third set of questions regards the role of the media and journalism in Irish society. With the explosion in communications this century, ideas about the role of the journalist and the media in society have changed more than once.[19] We already remarked that 'loyalty to the community' might well describe the role of Irish journalism earlier in the century. But with the emergence of a more pluralist kind of society, something like 'non-partisan objectivity' might capture the role of the media – letting the facts speak for themselves, the media as 'mirror' to society (as the Director General of RTÉ put it at a conference on media and morality in 1989).

Again, when one realises the extent to which the media may be controlled by powerful economic and/or political interests, so that objectivity is itself threatened, another statement of the role emerges, that of 'social responsibility' – symbolised by the investigative journalism of Watergate. Finally, with the rights movements from the 1960s, the radical challenging of institutions yielded an 'advocacy' style of journalism – where journalism is biased, but in the precise sense of seeking to develop political literacy and raise social consciousness.[20]

Perhaps there are other possible roles too. One suspects that entertainment has become more and more the role of the media.

Even the news has to be entertaining; but in the process the news may itself become entertainment. Where has the plight of the Kurds gone? Here, 'gone from the screen' comes to mean 'gone' – but how can so much suffering disappear so quickly? In this role, there can be a strong contrast between journalists themselves being personally affected by what they report and the essentially unconcerned voraciousness of the media itself.

The word 'liberal', which recurs in the self-characterisation of Irish journalists, seems central to this question of the role and identity of journalism and the media in Ireland. However, it is not easy to be precise about the meaning of the word. In the *Irish Times*, for instance, Michael Finlan asks about liberalism: 'in a broad sense, is it not simply another term for tolerance, a most commendably Christian virtue?'[21] That, however, hardly explains what Andy Pollak calls the 'inevitable tension' between the liberal media and the church. Pollak is referring here to the liberalism of journalists specifically, in terms of the free flow of ideas essential to their work. On another tack, Mary Holland recently spoke of the 'liberal agenda' in terms of 'a whole range of politically difficult social issues... including moves towards the introduction of civil divorce, the decriminalising of homosexuality, and legislation to make condoms more widely available.'[22]

One wonders to which of these meanings the *Irish Times* was referring when it claimed that 'newspapers and RTÉ are accused [by the church] of sharing a 'liberal agenda' which is supposedly at variance with the prevailing values of Irish people in general'?[23] At any rate, it is evident that liberalism has a number of meanings in our context. It refers to the break from an authoritarian society where, in Joyce's words, 'Christ and Caesar are hand in glove'. It refers to the pluralist society's ethic of tolerance. It refers to a journalism characterised by open debate and freedom of expression. It refers to a programme of moral/social changes of the kind outlined by Mary Holland. The word has other meanings also.[24] Because the concept is not unambiguous, one's comments must be nuanced.

On the one hand, one can say that if church people do not understand the goodness of liberalism, and what it has liberated us from, then their view of the current cultural situation in Ireland is going to be severely distorted. Here we are understanding liberalism as a style of truth-telling, inspired and formed by the conviction both that truth is to be found and that one finds it best in utter freedom.

On the other hand, one can suggest that liberalism's ethic of tolerance may not be the only alternative to the confessional society of the past. For this ethic is pathetic in a way – it can suggest a journalism which panders to intellectual fashion, and which has no truth of its own. One symbol of this is the phone-in vote that follows some radio debates – the nearest we can approximate to truth?

Neutrality is one of the values here, but one must differentiate between the neutrality that means fair access to all viewpoints, and the neutrality that is amoral. To quote again the *Irish Times* response to Cardinal Daly:

> But the media must be more than a check or a brake. They should also have a general vision of the society they serve and they must have the freedom to enunciate that vision. By and large, it is true, the Irish media support a view which is pluralist and liberal. [25]

In the amoral kind of neutrality, there is a tension between the two aspirations articulated here, the one of being liberal, the other of having a vision of society. Not always, but frequently, the liberal ethic of tolerance means that there is no vision, only fashionable views and ideas. In that form of liberalism, the journalist appears as the one who reflects the ideas in fashion, and who may feel compelled even to deride those ideas that are not. When considering the media's 'liberal agenda', one must also inquire into a possible link here between liberalism and cynicism.

Finally, there is the point of debate as to where Irish people generally stand on all this. If it is true that the official church thinks that the moral and religious ethos in Ireland has not changed, and if it is true that it expects the media to reflect an ethos that is no more, then one must have sympathy with some of the sentiments expressed by the liberal media. At the same time, if either church leaders or journalists themselves simply expect the media to reflect the sensibilities of the majority, that too is questionable.

A Meeting Point

Thus far, we have sketched some of the self-questioning that church and media could each engage in. On the one hand, the church might ask how well it recognises the changed cultural and ethical situation in Ireland; whether it still expects preference and deference from the media; and to what extent it lacks credibility when it comes to truth and communications within its own community, thereby weakening the credibility of the gospel.

On the other hand, media-journalism can ask whether they are governed by competitive, commercial interests to the detriment of their public service role; to what extent bias takes from objectivity, including in the treatment of the church; and whether the role and identity of media and journalism in Irish society are not quite confused, and sometimes impoverished by an inadequate notion of liberalism.

There is a meeting point in all this, and therefore a possibility at least of dialogue. The meeting point has to do with power. The church is experiencing the erosion of its influential position in Irish society, while the media have assumed a power that many now recognise as awesome. One bishop coined the phrase 'from Maynooth to Montrose' to capture this shift. And it may well be that power is what each criticises and perhaps even resents in the other – in an encounter where each finds itself reflected in the face of the other.

Either it can remain a power struggle, or the relationship can become something other. This 'something other', the possibility for a transformed relationship, might begin in a reworking on both sides of their implicit philosophies of communication. From there it might lead, as we will suggest, into at least one common focus of concern. This common focus for church and media in Ireland today is the challenge to both of what might be called a 'radical' perspective. For the church, on the one hand, it is the challenge to transcend an anti-liberal stance. For journalism, on the other, it is a challenge to transcend the liberal ethic of tolerance. To both, the challenge is that of seeing beyond the horizon of liberal-conservative, so as to become committed to the radical issues in Irish society.[26] The rest of this essay will elaborate on this challenge for the church first and then for journalism.

Challenges to the Church

It is not the church's task to resist the liberal agenda by trying to conserve or preserve the past. Just as liberalism seeks to go beyond traditionalism, so the church today is called to go beyond liberalism to radicalism. It can do that by getting in touch anew with its own sources. For, Christian sources encourage us to think of history and of reality in terms of communication, and they impress upon us the vision and the exigence of a certain quality of communication.

The Christian tradition sees history as a history of communication, very much in the sense that is proposed by Rosemary Haughton:

> The mental picture I am proposing is... a picture of life as given and received in exchange, without ceasing, forever. Life in this context means all of reality... it involves thinking of everything not just as part of an infinitely complex web, but as a moving web, a pattern of flowing, a never-ceasing in-flow and out-flow of being. But to say that is not enough; the language is still wrong because the word 'being' has for us a 'stopped' quality. For that word, let us substitute another: love. [27]

Existence is exchange; and a deeper existence is a deeper and more faithful exchange. As one author put it, 'Surely history consists primarily in speaking and being answered, in crying and being heard.' In this spirit, Christianity sees history as the history of a divine-human exchange, a divine-human dialogue. This is a view which reaches back into the Hebrew Scriptures, to the dialogue that was initiated by God with a people who were without voice in society, who could only cry. 'I have seen the affliction of my people who are in Egypt, and have heard their cry because of their taskmasters. I know their suffering...' (Ex 3: 7).

It is important to dwell on the meaning of communication that is suggested here. First of all, it suggests that God is to be thought of more in terms of listening rather than of speaking – as the Dutch theologian Schillebeeckx proposes:

> As human beings, we know that silence is an element of any dialogue, of any talking... God is silent in our earthly life. God listens to what we have to say to him... Should the living God not be extremely interested in us all our lives, listen silently to our life story until we have expressed everything... Do we not all dislike being constantly interrupted before we have finished? Nor does God interrupt us, but for him the whole of our life, however important, is just a breath, and God also takes it seriously; that is why he is silent: he is listening to our life story.[29]

Secondly, because listening is an intense form of activity, this is the image of an active God, engaged in the activity of bringing people into greater being through the experience of being listened to. Listening gives a voice to the voiceless; it 'hears into speech' those who have no voice, and thereby bestows on them an increase of being – of existence through exchange.

Thirdly, this is a communication conducted in fidelity. To communicate in this way is to promise to be with the other and to constantly hear them into speech. This in turn makes for a picture of morality as a matter of the kind of fidelity in communication that makes community possible. It is such fidelity, and not some impoverished idea of 'the facts', that provides the criterion of 'truth' in communication.[30]

Christians find in Jesus the incarnation of this divine mode of communication. We speak of communication as 'mediated', and here we find that even divine-human communication is mediated, in the person of Jesus. And when one considers the stories of the gospels, one finds confirmed the picture painted above. Again and again in the listening activity of Jesus, one finds those who cry being listened to, the voiceless in that society being heard into speech.

We can see in this also a kind of 'redemption' of the media of communication. Those media – not just the mass-media, but also the everyday 'media' of word, gesture, facial expression, body-language, touch – are meant to be the way towards communion, but tragically they are abused – the word lies, the kiss seduces, the gesture betrays. But in Jesus we can see most powerfully the truth of communication being recovered, the meaning and purpose of these media being recreated.

Christians inspired by Jesus seek to live out of and realise this vision, such that communication becomes a central theme of their existence:

> Human history and all human relationships exist within the framework established by this self-communication of God in Christ. History itself is ordered toward becoming a kind of word of God, and it is part of the human vocation to contribute to bringing this about by living out the ongoing, unlimited communication of God's reconciling love in creative new ways. We are to do this through words of hope and deeds of love, that is, through our very way of life. Thus communication must lie at the heart of the Church community. [31]

But according to biblical perspectives, this communication is characterised by a particular fidelity to the voiceless – to the victim, the little one, those out in the cold, the one who has lost out, the one who has no say – people who can no longer speak, people who cannot be heard, the people who were the preoccupation of Jesus' heart. Thus we can envisage a community of faithful communication that hears into speech all those who are voiceless, speechless, inaudible.

This is the way to credibility for the church, namely, that the church demand of itself first what it would demand of the communications media – free speech, open dialogue, listening to all voices, listening to the voiceless in particular. One may find support for this in the stress of the recent instruction of the Pontifical Council on 'the importance of the fundamental right of dialogue and information within the Church'. It sees this as a matter both of 'maintaining and enhancing the Church's credibility' and more deeply of 'realising in a concrete manner the Church's character as *communio*, rooted in and mirroring the intimate communion of the Trinity.' This *communio* is characterised by 'a radical equality in dignity and mission', which will 'express itself in an honest and respectful sharing of information and opinions.'

But in proposing the category of the voiceless as foremost, one must think of the laity in the church above all. For so many people in the church, their experience has been an experience of silence, of having to listen while others in authority talk and explain their experiences to them. The only future now possible is that such people (or what is left of them) be listened to and allowed to speak, in a way that would make reality of the words just quoted.

It could be fascinating in this context to analyse the religious experience and language of lay Catholic women and men. Might it be that the experience of silence has meant that these women and men in large part lack a language in which to articulate and communicate their religious experience? Might this in turn have not a little to do with their difficulty in communicating with their 'drifting' sons and daughters? Might it also be connected to to the quality of religious expression one finds sometimes in popular spirituality and local devotions? And might it be that the significance of the popular theology courses in which adults are increasingly participating is not so much about learning theology, but about learning to speak?

Finally, the challenge of listening applies also beyond the church itself. Listening implies a humility that can hear the truth even in unlikely places. In a culture of pluralism, that means developing the capacity to hear the word of God outside the church, a capacity to listen to the one who is not 'one of us' but who has no less a piece of the truth because of that. Something along these lines might be a starting-point in the church's effort both to redefine its place in Irish culture and to rediscover itself as an embodiment of the listening God.

Challenges to Media/Journalism
Media and journalism likewise need to undergo a conversion to something more radical in their practice of communication. And we would suggest that the conversion involved focuses, like that of the church, on the theme of the voiceless. A useful way into considering this is offered by a comparison of the Code of Professional Conduct of the National Union of Journalists with the Ethical Code of the International Catholic Union of the Press.

The NUJ Code stresses such principles as accuracy of information, straightforward means of obtaining information, sensitivity to human grief, respect for confidentiality, non-discriminatory reporting, the independence of journalists from influences on them whereby truth might suffer. The theme throughout is one of professional responsibility and integrity. Its relevance is all too obvious when one considers for instance the excesses of the tabloid press in Britain. Nevertheless, the fact that the code is journalist-focused is in notable contrast to the focus and perspectives of the second code to be considered.

The code of the International Catholic Union of the Press puts the work of the journalist in the context of people's right to receive objective information. Thus the journalist is seen as socially and not just professionally responsible – paragraph four speaks of the 'social role of the journalist'. Later paragraphs expand on this in terms of defending human rights, contributing to justice and peace, struggling against poverty, illiteracy, discrimination, oppression.[33]

This offers a wider basis for defining the role of the media. Not alone have journalists a responsibility to provide accurate information and resist the tendency towards manipulative journalism. They also have a responsibility to 'the human cause', articulated in terms of justice, peace, rights. In a sense these are opposite kinds of responsibility. In giving adequate and accurate information, the journalist/media must aim for neutrality and seek to minimise bias. But in the second responsibility they are not neutral. Living in a pluralist society does not mean ethical relativism. There are key human values that are not a matter of personal taste, but which are (or should be) the foundation stones of truly human society. These are presented as the compelling concern of the journalist.

What these and earlier considerations amount to is the conclusion that an ethical code for journalists must go beyond the individualist to the social and the structural. It must not be just a code about the behaviour and probity of individual journalists, but a code about their relationship to the society and the system they are part of. A useful conclusion might be to see journalism as a forum for accountability in society. Different perspectives are accommodated and fairly presented, but not as a kind of open market. They are presented critically, so as to become transparent when placed against the vision of a society of justice and peace. Thus journalists are stimulating in-depth reflection, assisting the development of political and ethical literacy in the readership.[34]

One recalls some comments of Brendan Ryan, to the effect that any indifference on the part of the Irish media to ethics and values makes for the 'liberation of the powerful and wealthy from the inhibitions of morality, ethics and values'. Opting out on the part of the journalist leaves the way unhindered for a 'ruthless individualism'. 'The media are there to inform us and indeed to protect us from abuse and manipulation. To do this they must stand back, learn and listen.' There is needed 'a renewed sense of media ethics, a willingness to confront issues in terms of ethics and principles.'[35]

This challenge to media and journalism today might usefully be cast as the challenge of the ethical imagination. Ryan's image of standing back brings to mind a passage in *More Kicks than Pence*, where Michael O'Toole speaks of how his difficult experience working with one newspaper reinforced in him 'the very definite feeling of always being an outsider.' And he went on, 'that is no bad thing for a journalist.'[36] Irish journalists might well see themselves as outsiders, standing back, much like Socrates in Athenian society, goading and challenging the ethical imagination.

On this theme, Michael Ignatieff wrote a piece entitled 'The Media admires itself in the Mirror'. He was referring to a tendency to self-absorption which he observed in the media, as a result of which journalism was losing its 'social imagination', the imagination whereby it 'mediates' the real world to its audience. In place of the social imagination, he saw journalism capitulating to entertainment and gossip.[37]

The outsider O'Toole speaks of stands for the social and ethical imagination of journalism. For the outsider is not in anybody's pocket, whether it be the pocket of the editor or the owner or the advertiser or the politician or the church or the liberal society. Perhaps one could reread in this light the paragraph in the NUJ code that says 'A journalist shall not accept bribes nor shall he/she allow other inducements to influence the performance of his/her professional duties'.

The outsider, rather, is committed to the truth that transcends all agendas and all parties and all interests. The words of Reinhold Niebuhr come to mind: 'justice cannot be approximated if the hope of its perfect realisation does not generate a sublime madness in the soul'.[38] It is this madness that is needed, rather than the different kinds of madness found in liberalism and traditionalism. It is the madness of the imagination that is absorbed by attention to the ethical demands of the other.

This imagination will be reflected in how media and journalists see their audience. The journalist as insider sees the audience as consumers of a product. But the journalist as outsider sees the audience as subjects s/he enters into communion with in an exploration for the truth. In particular, the journalist as outsider notices in that audience the ones who are speechless, or whose cries have been rendered inaudible by the noise of the powerful and the laughter of the prosperous. Such a journalist seeks to hear into speech those who have no voice.

Perhaps this is the reference-point against which journalism can understand its role and function in society, namely, what might be called a preferential attentiveness to the voiceless. In this context, notions such as loyalty to the community, objectivity, social responsibility, advocacy and forum for accountability can be invested with new content and inspiration. Here, it is encouraging to read Irish journalists recently emphasising the need to advert to and accommodate in the news alternative, marginal perspectives.[39]

Pope John Paul II has remarked that the communications media are 'the admission ticket of every man and woman to the modern marketplace'.[40] The challenge to the social and ethical imagination of the journalist is to ensure that each person actually gains admission, that each voice is let speak. One way of realising this would be to encourage alternative popular communication, such as local radio, local press, popular theatre, popular resource and documentation centres. Such initiatives give speech to the speechless; they can empower people, convince them they have something worthwhile to say. They can democratise communication, allowing people tell their stories rather than have their stories composed and imagined for them. Thereby they bring to attention alternative issues to those highlighted by the powerful media. Thereby they can recreate a multi-perspectival world.[41]

Conclusion

Were church and media to engage in the kind of self-questioning suggested in the first half of this paper, each would have good reasons for a humble approach to their mutual relationship, as well as a pressing agenda for self-transformation. But perhaps more significantly, if each were to enter into the kind of perspectives suggested in the second half of the paper, they might find something significant they had in common. In other words, when church and media imagine a best possible version of themselves as communities of communication, they find that in many ways they share a common cause. If this argument is valid, then for church and media to relate to each other in fear and suspicion implies that roles have been radically misunderstood or distorted.

We have concluded from this that one way forward in the church-media relationship in Ireland lies in the cultivation of the social and ethical imagination. The voice of the church and the voice of the media – each of which tends to regard the other as too loud and powerful - meet each other when faced with the silence of the voiceless. And faced with the voiceless, the liberalism of journalism and the traditionalism of the church are transcended in the more radical challenge to develop an imagination capable of responding to the ethical reality of 'the other'.

Notes:

1. *Irish Times*, 1/6/92
2. Michael O'Toole, *More Kicks than Pence* (Dublin: Poolbeg Press, 1992), 10-11
3. *Irish Times*, 1/6/92
4. Pontifical Council for Social Communications, *Pastoral Instruction of Social Communications*, *'Aetatis Novae'* (Vatican, 1992), n. 4. The text of the instruction can be found in *Catholic International*, vol. 3, no. 10 (15-31 May, 1992)
5. Cf. particularly *Aetatis Novae*, 8-11
6. Andy Pollak, 'The Church and the Press – Living with Liberalism'. *The Furrow* 42 (June 1991), 351
7. Gabriel Daly, 'Table d'Hôte Catholicism'. *The Furrow* 42 (July-August 1991), 412-414
8. Vatican Council II, *Pastoral Constitution on the Church in the Modern World*, *'Gaudium et Spes'* (Vatican, 1965), n. 19. The translation is taken from A. Flannery (ed.), *Vatican Council II: The Conciliar and*

Post-Conciliar Documents (Dublin: Dominican Publications, 1975), 919.
9. Michael O'Toole, *More Kicks than Pence*, 185. He goes on (190) to speak of newspapers that 'want to analyse and pontificate on every industry in the country yet shy away from any analysis of their own affairs'. On the other hand, there are encouraging signs in the self-criticism of some in the newspaper world that followed on the Maastricht referendum – cf. Vincent Browne's pieces in the *Sunday Tribune*, 7/6/92 and 21/6/92, and those of John Waters in the *Irish Times*, 20/6/92 and 23/6/92
10. *Aetatis Novae*, 5
11. 'Guardians of the truth.' *Irish Independent*, 27/6/92
12. *Sunday Tribune*, 7/6/92
13. Quoted in Jim McDonnell, 'Mass media, British culture and Gospel values'. H. Montefiore (ed.), *The Gospel and Contemporary Culture* (London: Mowbray, 1992), 166
14. *Irish Times*, 1/6/92; *Sunday Tribune*, 7/6/92
15. Browne's comments appear in the *Sunday Tribune*, 21/6/92, Waters' in the *Irish Times*, 20/6/92 and 23/6/92
16. 'The Church and the Press', 352
17. *Sunday Tribune*, 7/6/92
18. *More Kicks than Pence*, 184. Andy Pollak's article also discusses this tension.
19. On the following, cf. *Communication Research Trends* (London: Centre for the Study of Communication and Culture), vol. 1 (Spring 1980), no. 1.
20. In relation to Ireland, Michael O'Toole comments on the advent of television leading Irish journalism away from subservience to a more confrontational role (*More Kicks than Pence*, 80-81, 184).
21. *Irish Times*, 5/6/92
22. *The Observer*, 21/6/92
23. *Irish Times*, 1/6/92. Likewise, Michael Finlan speaks of church suspicion that RTÉ and the daily newspapers 'are dominated by a liberal ethos that is starkly at variance with the thinking of most Irish people who are seen as being more or less conservative and Christian in their outlook' (*Irish Times*, 5/6/92).
24. See, for example, Fintan O'Toole, 'Releasing Radicalism.' National Council of Priests of Ireland, *Good News in a Divided Society* (Dublin: Dominican Publications, 1992), 109.
25. *Irish Times*, 1/6/92.
26. Cf. Fintan O'Toole, 'Releasing Radicalism', for a similar sense of the inadequacy of and the need to go beyond the parameters of liberal-conservative.
27. Rosemary Haughton, *The Passionate God* (London: DLT, 1981), 21
28. Walter Brueggemann, *The Prophetic Imagination* (Philadelphia: Fortress Press, 1978), 22

29. Edward Schillebeeckx, *Church: The Human Story of God* (London: SCM Press, 1990), 131
30. John Waters gives a vivid illustration of what this means concretely for journalist: *Jiving at the Crossroads* (Belfast: The Blackstaff Press, 1991), 88-89
31. *Aetatis Novae*, 6
32. *Aetatis Novae*, 10
33. 'Ethics in Journalism: Principles of the International Catholic Union of the Press.' *Intercom*, May 1989, 5
34. Andy Pollak gives a definition along these lines: 'to bring the light of publicity and accountability to bear on those holding power, wealth and authority so as to make them more answerable for their actions to the public...' ('The Church and the Press', 350). In a similar vein, O'Toole quotes W.H. Auden's model journalist; 'the brave and honest reporter who unearths and makes public unpleasant facts, cases of injustice, cruelty, corruption, which the authorities would like to keep hidden, and which the average reader would prefer not to be compelled to think about' (*More Kicks than Pence*, iii). However, such definitions need to be completed by an articulation of the vision of society against which the critique is to be carried out.
35. *Alpha*, 16/3/89
36. *More Kicks than Pence*, 51-52
37. *The Observer*, 20/7/92
38. Reinhold Niebuhr, *Moral Man and Immoral Society: A Study in Ethics and Politics* (New York: Charles Scribner's Sons, 1932), 277
39. Vincent Browne, *Sunday Tribune*, 21/6/92; John Waters, *Irish Times*, 23/6/92
40. John Paul II, 'Without Compromise – with Sensitivity: Papal Message for World Communications Day 1992.' *Catholic International* vol. 3, no. 10 (15-31 May, 1992), 459
41. Cf. John Waters, *Jiving at the Crossroads*, 81ff, 162ff, for a contrast between the effects of national and local radio on a particular community.
42. *Aetatis Novae*, 16 sees a role for the church here also. In the context of the exclusion of some groups and classes from access to the media (14), the church may be called upon 'to promote alternative community media' which 'are open to people's involvement and allow them to be active in production and even in designing the process of communications itself'.

Morality and Culture in Dialogue

✠ *Donal Murray*

The dialogue between morality and culture in our time centres chiefly around the idea of freedom. The complexity of that dialogue might be summed up by pointing to two of the ways in which that dialogue is commonly expressed: the idea, on the one hand, that moral rules limit the freedom and the personal autonomy which are keystones of our culture and, on the other hand the idea that the vindication of freedom is itself a moral demand which fuels concern for poor and oppressed members of the human family, a concern which is also one of the great moral issues underlying contemporary Western culture. Moral obligations, therefore, appear, often to the same people, both as the enemies and the champions of freedom.

The central necessity for a fruitful dialogue is to tease out the meaning of freedom and to unmask the often undetected differences which risk producing a dialogue of the deaf. There is for instance, a common assumption that people who enter unrestrainedly into what one might call the permissive society are liberated, like prisoners emerging from a dungeon. From another point of view, one might be inclined to suspect that they are rather more like people leaping from the confines of an aircraft at 30,000 feet shouting, 'Free at last !'

Living in Private Rooms

All freedom is at root, personal freedom. One must, however, ask whether this is precisely the same as what we think of as individual autonomy. In the early seventies, Lionel Trilling proposed the thesis that 'at a certain point in history men became individuals'. This change can be detected, he suggests, by the emergence of the impulse to write autobiography! At first sight it seems an absurd idea – surely people were always individuals! But the point he wishes to make is that, up to a certain period, a person

> did not suppose that he might be an object of interest to his fellow man not for the reason that he had achieved something notable or been a witness to great events but simply because as an individual he was of consequence. It is when he becomes an individual that a man lives in private rooms; whether the privacy makes the individuality or the individuality requires the privacy the historians do not tell us. [1]

One of the greatest values of our culture is that of *sincerity*– that is the value of a person being true to him or herself. To be true to oneself involves understanding oneself. The first issue therefore, that arises in the dialogue of culture and morality is how one is to understand the person, the subject of freedom. How far do we see the person as an individual in a private room, emerging from time to time to exercise freedom and retiring into the private room which is his or her natural habitat? Or do we think of the person as a subject who is, from the beginning related to others, who cannot be understood at all except in terms of the relationships through which he or she is created and formed, sustained or broken, challenged and enabled to grow?

In the private room, the primary question will tend to be, 'Have I been true to myself? Have I been authentic? ' This is not necessarily the same as asking, 'Have I been true to the people whom my actions "address", who are acknowledged or rejected by the way I use my freedom?'

> 'This above all ,' Polonius said, 'to thine own self be true
> And it doth follow as the night the day,
> Thou canst not then be false to any man.'

We might profitably ask ourselves whether it is a question of one following the other. If the two things do go together, which they do, is it not rather because they are incapable of being separated? Being true to others is not the consequence of being true to oneself, it is more like the meaning of being true to oneself. This is certainly implied by the anthropology of Vatican II which declares that the human being can find his or her true self only by the sincere giving of self (*Gaudium et Spes* 24). Freedom does not find its deepest expression in the private room but in responding to others.

> The human person, in fact, is essentially a social being, and without relationships with others can neither live nor develop his or her gifts. [2]

In the past, a person's idea of him or herself did not begin in private rooms, which after all did not exist. The person was significant, not as an abstract individual, but as somebody with a place in the whole network of relationships which made up the neighbourhood or clan. Nowadays, it seems, the communities to which an individual belongs are weaker and less significant. The individual tends more and more to see him or herself standing alone in the face of the vast and impersonal machine which is the state and in the face of the structures, such as they are of international politics and economics. The forces which shape the individual's world seem to be far beyond his or her control. The starvation of the Third World, the destruction of the environment, the future of Eastern Europe and so on – all are problems before which the individual feels overwhelmed.

That is the paradox which is raised by the notion of individual autonomy: the isolated individual's characteristic attitude is not one of freedom but of helplessness. This is because we have to a great extent lost or failed to appreciate the realities and the contexts in which real human growth can occur. The paradox can only be resolved when it is recognised that as Jonathan Sacks put it:

> The Enlightenment and the intellectual and social process to which it gave rise have had a devastating effect on the traditions which give meaning and shape to life lived in community. They have focussed relentlessly on two entities: the individual, detached from historical context, and the universal, politically realised in the secular state. They have left little space for that third essential component of our social ecology: particular and concrete communities of character, of which religions were and are the most potent examples. To put it briefly and bluntly, neither the individual nor the state is where we discover who we are and why. [3]

The individual living in a private room, on emerging, finds more

and more that he or she has stepped out into the soulless interme-
diary communities in which human beings grow in their commitments, their relationships and their understanding of themselves
and their lives. The inevitable result is a sense of powerlessness
arising from a lack of confidence about who we are and why.

Polonius has got it wrong. There cannot be a real distinction between being true to oneself and being true to others. The idea that
the ultimate moral criterion is integrity, or authenticity, or sincerity
is common in out culture. It is true, but only on condition that one
understands that the self to which one is true can find itself only
in giving itself.

As Archbishop Connell expressed it in last year's Lenten Pastoral:

> This is something we have learned from Christ: integrity is
> nothing other than the perfection of love … Integrity goes with
> the surrender of self: what one might hesitate to sacrifice for
> the sake of impersonal standards may freely be given out of
> love.[4]

The moral call is not, therefore, something which restricts and
limits one's freedom to be true to oneself . It *is* the call to be true to
oneself. But that means recognising what one is – a being who lives
and flourishes through love.

The image which we may sometimes have of the autonomous individual in splendid isolation, unaffected by contact with other
individuals, emerging to act with perfect awareness and freedom
is an illusion. Such a being could never learn to express itself, never
develop a moral sense, never even become aware of itself in any
recognisable sense as a person. The first idea of dialogue points us
in the direction of the chief contexts in which a person becomes
more fully and consciously human. These are neither the private
room of some kind of existential loneliness nor the impersonal
arena of the state. They are the many often overlapping, groupings and communities, first among which is the family, in which
people grow as persons and as social beings:

> Apart from the family, other intermediate communities exer-
> cise primary functions and give life to specific networks of soli-
> darity, These develop as real communities of persons and
> strengthen the social fabric, preventing society from becoming

an anonymous and impersonal mass, as unfortunately often happens today. It is in interrelationships on many levels that a person lives, and that society becomes more 'personalised'. [5]

If one begins in the private room, the apparatus of the state, and indeed everything outside the private room, will be seen as operating on the individual from outside and therefore as impositions. If one begins, however, with the person who is formed and who develops through relationships inspired by love and loyalty, trust and truthfulness, then these moral obligations are not imposed from outside. They are part of what one is, or, better, of who one is.

In the context of the family and of grouping in a more human scale, one can begin to see the obligations which express themselves not so much in 'having to' as in 'wanting to'. That is why integrity or sincerity is indeed a basic value and why dialogue about its meaning is worth pursuing. Through reflection on its meaning, people of our day can 'be helped to discover that there is one demand – and it includes all others – that offers no violence to freedom, because it is the demand of a personal love.'[6] Even the broader and seemingly more impersonal demands of the wider society and world can be seen as the basic 'family' attitudes of fairness, loyalty and honesty writ large.[7]

The second conclusion that one may draw is that society is impoverished if the role of these intermediate groupings in moral and human growth is not appreciated. One result of failing to recognise this role is the emergence of the absurd notion that the state should be regarded as a prime mover in the field of education. The state has, of course, the right to ensure that people are properly prepared for their role as citizens. The idea that the state can form and prepare a person for all the richness and variety of human living is, however, a nonsense. The state, as such, does not know 'who we are and why'; it can give no adequate answer to the question either what a person is or of the question of the purpose of human life.[8]

The tendency to think that the only important poles in modern culture are the individual and the state leads inevitably to a society which is increasingly soulless. All that makes us human, all the contexts in which we really belong, are devalued. We are left alone at the mercy of economic trends, technological novelties and international politics; at the same time we are uncomfortably aware that we lack the moral strength and the community cohesion to be able to evaluate wisely and to control effectively what these forces are doing to our lives. In the end, we find that they are preventing us from being ourselves.

How can it be otherwise if our shared values are weak and the shared human experience which most significantly makes us what we are is regarded as of marginal importance? We need to be ourselves, but we have grown in self-understanding by the sharing of ourselves with others.

The Pluralist Paradox
The second area of dialogue is suggested by another key value of our culture, that of *tolerance.* We need to tease out its meaning. As in the case of sincerity, tolerance is obviously very closely linked with our understanding of freedom.

There is a notion of tolerance which merely reflects the 'authenticity' of the individual in the private room. That is what would be implied, for instance, in the idea that an individual's private beliefs are of no possible concern to anybody else, that to show interest in another person's beliefs and values would be an intrusion into his or her private room.

The strange thing is that such an attitude appears in practice to produce the opposite result to that which it intends. One reason for this is obvious enough. It is an attitude which does not encourage the differing moral standpoints to understand one another. It may, in fact, despair of their understanding one another.

It is at least partly based on the experience of incomprehension which is familiar to us nowadays, not least in Ireland. One can see that some of the participants on both sides of debates on questions like abortion and divorce regard each other as entirely lacking in human feeling and in moral sensitivity. Close analysis of the arguments will show that , very often, these participants are operating out of different and incompatible moral philosophies:

> From our rival conclusions we can argue back to our rival premises: but when we do arrive at our premises argument ceases

and the invocation of one premise against another becomes a matter of pure assertion and counter-assertion. Hence perhaps the slightly shrill tome of so much moral debate.[9]

The pluralism of tolerance which is satisfied simply to walk away from such disagreements muttering uncomprehendingly that there is no accounting for taste, is a recipe for bitterness:

> Once we lose a common language , we enter the public domain as competing interest groups rather than as joint architects of a shared society ... At its extreme [this environment] produces a clash of fundamentalisms, some liberal, some conservative, neither with the resources to understand the other. [10]

There is another, and more basic, reason why this merely passive tolerance tends not to produce the desired result. For one person to say to another 'Your beliefs, whatever they are , are alright with me; it does not matter to me in the slightest what you believe' is not very satisfactory, nor even very polite! The trouble is that a person's beliefs may well matter very much indeed to him or her. Freedom is understood and exercised only as a shared and reciprocal reality. To regard another person's criteria for decision making, another persons values, other than with respect and positive interest is to devalue one's own freedom.

A passive tolerance allows the other person to believe whatever he or she wishes, but strongly suggests that these beliefs should, so far as possible, not be brought to the notice of those for whom they are a matter of indifference. Where does that leave somebody who, while recognising that his or her beliefs should not be intrusively or inappropriately paraded, nevertheless regards them as relevant to every area of life? Where does that leave people who feel that it would be a betrayal of their convictions to leave them behind in the 'private room?'

The fact is that, in whatever context it takes place – economic, political, social, home, neighbourhood – every exercise of human freedom has to do with morality. People have been heard recently to suggest that no problem of conscience arises in connection with the Referendum on the Maastricht Treaty. The fact is that *every* decision a person makes is either responsible or irresponsible, moral or immoral. Seriously to suggest that there are areas of life where the question of moral responsibility does not arise would be to impoverish the notion of freedom and to dehumanise our idea of ourselves and of our society.

The reality is that we are engaged in a common moral quest where the conscientious convictions of one person may help others to learn the truth. If another person's convictions are of no interest to me, then I am failing to see, as Vatican II stated that I should, that I am

> joined to the rest of humanity in the search for truth and for the right solution to so many moral problems which arise both in the life of individuals and from social relationships. [11]

Sometimes, pluralism and tolerance are presented as if the ideal were that all traditions should meet and merge into some kind of amalgam which would, no doubt, turn out to be a lowest common denominator. Others speak as if pluralism meant that the traditions should, as far as possible, remain private and avoid having to meet in order to preserve their own identities uncontaminated.

When we begin to reflect on what a real, active tolerance would call for, we find that, like sincerity, it has depths which may initially have escaped us. A fuller and richer understanding requires that the various beliefs and traditions should meet and engage in dialogue with respect for the integrity of each:

> How can the culture which is predominant in a given society accept and integrate new elements without losing its own identity and without creating conflicts? The answer to these difficult questions can be found in a thorough education with regard to the respect due to the conscience of others; for example, through greater knowledge of other cultures and religions, and through a balanced understanding of such diversity as already exists. [12]

Disagreement about moral approaches and moral obligations can often lead only to embarrassed silence. The result can be that moral discussion is increasingly seen as inappropriate to the public domain. Once there is disagreement on any significant scale about a moral issue it is felt that society, the state and the law have no further role:

Given this approach one should abandon the criterion of social values when considering legislation and should substitute for it a kind of sociological empiricism or counting of heads with a view to accommodating everybody and permitting everything.[13]

It would, of course, be entirely wrong that any group should try to coerce other people into obeying religious and moral rules in order to make the others conform to the norms of the more powerful group. But it is also important to recognise that to acquiesce in a constant retreat of moral considerations into a more and more private sphere is to acquiesce in an increasingly superficial understanding of human society. The solution does not lie in a silent withdrawal but in learning the criteria and language which will allow us to build society on something more than the empty 'values' which remain when moral discussion retreats: 'success and self-expression, the key values of an individualist culture.'[14]

It is necessary to question the idea that the best citizens of a modern democracy are those who keep their moral opinions to themselves and who regard all moral opinions with an equally detached neutrality:

Nowadays there is a tendency to claim; that agnosticism and sceptical relativism are the philosophy and basic attitude which correspond to democratic forms of political life. Those who are convinced that they know the truth and firmly adhere to it are considered unreliable from a democratic point of view, since they do not accept that truth is determined by the majority, or that it is subject to variation according to different political trends ... As history demonstrates, a democracy without values easily turns into open or thinly disguised totalitarianism.[15]

The concrete result of squeezing moral discussion out of public debate is that the government is expected to be morally neutral:

So governments are there to treat AIDS, child abuse, homelessness and addiction and not to disseminate a morality that might reduce them in the first place. [16]

This is a failure to appreciate that there is more to society than the relationship between the state and the private individual. The moral vitality, indeed the humanity, of social life, require that there should be many groupings with moral convictions and religious beliefs. These groups are both entitled and obliged to contribute in the light of these convictions to the discussion as to the best path for society to take whether in its laws or simply in its attitudes and public opinion. There should be a great deal of moral discussion in any healthy society. A society where moral values are not at the heart of the whole approach to social living is a society which is lacking an essential human dimension:

> We live indeed in a pluralist society. But this does not mean that we accept all patterns of moral values equally, that we are completely and emptily permissive. We may still – and I argue should – judge between them, condemning and praising some and being indifferent or permissive towards others; but we must now do so with a much more deliberately cultivated knowledge of how other subgroups live and what they believe in and why, and a greater tolerance of a wider degree of diversity than in the past. There may still be limits to tolerance. [17]

Tolerance is not about damping down moral reflection and debate, it is about the attitude of respect with which the moral convictions of others are approached and the seriousness with which moral questions are addressed. A superficial caricature of pluralism would see the existence of a variety of moral approaches as a signal that discussion of moral issues should be avoided wherever possible; each approach should be allowed to go its own way with as little friction as possible. Active tolerance, on the contrary, sees the dialogue of morality and culture as a duty which is more pressing precisely to the degree that a variety of moral outlooks exists in society.

The Moral Environment

A third area of dialogue which is suggested by our culture is *concern for the environment*. It is not so long ago that decisions about industrial and technological developments could be made without any reference to the effect that they might have on the world's resources. Nowadays it is inescapably clear that we cannot operate in a vacuum.

The myth of progress was based on the illusion that the resources of the earth are unlimited. It is now clear that the continued pursuit of that myth would threaten the very ability of the planet to support human life. Freedom, understood as the capacity to deal with the world in whatever way one wishes, turns out to be a way of enslaving ourselves by creating for ourselves an increasingly uninhabitable environment:

> Faced with the widespread destruction of the environment, people everywhere are coming to understand that we cannot continue to use the goods of the earth as we have in the past. [18]

It is frequently suggested that this exploitative attitude towards the material world is a consequence of the Judaeo-Christian approach to creation. The text of Genesis is quoted, granting human beings dominion over all creatures and instructing them to subdue the earth. This is by no means a complete or balanced reading of the biblical texts. In any case, exploitation of the environment, generally speaking, arises rather more from greed than scriptural exegesis!

There is, however, another underlying factor which is of more immediate interest in this context. That is the idea that freedom is some kind of creative core in a person which strives to overcome the limitations imposed on it by surrounding circumstances. The world outside oneself is a restriction to be overcome, to be conquered, to be bent to one's will.

Once again, we need to go back to an understanding of human freedom. Human freedom is not an ability to do whatever one wishes with no reference to what is possible, to what resources are present, to what other factors may be operating. Human freedom is the ability to deal with a situation which one does not create, but which one finds. It is the ability to use resources which are already there or are capable of being developed. We are able to uncover and to choose among the possibilities which are present; we cannot make something out of nothing:

> Human intervention is not 'creative'; it encounters a material nature which like itself has its origin in God the Creator and of which the human person has been constituted the noble and wise guardian. [19]

This consideration concerns every exercise of freedom, not merely those which have an immediate bearing on the scarcity of natural resources. Every free act takes place in various environments, ecological, social, cultural and so on. Being truly free does not mean ignoring those environments but rather recognising them so that one's action genuinely deals with reality, not with an illusion, so that the implications and consequences of one's decision are as clear as possible.

It might be argued, in fact, that the characteristic of the freest actions is found not so much in a struggle with the environment, but in harmony with it. The really free action, for instance, in sport, in art, in handling any instrument from a chisel to a computer, is the one which 'makes it look easy'. The real artist, however, does not give the impression of struggling with the medium but of being entirely at home in it.

This leads to a further reason why a reflection on our cultural keynotes demands a breaking out of the private room. Freedom is not a private centre dealing with an alien world; freedom is from the beginning and always about living in reality and dealing with reality as it is.

This involves not merely breaking out, so to speak, in terms of space, but also in terms of time. Human freedom cannot start from nowhere, nor can it start from no beginning. Wherever we want our lives to go they must get there from here. We may seek to change what our lives have so far made us; we cannot, however, start again as if the past had never happened. My past has to be integrated into my future. Even events which one now regrets can be part of the path towards what one wishes to become, but only if one acknowledges them.

That also is the mark of the true artist, that he or she can integrate the past. The artist critically interprets the past and makes it creatively present.[20] The most creative art is not the product of isolation from other people nor of insulation from tradition. That was the theme of T. S. Eliot's essay, 'Tradition and the Individual Talent' [1919] where he points to:

> ... our tendency to insist, when we praise a poet, upon those aspects of his work in which he least resembles anyone else. In

these aspects or parts of his work we pretend to find what is individual, what is the peculiar essence of the man ... Whereas if we approach a poet without this prejudice we shall often find that not only the best, but the most individual parts of his work may be those in which the dead poets, his ancestors, assert their immortality most vigorously.[21]

That has its parallel in the area of moral decision making – in the temptation to believe that the freest action is one which is least affected by the traditions that have formed one's culture and least influenced by the surrounding realities. It may rather be that the most individual and the most free actions are those in which the dead generations assert their immortality. To know who one is, to know the culture in which one has come to awareness and freedom is a necessary part of being truly free. We are not enslaved by knowing and understanding our traditions; we are enslaved rather by what we do not know and do not understand. The person who does not appreciate the tradition cannot understand its influence, cannot build upon it and indeed cannot evaluate it and challenge it when that is required:

> To challenge does not necessarily mean to destroy or reject a priori, but above all to put these values to the test in one's own life, and through this existential verification to make them more real, relevant and personal, distinguishing the valid elements in the tradition from false and erroneous ones, or from obsolete forms which can be usefully replaced by others more suited to the times. [22]

To say that human activity can never be performed in a vacuum, that it is always within a situation, does not, of course, imply that every situation is equally conducive to freedom. The dialogue between morality and culture cannot ignore the moral environment, the 'human ecology' (*Centesimus Annus* 38).

That dialogue involves looking at the human environment in terms of its capacity to foster 'the development and expansion of the human spirit', or, on the contrary, to 'deprive the human spirit of the genuine truth of its being and life'.[23] The moral climate of society – a product of family life, education, laws, customs, social and religious groupings, public debates and attitudes – is not neutral; it is vital to the well being of citizens.

It is undoubtedly true that modern societies provide a very diverse, indeed confusing, moral environment. The area of agreement on particular moral issues appears steadily to diminish. This may have a certain inevitability, but one should not too easily assume that of itself it makes society more free. The widespread acceptance of standards of behaviour can provide a context in which people can more easily develop their moral potential. An environment in which people are expected to behave with integrity in business, fidelity in marriage, faithfulness to their promises, is one which fosters responsible freedom.

How far that expectation should be expressed in legal provisions, how it can be fostered by public attitudes, by education, by the ethos of groups within the community is something that each society must work out for itself. How society can best provide for those who do not accept the validity of these expected standards is a challenge that must also be faced. What remains true is that a society which had few if any such expectations would be a moral desert.

The Search for Truth

The culture in which we live, and which is part of what we are, is one which asks many questions about the realities and the activities which it encounters: 'Will it work?'; 'Does it make people feel good?'; 'Is it likely to cause pain to anybody?'; 'What effect will it have on our standard of living?'; 'How does it rate in the opinion polls?' One question which tends to be submerged is the crucial one: 'Does it correspond to the truth?'

We might sum up the points that we have been looking at by reflecting on a final keynote of our culture, the question of *conscience*. Conscience is our attempt to seek and find the truth. A conscience judgement is an honest belief that one has discovered the truth. That at least is how it has been seen in the Catholic tradition. The approaches that we have looked at would tend to see conscience differently.

In the 'private room' the question is simply whether I am being sincere. If, however, conscience is a search for the truth, then there is another question, namely, have I in fact reached the truth? The difference between these two questions is evident to anybody

226

who has ever made a mistake in good conscience: it is entirely possible to be sincere and yet be mistaken. By definition of course, the sincere person cannot know, at the time, that he or she is mistaken. But a mistake may be clearly recognised after the event as each of us can testify from our own experience.

In the exercise of my freedom, I am not answerable only to myself. To be sincere means that I believe I have done all I reasonably can to reach the truth. It means that I am as satisfied as I can be that I have reached the truth. It means that I have done my best to recognise and respect the demands made upon me by other people and by the realities of my situation. It means that I have sought to respect the reality of myself, not as some kind of hermetically sealed individual but in the relationships and the interdependence with other human beings which make me what I am. If I have been insincere, then my decision lacks any value; if I have been sincere, then, clearly I am obliged to do what I have concluded is right. The judgement which I have made, however, is not just about my own feelings nor even about my sincerity, but about the people and the world outside my private room. That judgement must ultimately be measured by whether it is true or false.

The walls of the private room are broken by another consideration. The person who goes into his room and shuts the door remains answerable to God 'who is in that secret place' (Mt. 6: 6):

> Interiorly, the human being surpasses the whole universe of material things. It is to that deep interiority that a person turns when entering into his or her heart. There, God who probes the heart awaits; there a person decides his or her own destiny beneath the eyes of God. [24]

A further deepening of the notion of conscience and of freedom occurs when we recognise that the person, in those profound depths beneath the eyes of God, cannot simply be identified with the autonomous individual who appears in the first superficial glance of self-reflection. I think it was Karl Rahner who, in a salutary meditation on the last judgement, said that faced with the infinity of God we will see the full truth about ourselves and, what is more, we will recognise that the truth which we now see is something that we always knew!

The truth which conscience seeks is the deepest truth about ourselves. Thus a superficial sincerity is not the end of the matter. It is
simply not the case, as is sometimes suggested, that one would be
better off not to be aware of some moral obligation, because then
on would not have to fulfil it ! This fails to recognise that morality
is about doing justice to our own humanity and the humanity of
others. When we are mistaken, we are, however sincerely, doing
violence to ourselves:

> The person who is no longer able to recognise that murder is a
> sin is more completely fallen than someone who can still recog-
> nise the evil of his or her behaviour, because the former is
> further removed from the truth and from conversion ... [The
> Pharisee] is completely at peace with his conscience. But this
> silence of his conscience renders him impenetrable to God and
> to people. In contrast , the cry of conscience which gives no
> peace to the tax collector makes him capable of truth and
> love.[25]

Somebody once remarked that conscience is very well bred and
soon ceases to speak to those who do not wish to listen to it! Even
though conscience is silenced, however, it is never totally sup-
pressed:

> Just as it is impossible to eradicate completely the sense of God
> or to silence the conscience completely, so the sense of sin is
> never completely eliminated.[26]

There is more to us than meets the eye. There is more to us than
meets even our own eye. A proper understanding of conscience
and of the responsible exercise of freedom leads to a realisation
that the search for truth is never ending. It is a search which does
not find its goal simply in a real or imagined equilibrium within
one's own heart, but in an understanding of oneself, of the world
and of God which cannot finally be achieved in this life. In fidelity
to conscience, Christians are joined with the rest of humanity in
the search for truth.[27] Ultimately, the search for truth and the
search for God are one and the same.[28]

That is why tolerance cannot properly be seen as a passive non-
interference with what one sees as the harmless idiosyncrasies of
other people. Conscience is, as Vatican II called, our 'most secret

core and sanctuary': There a person is alone with God whose voice echoes in his or her depths.[29] Any person's search for the truth is sacred, even if the search has in a particular instance gone astray. More than that, the knowledge that one's insight into the truth is limited cannot but lead one to realise that there is wisdom to be gained by understanding another person's honest perception of it:

> How modest must the Christian be in regard to his or her limited insight! How quick to learn and how slow to condemn! One of the constant temptations in every age, even among Christians, is to make oneself the norm of the truth. In an age of pervasive individualism, this temptation takes a variety of forms. But the mark of those who are 'in the truth' is the ability to love humbly. That is what God's word teaches us: the truth is expressed in love.[30]

The recognition that the individual person is not the norm of the truth is the core of the challenge which needs to be faced in the dialogue of culture and morality. We need to recognise, in the first place, that the goal of conscience is the truth in its full profundity. That profundity is found only in love which alone allows us really to understand another person, which allows us to know ourselves not in some complacent, self-satisfaction but in the dynamic 'love of what God may make me'.[31]

That humble love will also recognise the respect that is due to the tradition which has made us and to the generations that may follow us. This is how we do justice to who we are, to the reality of the human person:

> ... above all a being who seeks the truth and strives to live in that truth, deepening [our] understanding of it through a dialogue which involves past and future generations.[32]

What we need as the foundation for the dialogue between morality and culture is the conviction that we are beings who seek the truth. That search is one in which we are engaged together. There may be as many opinions as there are people, but there is only one truth. It is right that we should respect the views of those who differ from us, but what we must not do is to deny that we are engaged in the same quest, that we are seeking the same truth.

That shared quest is precisely why it is right to respect, to listen to and to value the views of others.

There will be many disagreements. There will even be many situations of virtually total incomprehension. What would be disastrous however, would be to conclude that there is no truth, only opinion, that what is true for one person may be false for another – as if our actions and attitudes did not affect one another, did not speak to one another and express our attitudes to one another, did not take place in a world which we must share.

The most profound moral threat to our culture is that we are in danger of abandoning the notion that we seek the moral truth together and of settling for the idea that there is no accounting for moral taste. We are in danger of coming to the conclusion that the way to preserve unity and harmony in society is to damp down or to regard as 'out of bounds' discussion about contentious issues of morality, social and personal.

Social harmony gained at the price of suppressing our sense of seeking the truth, unity built on silencing our common concern about how to build a society in which people can flourish as human beings, would be an empty harmony and inhuman unity. It would be a society without a soul, a society hostile to human freedom.

Freed by the truth
Freedom and truth are inseparable: 'A human being becomes free to the extent that her or she comes to a knowledge of the truth and to the extent that this truth – and not any other forces – guides the person's will.'[33]

We become free to the extent that we resist any concept of freedom which 'fails to enter into the whole truth about humanity and about the world'.[34] That is the challenge; which can be detected in the questions our culture raises. It is the challenge of entering into the whole truth,
    about ourselves,
    about the other people who seek the truth with us,
    about the reality of the world,
    about God who meets us in the secret core and sanctuary of
    conscience

and about his Son who 'meets people of every age , including our own, with the same words, "You will know the truth and the truth will make you free."' [35]

Notes

1. Trilling, L. , *Sincerity and Authenticity*, Oxford University Press 1974, 24, 25
2. *Gaudium et Spes*, 12
3. Sacks, J., *The Persistence of Faith*, Weidenfeld and Nicholson 1991, 14
4. Connell, D. , *Christian Integrity*, Veritas 1992, 7
5. Pope John Paul, *Centesimus Annus*, 49
6. Connell, D. , *Christian Integrity*, 7
7. Murray, D. , *The Inner Truth*, Veritas 1980, 70 ff
8. Sheed, F., *Society and Sanity*, Sheed and Ward 1953, 3,4
9. Mac Intyre, A., *After Virtue*, Duckworth 1983, 6.
10. Sacks, J., *The Persistence of Faith*, 88
11. *Gaudium et Spes*, 16
12. Pope John Paul II, *Message for the World Day of Peace 1991*
13. Newman, J. , *Conscience versus Law*, Talbot Press 1971, 179-180
14. Sacks, J., *The Persistence of Faith*, 32
15. Pope John Paul, *Centesimus Annus*, 46
16. Sacks, op. cit. 42
17. Crick, B. , *Crime, Rape and Gin*, Elek Books , 1974, 14
18. Pope John Paul, *Message for the World Day of Peace 1990*
19. Congregation for the Doctrine of the Faith, *Instruction on Christian Freedom and Liberation*, 34
20. Steiner, G., *Real Presences*, Faber and Faber 1989, 11ff
21. Eliot, T. S. , *Selected Essays*, Faber and Faber 1953, 14
22. Pope John Paul, *Centesimus Annus*, 50
23. Pope John Paul, *Dominum et Vivificantem*, 60
24. *Gaudium et Spes*, 14
25. Ratzinger, J. , *Elogio della Coscenza*, *Il Sabato* 16 March 1991, my translation.
26. Pope John Paul, *Reconciliatio et Paenitentia*, 18
27. *Gaudium et Spes*, 16
28. Pope John Paul, *Message for the World Day of Peace 1991*
29. *Gaudium et Spes*, 16
30. Pope John Paul, *Message for the World Day of Peace 1991*

31. Marcel, G. , *Being and Having*, Fontana 1965, 77
32. Pope John Paul, *Centesimus Annus,* 49
33. CDF, *Instruction on Christian Freedom and Liberation* , 26
34. Pope John Paul, *Redemptor Hominis,* 12
35. *Redemptor Hominis,* 12

Contributors

DERMOT A. LANE is a priest of the archdiocese of Dublin. He has been on the staff of Mater Dei Institute since 1970 and was Director of Studies from 1982 to 1992. He was recently appointed parish priest of Balally, Dublin 16.

WILLIAM RILEY is a priest of the Dublin archdiocese who has been a lecturer in Scripture at Mater Dei Institute since 1983. Among his publications are *Tale of Two Testaments, The Old Testament Short Story* (co-authored with Carmel McCarthy) and *King and Cultus in Chronicles*.

ANN KELLY is a graduate of Mater Dei Institute and has a postgraduate degree in Theology from Maynooth. She is at present lecturer in Religious Studies in St. Patrick's College, Drumcondra, Dublin 9, and co-editor of *Womanspirit:The Irish Journal of Feminist Spirituality*.

ANNE M. MURPHY is a religious of the Sacred Heart of Mary and is Head of the Music Department at Mater Dei Institute. She is a graduate in Music and Theology from St Patrick's College, Maynooth. Her research interests include the dialogue of faith and art in music.

JOHN DEVITT has been Head of the English Department in Mater Dei Institute since 1979. He has written extensively on literary and educational topics and is co-editor of the *Bronze by Gold* anthologies (1989-1991).

MICHAEL PAUL GALLAGHER S.J. was a lecturer in Modern Literature at University College, Dublin, for twenty years. Exposure to students led to an interest in unbelief and to the publication of various books on pastoral theology (*Help my Unbelief, Free to Believe, Struggles of Faith, Where is your God?*). In 1990 he moved to Rome, to work with the Pontifical Council for Dialogue with Non-Believers.

ANDREW G. McGRADY is a graduate of Mater Dei Institute and lecturer in the Education Department of the Institute. His doctoral studies into the development of metaphorical thinking were undertaken at the University of Birmingham.

DONAL HARRINGTON is a priest of the archdiocese of Dublin. He is Head of the Moral Theology Department at Mater Dei Institute and a member of the staff of Holy Cross College, Clonliffe. He is also a part-time co-ordinator with Parish Development and Renewal in the archdiocese.

✠ DONAL MURRAY is an Auxiliary Bishop of Dublin. He lectured in Mater Dei Institute in Moral Theology from 1969 to 1982. He is Chairman of the Episcopal Catechetical Commission in Ireland and also a member of the Pontifical Council for Dialogue with Non-Believers in Rome.

Hermeneutics is the art of understanding & interpreting different texts, events & human experiences.

Polysemy is the property of words which allows them to have more than one meaning.